Paradoxical Psychotherapy:

Theory and Practice with Individuals, Couples, and Families

Paradoxical Psychotherapy:

Theory and Practice with Individuals, Couples, and Families

GERALD R. WEEKS, Ph.D.

University of North Carolina—Wilmington

and

LUCIANO L'ABATE, Ph.D.

Georgia State University

 BRUNNER/MAZEL, *Publishers* • NEW YORK

Library of Congress Cataloging in Publication Data

Weeks, Gerald R., 1948-
  Paradoxical psychotherapy.

  Bibliography: p.
  Includes index.
  1. Paradox—Therapeutic use.   2. Logotherapy.
I. L'Abate, Luciano, 1928-   II. Title.
[DNLM: 1. Psychological theory.   2. Psycho-
therapy—Methods.   WM 420 W395p]
RC489.L6W43   616.89'14   81-17083
ISBN 0-87630-289-4   AACR2

Published by
BRUNNER/MAZEL, INC.
19 Union Square
New York, New York 10003

MANUFACTURED IN THE UNITED STATES OF AMERICA

Foreword

This book offers a number of firsts. Among other things, it is the first volume to:

1) Provide a comprehensive overview of paradoxical therapy, covering history, theory, technique, applicability, research and ethics.

2) Place its subject matter within a dialectical framework.

3) Attempt the difficult task of compiling an extensive catalogue of the various paradoxical methods that have been developed, accompanying each technique with detailed explanations and guidelines as to how and where to apply it.

4) Offer a wide selection of both brief and (more uniquely) extended therapy cases to which paradoxical methods apply.

5) Devote considerable space to the use of various kinds of paradoxical letters.

6) Explicate in detail the contraindications for the use of paradox.

7) Deal at length with a number of interesting and related side issues such as therapy "addicts" and "therapist killers."

The book is current, scholarly, illuminating and often humorous. It is chock-full of delightful therapeutic morsels in the form of clinical cases and vignettes. The authors challenge our thinking and our modus operandi. For instance, they openly and forthrightly define the symptom as a "friend"—perhaps another first in the literature. They offer many creative ways of relabeling behaviors and patterns heretofore considered only as "dysfunctional." They also remove much of the "magic" from paradox and provide a glimpse of the hard work that sometimes accompanies such an approach.

It will be difficult for a therapist not to be stimulated by this book— not to be excited at points and not to feel his or her options have been increased. Therapists both green and grey should be indebted to Weeks and L'Abate for years to come.

M. Duncan Stanton, Ph.D.
Philadelphia Child Guidance Clinic,
University of Pennsylvania

Preface

Paradoxical psychotherapy has rapidly become one of the most important approaches to family therapy and psychotherapy during the past few years. Clinicians have been attracted to it because it is a form of brief therapy which produces change as if by magic. In fact, its early practitioners have sometimes been referred to as magicians. Until recently, paradoxical therapy was surrounded by an aura of mystery because the principles and techniques of the approach had not been delineated.

The aim of this book is to present an overview of paradoxical therapy. An attempt is made to integrate current scientific knowledge in this area. This process involves explicating and extrapolating much that has been implicit in this approach. In short, paradoxical therapy is demystified.

Aside from presenting a comprehensive account of other research, the book presents our own working method. This method is delineated in such a way that others can replicate it both in clinical practice and research. The fact that our method can be replicated elevates paradoxical therapy from art to science. Otherwise, paradoxical therapy would either die slowly or remain unaccepted by most therapists.

Paradoxical Psychotherapy: Theory and Practice with Individuals, Couples, and Families is designed for all clinical psychologists. Applications are offered for the individual, marital, and family therapist. The book could be used by the clinician who is interested in learning about this approach or by the seasoned paradoxical therapist who wishes to gain an overall perspective. Academicians interested in the theory of paradoxical therapy and research will find that attention has been given to these issues.

This book is the first to offer an overview of paradoxical therapy. It helps to clarify the uneven growth of the theory, research, and practice of this approach. Our hope is that this book will help crystallize issues that will contribute to the systematic development of paradoxical therapy.

OVERVIEW OF THIS BOOK

Chapter 1 reviews the history of paradoxical psychotherapy proper and the use of therapeutic paradoxes in earlier systems of psychotherapy. It also reveals how paradoxical methods are embedded in many other systems of psychotherapy.

Chapters 2 and 3 examine the theoretical aspects of paradoxical therapy. Previous theories of paradox are described and a new theoretical basis for the practice of paradoxical therapy is proposed. The concept of dialectics is used to account for problem formation and resolution.

Chapter 4 investigates an area that has received very little attention. It offers criteria for when to use paradoxical therapy.

Chapter 5 offers suggestions on how to work paradoxically. These suggestions are both general and specific. The chapter contains our principles of paradoxical intervention.

Chapters 6 and 7 reveal the methods of paradoxical interventions. These two chapters provide a "mental template" for the clinician.

Chapter 8 focuses on two new and significant areas where paradoxes have been tried—the paradoxical treatment of depression and children.

Chapters 9 and 10 exemplify the use of paradox in a variety of situations. The techniques used are labeled and explained through the use of written paradoxical letters given to clients.

Chapter 11 reviews the research on all types of paradoxical treatment.

Chapter 12 clarifies some of the ethical issues which have been raised. It also suggests who should be trained in this approach and how.

G.R.W.

Contents

Acknowledgments

I wish to thank a number of people who helped bring this book to fruition. I would like to thank Dr. John T. Williams, Jr., Chairman of the Psychology Department at UNC-Wilmington, for his support and help in scheduling classes to permit research and writing time.

Superb editorial assistance was freely offered by Ron Burkhalter, Dr. Andy Jackson, and Carolyn Windham. Ron Burkhalter not only spent many hours reviewing the manuscript for its technical quality, but offered many challenging ideas regarding content.

Special thanks to Jackie W. Johnson and Thomas F. Ryan who were co-therapists for two of the cases reported herein.

My heartfelt thanks to Mrs. Martha Jo Clemmons for her many hours of deciphering my handwriting and typing one draft after another. She was assisted by Dianne Matthews and Jo Ann Teague.

I would also like to express my appreciation to my wife, Kathy, for her enduring patience, understanding, support and love.

GERALD R. WEEKS

We are both indebted to many others. These are our many colleagues and friends at Georgia State University and Harlem Valley Psychiatric Center who encouraged our interest in paradox and supported our clinical experimentation. We gratefully acknowledge the contributions of Joseph Frey, II, Edgar Jessee, Michael O'Shea, John Schoonbeck, Sadell Sloan, Pat Soper, Thomas Todd, and Victor Wagner.

GERALD R. WEEKS
LUCIANO L'ABATE

Paradoxical Psychotherapy:

Theory and Practice with Individuals, Couples, and Families

1

Introduction to paradoxical psychotherapy

Paradoxes have fascinated men since the sixth century B. C. when Epimenides of Megara devised the paradox of the liar, and Zeno of Elea formulated the paradoxes of infinity (Hughes and Brecht, 1975). Epimenides' mind-boggling liar paradox asserted that "all Cretans are liars." However, since Epimenides was also from Crete, then he too must be a liar. But if Epimenides is a liar, then the statement, "all Cretan are liars," must be a lie, which means that all Cretans tell the truth . . . except Epimenides was just proved to be lying . . . but since he is from Crete . . . ad infinitum. Interest in paradox waned following Zeno until the late nineteenth century revival of logic (Edwards, 1967). Recently, family therapists have developed an intense interest in a special type of paradox, leaving logical and semantic paradoxes to the domain of philosophers and linguists (Soper and L'Abate, 1977).

The purpose of this book is to examine the various ways in which the paradox may be applied in psychotherapy. While it is important to understand theory, the major emphasis of this book will be on how to use or apply paradoxical methods. Paradoxical psychotherapy is a relatively new, exciting, powerful, and non-commonsensical form of therapy. Its most outstanding characteristic is its departure from traditional psychotherapeutic techniques. Few therapists have been willing or able to practice paradoxical psychotherapy due to its uniqueness and the lack of any coherent guide. In fact, it could be stated from the outset that the guiding principle of a paradoxical therapist is: "If a therapist would do it, do the opposite." This principle is itself paradoxical, referring to traditionally trained therapists. Paradoxical methods have been used primarily by family or systems-oriented therapists. Haley (1963, 1976), Selvini Palazzoli and her group (1978a), and Watzlawick et al. (1967, 1974) are probably the best-known proponents of the paradoxical treatment of families. In addition, a review of the literature shows that the majority of articles published on paradoxical techniques have appeared in the family therapy journal *Family Process* (Weeks and L'Abate, 1978). This book will demonstrate how the paradox can be applied in individual, marital, and family therapy, with more emphasis on the latter two forms of therapy.

WHAT IS PARADOXICAL PSYCHOTHERAPY?

Logicians have distinguished three types of paradoxes (Watzlawick, Beavin, and Jackson, 1967). The first type is the *antimony*. These paradoxes are statements which are contradictory but provable. In other words, they are logical contradictions and are of interest only to logicians and mathematicians. The second type of paradox is the *semantic antimony* or *paradoxical definition*. Paradoxical definitions stem from hidden inconsistencies in the structure of our language. Epimenides' liar paradox is an example of a paradoxical definition. Bertrand Russell's theory of logical types also illustrated a paradoxical definition in that whatever comprised all of a collection cannot be one of the collection. In order to prevent these types of paradoxes from occurring, logical levels must be kept separate, and it must be recognized that going from one level to the next involves a quantum jump in a system.

The third type of paradox is the most important because it underlies paradoxical psychotherapy. This paradox is called the *pragmatic paradox*. Unlike a contradiction, a pragmatic paradox gives a person no choice. "Thus, if the message is an injunction, it must be disobeyed to be obeyed; if it is a definition of self or other, the person thereby defined is this kind of person only if he is not, and is not if he is" (Andolfi, 1974, p. 222). Accordingly, paradoxical therapy is based on the principle that a person is expected to change by remaining unchanged. The classic example of this principle and of the pragmatic paradox is the paradoxical injunction, "Be spontaneous." As soon as one attempts to act on this command, one cannot. It is only when one gives up that one can behave spontaneously. The most common form of the pragmatic paradox or therapeutic paradox is to prescribe the symptom—in other words, to encourage the client to become even more symptomatic.

The earliest research on the pragmatic paradox was conducted by the Palo Alto group (the Bateson project and the Mental Research Institute). In 1956, Gregory Bateson, Don Jackson, Jay Haley, and John Weakland published a classic paper called, "Toward a theory of schizophrenia." This paper pointed out the pathological aspects of paradoxical communication in producing schizophrenia and suggested that pragmatic paradoxes could be used therapeutically. At the time this paper was published, the term pragmatic paradox was not being used. Instead, the equivalent term "double-bind" was being used. The development of this work eventually revealed that a therapeutic double-bind is a mirror usage of a pathological double-bind (Watzlawick et al., 1967).

To understand a therapeutic double-bind fully, it is essential first to examine a pathogenic double-bind. In a pathogenic double-bind, a person is placed in a no-win situation. Bateson et al. (1956) asserted that repeated exposure to this kind of communication could produce schizophrenia. More recently, Sluzki and Eliseo (1971) have considered the double-bind a universal pathogenic situation accounting for neurotic as well as psychotic symptomatology.

For double-binding to take place, several conditions must be met over a period of time. The first requirement is that there be two or more persons who are closely connected (e.g., family members). Secondly, there must be communication around some recurrent theme. A single experience is not deemed effective. Thirdly, a primary negative injunction must occur. This verbal injunction usually occurs in two forms: a) "Do not do so and so, or I will punish you," or b) "If you do not do so and so, I will punish you." The learning context is one of avoidance of punishment. Fourthly, a secondary injunction is delivered which conflicts with the first and also threatens punishment. The secondary message is generally more difficult to grasp, recognize, or articulate because it is usually conveyed nonverbally. The classic example is a mother tightening up and folding her arms as she says, "I love you" to her child. Finally, a tertiary negative injunction is communicated which prohibits the victim of the bind from leaving the field or commenting on his/her untenable situation.

While a pathogenic double-bind places a person in a no-win predicament, a therapeutic double-bind forces a client into a no-lose situation. In the therapeutic double-bind, there is also some kind of intense relationship over a period of time. Within the context of therapy, the behavior the client wants to change or eliminate is prescribed or encouraged by the therapist, and the therapist implies that this reinforcement is the means of change. The client is placed in the double-bind of being told to change by staying the same. Watzlawick et al. (1967) stated, "If he complies, he no longer 'can't help it'; he does 'it,' and this, as we have tried to show, makes 'it' impossible, which is the purpose of therapy. If he resists the injunction, he can do so only by *not* behaving symptomatically, which is the purpose of therapy" (p. 241).

Finally, the client is not permitted to dissolve the paradox by commenting on it. In other words, in a therapeutic double-bind, a client gains control over the symptom by either giving it up (disobeying the injunction) or by enacting it intentionally or voluntarily. If the latter occurs, the client has gained control over the symptom in the sense that s/he now controls it, and not vice versa. This type of bind or paradoxical situation forces the client outside his or her pathological frame of reference.

Pragmatic paradoxes or therapeutic double-binds produce a unique kind of change. Watzlawick et al. (1974) maintained that paradoxical injunctions produce second-order rather than first-order change. First-order change refers to change within a particular frame of reference or system, such as the events which happen or change within dreams. Second-order change refers to a change in the frame of reference or system itself, such as a change from dreaming to waking. Second-order change is actually the process which allows the client to escape from the pathogenic double-bind. The solution is the new frame created by the client's escape from the bind. The therapeutic double-bind implicitly challenges the client's model of the world by forcing him/her into an experience which contradicts the self-destructive limitations of the present model. This experience serves as a reference structure by which the client expands his model of the world (Bandler and Grinder, 1975, p. 169).

HISTORY OF PARADOXICAL PSYCHOTHERAPY

The history of paradoxical psychotherapy proper begins with the work of the Palo Alto and Mental Research Institute group and was later formalized in *Pragmatics of Human Communication* by Watzlawick, Beavin, and Jackson in 1967. However, it is a mistake to believe that paradoxical techniques suddenly came into existence with this group. Paradoxical techniques have been used since the early days of psychotherapy. These techniques are embedded in many different systems of psychotherapy which are rarely credited today with having any impact on the development of paradoxical psychotherapy. Even more interesting is the fact that each system which employs paradoxical techniques provides a different theoretical explanation about why these techniques work. A comparative historical analysis of paradox helps us understand what has been tried and why these techniques have been effective.

According to Mozdzierz, Macchitelli, and Lisiecki (1976), Alfred Adler (1914) was the first person in Western civilization to use and write about paradoxical strategies. Mozdzierz et al. (1976) pointed out that paradox is dialectics applied to psychotherapy. Adler was strongly influenced by the work of Nietzsche, Vaihinger, and Hegel and believed dialectical thinking to be the modus operandi of his psychology (Ansbacher, 1972).

Mozdzierz et al. (1976) delineated what they call Adler's (1956) nonspecific paradoxical strategy and identified 12 specific paradoxical techniques which they claim stem from Adlerian psychology. Adler's (1956, p. 337) nonspecific paradoxical strategy was to avoid power struggles with clients. He stated that clients will attempt to depreciate the therapist by doing things such as expressing doubt, criticizing, forgetting, being late, making special requests, and having relapses. Adler viewed neurotic symptoms as teleologically uncooperative symptoms, or inadequate ways of dealing with the demands of life, especially social cooperation or social interest. The use of paradoxical strategies shifts the patient's symptomatic uncooperative behavior to cooperative behavior between the therapist and client. Adler advised the therapist of the ways to "never force a patient," such as renouncing his/her own superiority, being constantly friendly, keeping a cool head, and never fighting with a client. In other words, he suggested going with or accepting the patient's resistance. The following case illustrates this idea.

> A girl of 27 who came to consult me after five years of suffering said: "I have seen so many doctors that you are my last hope in life." "No," I answered, "Not the last hope. Perhaps the last but one. There may be others who can help you too." Her words were a challenge to me; she was daring me not to cure her, so as to make me feel bound in duty to do so. This is the type of patient who wishes to shift responsibility upon others, a common development of pampered children. It is important to evade such a challenge. The patient may have worked up a high tension of feelings about the idea that the doctor is his "last hope," but we must accept no such distinction. To do so would be to prepare the way for a disappointment, or even suicide (Adler, 1956, p. 339).

It is also interesting to note that Adler (1956) was the first theorist to deal with depression paradoxically. He recognized the interpersonal dynamics of depression and used a paradoxical technique which is today called restraining. He would instruct the depressed patient to:

> "Never do anything you don't like." This seems to be a very modest request, but I believe it goes to the root of the whole trouble. If a depressed person is able to do anything he wants whom can he accuse? What has he got to revenge himself for? "If you want to go to the theatre," I tell him, "or to go on a holiday, do it. If you find on the way that you don't want to, stop it." It is the best

situation anyone could be in. It gives a satisfaction to his striving for superiority. He is like God and can do what he pleases. On the other hand, it does not fit very easily into his style of life. He wants to dominate and accuse others; if they agree with him, there is no way of dominating them. . . . Generally the patient replies, "But there is nothing I like doing." I have prepared for this answer, because I have heard it so often. "Then refrain from doing anything you dislike," I say. . . . I know that if I allow it, he will no longer want to do it. I know that if I hinder him, he will start a war (Adler, 1956, p. 346-347).

Some of the specific Adlerian-based techniques Mozdzierz et al. (1976) described are: 1) *permission*—giving the client permission to have a symptom; 2) *prediction*—predicting the client's symptoms would return, or that he would have a relapse; 3) *proportionality*—getting the client to exaggerate symptoms or have the therapist take them more seriously than the client; 4) *pro-social redefinition*—redefining or reinterpreting symptomatic behavior in a positive instead of negative way; 5) *prescription*—directing the client to engage in his symptomatic behavior; and 6) *practice*—asking the client to refine and improve his symptomatic behavior.

The second theorist to explore the technique of symptom prescription was probably Knight Dunlap in 1928 (Watzlawick et al., 1967; Raskin and Klein, 1976). Dunlap (1928, 1930) developed a procedure he called "negative practice" for such symptoms as nail biting, enuresis, and stuttering. He would direct the client to practice the symptom under prescribed conditions with the expectation of losing the habit. Dunlap (1946) never developed an adequate rationale for the technique of negative practice. However, his description of negative practice is very similar to the present-day concept of paradox and offers an implicit theoretical basis. Dunlap (1946) stated: "The general principle of negative practice is that of making an effort to do the things that one has been making an effort not to do, instead of making an effort to avoid doing the things that one has been doing. . . . The principle involved might be formulated as bringing under voluntary control responses which have been involuntary. . . . This is merely a description of the results of negative practice and is not an explanation" (p. 194).

Dunlap changed his original views toward the application and effectiveness of this technique in his later work. In his early work he believed the technique could be used to treat a variety of disorders, but by 1932 he believed it would only be applicable to small motor habits.

The principle of negative practice is often called "massed practice" by modern behavior theorists. Hull (1943) provided a theoretical explanation of massed practice with his construct of "reactive inhibition." He stated that the repetition of a behavior in rapid succession was aversive to an organism, and the rest period which follows is pleasurable or negatively reinforcing. The fatigue plus the negative reinforcement become paired with not performing the symptom and inhibit its further occurrence. A review by Rimm and Masters (1974) of the research on negative practice showed the technique produces mixed outcome.

There are two other more recent behavioral techniques which can be construed as paradoxical. One well-known technique is implosion. Implosive therapy attempts to eliminate avoidance behavior through the process of extinction. It is commonly used to treat phobias but has been applied to such problems as sexual deviations, loss of impulse control, guilt, aggression, and fear of rejection. Implosive therapy requires the client to imagine the scenes of the avoided behavior from least to most anxiety-provoking without being permitted actually to engage in any avoidance behavior. For example, an individual who feels hostile and angry toward someone might be told to imagine verbalizing those thoughts and culminate in imagining that he is a wild animal ripping his victim apart. Stampfl and Levis (1967) presented the first complete description of implosion, and the technique has been shown to produce mixed outcome (Rimm and Masters, 1974).

Stimulus satiation is the most recent behavioral technique related to paradoxical psychotherapy. This technique involves repeated exposure of the desired stimulus to the client. The best known case was reported by Ayllon (1963). A psychotic patient had developed the habit of hoarding towels. The staff was instructed to give her more and more towels over five weeks. By the sixth week the patient was not only refusing more towels but removing them from her room.

Of all the historical percursors of paradoxical psychotherapy, Victor Frankl's work is the most explicitly paradoxical. Frankl developed an existential approach to psychotherapy which he called logotherapy. The goal of logotherapy was to make man consciously accept personal responsibility. One of the main techniques of logotherapy is paradoxical intention. Frankl (1975) claimed he was using paradoxical intention as early as 1925, but he did not formally describe it until 1939 (Frankl, 1939). The first major English presentation of his work appeared in 1965 in a book entitled, *The Doctor and the Soul: From Psychotherapy to Logotherapy*. Paradoxical intention involves directing the patient intentionally to will the symptom to occur. Frankl (1967) stated:

> The reader will note that this treatment consists not only of a reversal of the patient's attitude toward his phobia inasmuch as the usual "avoidance" response is replaced by an intentional effort—but also that it is carried out in as humorous a setting as possible. This brings about a change of attitude toward the symptom which enables the patient to place himself at a distance from the symptom, to detach himself from his neurosis. This procedure is based on the fact that, according to the logo-therapeutic teaching, the pathogenesis in phobias and obsessive-compulsive neurosis is partially due to the increase of anxiety and compulsions by the endeavor to avoid or fight them. A phobic person usually tries to avoid the situation in which his anxiety arises, while the obsessive-compulsive tries to suppress, and thus fight, his threatening ideas. In either case the result is a strengthening of the symptom. Conversely, if we succeed in bringing the patient to the point where he ceases to flee from or to fight his symptoms, but on the contrary, even exaggerates them, then we may observe that the symptoms diminish, and that the patient is no longer haunted by them (pp. 146-147).

Paradoxical intention was based on the principle that anxiety neurosis and phobic reactions are characterized by anticipatory anxiety. Moreover, it is anticipatory anxiety which produces the conditions the patient fears. Paradoxical intention is designed to interrupt the vicious cycle by reducing or eliminating the anticipatory anxiety, hence the neurotic condition. Frankl emphasized that he was not merely treating the symptom but was changing the patient's attitude toward his neurosis. He called this change in attitude an existential reorientation. He also stated that humor was an essential ingredient in the patient's being able to detach himself from his neurotic condition. In many of his cases the patient begins laughing at himself as soon as he is instructed to will the symptom. One of Frankl's (1967) frequently cited cases illustrates these principles:

> A young physician came to our clinic because of severe hidrophobia. He had been troubled by disturbances of the autonomic nervous system for a long time. One day he happened to meet his chief on the street, and as the young man extended his hand in greeting, he noticed that he was perspiring more than usual. The next time he was in a similar situation he expected to perspire again, and this anticipatory anxiety precipitated excessive sweating. It was a vicious circle; hyperhidrosis provoked hidrophobia and hidrophobia, in turn produced hyperhidrosis. We advised our patient, in the event that his anticipatory anxiety should occur, to resolve deliberately to show people whom he confronted at the time just how much he could really sweat. A week later he returned to report that whenever he met anyone who triggered his anticipatory anxiety, he said to himself, "I only sweated out a liter before, but now I'm going to pour out at least ten liters!" (p. 146).

In 1967 Frankl reasserted his belief that paradoxical intention is a nonspecific method. It can be applied to any number of neurotic and psychotic conditions irrespective of etiologic basis. He also stated that it may be possible to alleviate just the symptoms without taking account of the deeper or underlying cause, and while paradoxical intention tends to be a short-term therapy, it can also be longer if the therapist wishes to help the patient develop a more complete understanding of his or her existential possibilities.

The use of paradoxical intention in the United States has been popularized by a number of Frankl's students and followers. Louis Barber, Joseph Farby, Reuven Bulka, Hans Gerz, Elisabeth Lukas, and William Sahakian are just a few who have proselytized the work of Frankl. The reader interested in recent developments in logotherapy should consult a recently edited book entitled *Logotherapy in Action* (Fabry et al., 1979).

The fourth major therapist to develop a paradoxical approach to treatment was the psychiatrist John Rosen in his *Direct Psychoanaly-sis*. Rosen's (1953) book described "the treatment and cure of psychotic patients" (p. 1). His first description of this method was published in a paper in 1946 called "A method of resolving acute catatonic excitement." By 1953 he had formalized a complete system of psychotherapy which emphasized a procedure called "re-enacting an aspect of the psychosis" (p. 27). In short, whenever a patient would begin to act in a bizarre manner, Rosen would direct the patient to proceed to act out the psychotic episode in its most florid state. Rosen's (1953) clearest explanation of why this method worked is summarized as follows:

> Whenever your hunch tells you they are in danger of repeating some such irrationality, you beat them to the draw by demanding that they re-enact just exactly the piece of psychotic behavior that you fear they may fall into again. Perhaps your boldness indicates to the patient that you are willing to take a chance of making him act crazy because you are convinced that he no longer can. Perhaps it has something to do with the patient's sense of shame when you ask him to do something foolish and remind him that he used to do this foolish thing. Sometimes the patient makes an attempt to re-enact the symptom which comes out very feebly, obviously not spontaneous, and sometimes he will say he did it to humor you. When the patient has clearly lost his touch, the therapist has reason to rejoice (p. 27).

When a psychotic patient was no longer seeing visions or hearing voices, Rosen would ask the patient to remember when he was hallucinating and try to elicit the patient's cooperation in seeing or hearing things again. This strategy, of course, was intended to discourage the reappearance of his symptom in addition to helping the patient reject the symptom as crazy. Rosen believed the road to reality was the reverse of the road to psychosis. The patient must work his way back in stages which resembled the stages in the development of the psychosis.

Aside from re-enacting an aspect of the psychosis, which is analogous to symptom prescription, Rosen (1953) used two other paradoxical techniques. The first technique was magical gestures. This ploy involved joining with the patient in his psychosis and exaggerating it. The other technique was called "misery loves company." When a client denied his psychotic symptoms, Rosen would enact them and proclaim he had the same symptoms when he was crazy. This technique had the effect of giving the client permission to have his symptom without the accompanying anxiety and demonstrated to the client that the symptoms would disappear since the therapist was not crazy.

Rosen (1953) claimed to have had remarkable success in treating psychotics. In one study, Rosen claimed that 36 out of 37 schizophrenics recovered to the extent of achieving the emotional stability of normal individuals. A later analysis of his work showed that out of 100 schizophrenics, 27 responded with marked improvement. Those who responded most quickly had received no ECT, had limited hospitalization, and could verbalize in a conventional manner. Rosen's faith in direct analysis was reflected in his statement that he could not concede to the hypothetical hopeless case.

Paradoxical techniques are also embedded in two recent theories of psychotherapy, although they are not labeled paradoxical. Gestalt therapists sometimes use a technique known as exaggeration. According to Levitsky and Perls (1970), this technique involves asking the client to repeat and amplify a movement or gesture. The assumption is that a gesture may be an abortive or incomplete attempt to communicate. Enright (1970) offered an excellent example of the application of exaggeration. A woman was making short rapid movements with her finger against her arm. When she amplified the movement it turned out that she was pantomining the form of a cross. At that moment she realized she had hung herself on a cross. She had set herself up to be a martyr.

Other gestalt techniques can also be viewed paradoxically, although most gestalt therapists deny and reject the idea that they use paradoxical methods. Beisser (1970) has stated that at the heart of gestalt therapy is a paradoxical theory of change. He asserts "that change occurs when one becomes what he is, not when he tries to become what he is not" (p. 77). Thus, the gestalt therapist helps the clients be "where and what he is." The gestalt therapist assumes the paradoxical role of not being a changer.

Another unique form of therapy which uses paradoxical methods was developed by Farrelly (Farrelly and Brandsma, 1974). This approach is called provocative therapy since the goal of treatment is to produce a strong emotional or affective response in the client. Farrelly's approach best represents the use of symptom exaggeration. The key element in this therapy is humor. Humor is generated through the use of exaggeration, mimicry, ridicule, distortion, sarcasm, irony, and jokes. One of Farrelly's favorite techniques is to prescribe the symptom in some humorous way, such as telling a suicidal patient to place her arm in a vise in order to cut it off with a hacksaw. He also mimics clients' symptoms in a larger-than-life style, but shows selective control over the symptom. For example, his arm may suddenly become paralyzed just like his client's arm, but it becomes temporarily functional when he reaches for his coffee cup.

Farrelly and Brandsma (1974) offer two hypotheses in explaining why provocative therapy works. The first hypothesis is that when a client is provoked by the therapist within his or her own frame of reference, s/he will change in a direction opposite from the therapist's definition of the client. The second hypothesis is that when the therapist provocatively urges the client to continue his/her self-defeating behaviors, the client will discontinue those behaviors and behave more appropriately. These two hypotheses accept the usefulness of negativistic tendencies. They are in fact identical with the theory of change espoused by Watzlawick et al. (1974).

Of course, two of the most important precursors of paradoxical psychotherapy were Milton Erickson and the Bateson project or Palo Alto group. This group postulated a theory of the double-bind, as we previously described it, as a mirror image of the therapeutic double-bind or paradox in psychotherapy. The members of the Palo Alto group have published a number of significant books describing the use of paradox. These include Watzlawick, Beavin, and Jackson, 1967; Lederer and Jackson, 1968; Haley, 1963, 1973, 1976; and Watzlawick, Weakland, and Fisch, 1974. In 1967, John Weakland, Paul Watzlawick, Richard Fisch, and Arthur Bodin formed the Brief Therapy Center of the Mental Research Institute under the direction of Richard Fisch. The Brief Therapy Center uses paradoxical interventions in treating a variety of problems.

The other most important precursor of paradoxical psychotherapy was Milton H. Erickson. Erickson's influence on the development of paradox has been somewhat indirect in that most of Erickson's therapeutic work has been presented by Jay Haley. Jay Haley first met Erickson during the second year of the Bateson project. He developed a close relationship with Erickson and in 1973 presented a unique collection of Erickson's therapeutic work. Haley found that Erickson was a master in the use of paradoxes in both hypnosis and psychotherapy. In *Uncommon Therapy* (1973) he described several common paradoxical techniques Erickson used. Basically, Erickson attempted to produce change by relabeling what people do in positive ways. He effected change through implicit and indirect influence rather than using direct methods.

Hypnosis, in general, could be considered a precursor of paradoxical psychotherapy. Even hypnotists less masterful than Erickson employ a variety of paradoxical procedures. Hypnotists use reframing, emphasize the positive, go with resistance, and place the subject in double-binds. In general, a paradoxical injunction is given to a subject by the hypnotist who communicates two levels of messages: 1) Do as I say; 2) don't do as I say but behave spontaneously. The subject adapts to the conflicting set of directives by undergoing a change and behaving in a way described as trance behavior (Haley, 1963, 1973; Andolfi, 1974; Sander, 1974). The hypnotist's techniques are very similar to those of the therapist who first directs his client to do things he can voluntarily do and then requests or communicates an expectation of spontaneous change (Haley, 1973).

Erickson and Rossi (1975) identified a number of double-binds used in hypnosis as well as in therapy. The first involves offering a free choice among comparable alternatives, one of which must be chosen (i.e., "Would you like to go into a trance now or later?"). In a second, rather complex double-bind, a request ostensibly made at the conscious level effects a change at the unconscious or subconscious level (e.g., "If your unconscious wants you to enter a trance, your right hand will lift. Otherwise your left hand will lift.") A third double-bind uses time as a binding agent (e.g., "Do you want to get over that habit this week or next? That may seem too soon. Perhaps you'd like a longer period of time, like three or four weeks?"). The fourth double-bind—the reverse set double-bind—was frequently used by Erickson in enabling patients to reveal material by enjoining them not to. The fifth therapeutic double-bind used by Erickson is the nonsequitur double-bind where he casually inserts a variety of increasingly absurd comments in a binding form. There is a similarity in the content of the alternatives offered but no logical connection (e.g., "Do you wish to take a bath before going to bed, or would you rather put your pajamas on in the bathroom?").

The most recent development in paradoxical psychotherapy has been made by a group of Italian psychiatrists, the Milano group. In a book entitled *Paradox and Counterparadox,* Selvini Palazzoli, Cecchin, Prata, and Boscolo (1978a) adeptly illustrate the use of paradox with families of schizophrenics and other severely psychotic patients.

Paradoxical psychotherapy is still relatively new and has not gained widespread acceptance. As a distinct form of therapy, paradoxical therapy is probably less than 15 years old. In the past five years interest in this approach has certainly mushroomed. Conferences, seminars, journal articles, and books on paradoxical therapy have increased sharply. Unfortunately, there are still many problems with learning how to work paradoxically. Paradoxical psychotherapy has no underlying theory to guide its development and practice. The working principles of the approach have been poorly delineated and there has been little empirical investigation on the process or outcome of this therapy. These issues are the substance of our book. In the next chapter we will begin examining the paradoxical view of human behavior in terms of a dialectic metatheory.

2

Human nature and the paradoxical theory of change

Theories of psychotherapy almost always have some theoretical foundation or accompanying theory of personality (Corsini, 1979). A theory of personality provides a rationale for the system of psychotherapy. The personality theory generally makes explicit assumptions about the nature of man, the structure of personality, and how structures work together or may fail to work together. In some cases, the theory of personality seems to have been developed first, and then the theory of psychotherapy, while in other cases the reverse seems to be true (Hall and Lindzey, 1970). Paradoxical psychotherapy clearly falls in the latter category. In the over 100 articles and books written about this kind of therapy only two works (Watzlawick et al., 1967, 1974) attempt to provide any kind of adequate theoretical explanation. We will review the theoretical basis already available for this approach to therapy and then offer our efforts in grounding this type of therapy in theory.

THE PARADOXICAL THEORY OF CHANGE AND COMMUNICATION

Paradoxical techniques are designed to produce a special kind of change. Watzlawick et al. (1974) discuss two levels of change—first- and second-order change. First-order change refers to change within

18

a given system. In other words, the system itself remains unchanged, while its elements or parts undergo some kind of change. First-order change appears to be linear, stepwise, or mechanistic (Adams, 1977). It is a change in quantity, not quality. First-order change involves using the same problem-solving strategies over and over again. Each new problem is approached mechanically. If the problem resists resolution, more old strategies are used and are usually more vigorously applied. There is either more of a behavior or less of a behavior along some continuum. For example, a father might attempt to deal with his son's chronic misbehavior by using more and more punishment. This approach to the problem reflects the concept of first-order change because the structure of the interactions between the father and son remains constant.

Second-order change refers to a change of the system itself. The system is transformed structurally and/or communicationally. Second-order change tends to be sudden and radical; it represents a quantum jump in the system to a different level of functioning. This type of change is discontinuous and qualitative. It is not logically predictable and often appears abrupt, illogical, and unexpected. Paradoxical interventions produce second-order change, sometimes called paradoxical change (Weeks and Wright, 1979). In the example given for first-order change, the father tried the same solution over and over again. A second-order change solution to the same problem would involve trying something radically different or unexpected, such as encouraging the son to misbehave whenever he thinks his father is feeling sad, or when he thinks his parents might fight.

In the first chapter we pointed out how Adler (1956) believed dialectics served as the theoretical basis for paradoxical therapy. Watzlawick, Weakland, and Fisch (1974) have asserted that their theory of change is also related to dialectics. They summarized this relationship as follows:

> An event _a_ is about to take place, but _a_ is undesirable. Common sense suggests its prevention or avoidance by means of the reciprocal or opposite, i.e., not- _a_ (in accordance with group property _d_), but this would merely result in a first-order change "solution." As long as the solution is sought within this dichotomy of _a_ and not- _a_ , the seeker is caught in an illusion of alternatives and he remains caught whether he

chooses the one or the other alternative. It is precisely this un-questioned illusion that one has to make a choice between a and not- a , that there is no other way out of the dilemma, which perpetuates the dilemma and blinds us to the solution which is available at all times, but which contradicts common sense. The formula of second-order change, on the other hand, is "not- a but also not not- a ". . . . Philosophically the same principle is the basis of Hegelian dialectics with its emphasis on the process that moves from an oscillation between thesis and antithesis to the synthesis transcending this dichotomy (p. 91).

Paradoxical change is also grounded in principles of communica-tion and cybernetics (Wiener, 1948). The key concept is feedback. According to Watzlawick et al. (1967), if in a chain of events a produces b , b produces c , and so on, we are dealing with a linear deterministic system. If, however, c leads back to a , we are dealing with a circular system and a circular system behaves differently from a linear system. In a circular system there are two types of feedback, negative and positive. Negative feedback inhibits change in a system or produces a constant state. This kind of feedback is error-activated, much like the thermostat in a house. Negative feed-back maintains the status quo or homeostasis of living systems. The other type of feedback is positive feedback. This type of feedback op-poses negative feedback in that it promotes change or disequilibrium. It is commonly called deviation-amplifying feedback. Paradoxical injunctions are actually deviation-amplifying or positive feedbacks in-troduced into the system. The deviation-amplifying feedback, if prop-erly conceived, should topple the dysfunctional system of behavior by forcing it to recalibrate.

Foley (1974) has stated that the role of the "identified patient" sometimes represents negative feedback. A child behaving as an identified patient may act out whenever his parents become conflicted in order to prevent the family's dissolution.

Change in a system of behavior always occurs with respect to some degree of homeostasis. The system remains intact through the combi-nation of both positive and negative feedback. The deviation-amplify-ing feedback introduced in a dysfunctional system leads to a second-order change in the system. Positive feedback forces the system to a point where the old rules are experienced as obsolete. At this point the system becomes temporarily confused and attempts to solve the problem by reconstituting itself in a different way. The system changes itself in a qualitative way behaviorally and/or phenomenologically.

A DIALECTICAL THEORY OF PARADOXICAL PSYCHOTHERAPY

Weeks (1977) began to formulate a dialectical approach to psychotherapy and proposed that dialectics would serve as the theoretical foundation for paradoxical therapy. He stated that a dialectical approach to therapy seemed well-justified since the essence of dialectics is change. He also found many consistencies between dialectic theory and the assumptions implicit in the paradoxical theory of change. As we pointed out earlier, Watzlawick et al. (1974) recognized the similarities between their theory of second-order change and Hegelian dialectics.

We have argued that every therapist, either implicitly or explicitly, brings a theory of personality to the therapy room. This theory, like all theories, simplifies and guides the process of therapy. It determines the therapist's style, choice of techniques, and reactions to the expectations for clients. The client is always the client-as-he-appears-through-the-theory. Dialectical theory provides us with an image of man which is congruent with paradoxical therapy. Rychlak (1968, pp. 471–473) offered the clearest conceptualization of the dialectical image of humans. A summary of some of his points follows: a) Persons meet experience with meaningful conceptions or basic premises, and fashion it at least as much as experience fashions them. b) Persons' experiencing of their environment, which frames their understanding, is at heart a search for meaning. c) Persons store information obtained from the past in memory, but they also create meaning for the future by reasoning for the sake of older meaning. d) The mental mechanism for a deliberate creative human act begins in dialectical opposition, which generates at some point an alternative not now realized. e) Once a thought is projected, it takes on the character of a value. f) People can make the possibilities they dream into reality by living them.

This dialectical image stresses internal as well as external contradictions and conflicts. Struggle is an intrinsic part of being human. Development proceeds through the resolution of contradictions and the eventual emergence of new contradictions (Riegel, 1976). This conception of being human is one of an active agent in the world—an agent who creates his/her world and is in turn created by it. Persons are not assumed to possess stable, absolute, or universal traits, qualities, competencies, etc. They are viewed as changeable and forever changing. People frequently seek out disequilibrium rather than equilibrium. They are propelled forward through ever-present internal negations, i.e., they are always becoming that which they are not, and not that which they are.

THE DIALECTICS OF CHANGE AND PARADOXICAL THERAPY

There is a philosophical link between paradoxical therapy and dialectics in that they view change similarly. Change is the essence of dialectics. Unfortunately, many readers may believe reference is being made to the famous triad of thesis, antithesis, and synthesis. Hegel was in fact opposed to the use of these simplistic terms; they misrepresent his philosophy because of their static and mechanical quality. To understand Hegel's theory of change, dialectics must be examined as the study of being. Marcuse (1954) succinctly summarized Hegel's ontology:

> To know what a thing really is, we have to get beyond its immediately given state (S is S) and follow out the process in which it turns into something other than itself (P). In the process of becoming P, however, S still remains S. Its reality is the entire dynamic of its turning into something else and unifying itself with its "other." The dialectical pattern represents, and is thus "the truth of," a world permeated by negativity, a world in which everything is something other than it really is, and in which opposition and contradiction constitute the laws of progress (p. 49).

Buss (1976) summarized change and development as follows:

> Being is defined in terms of Becoming, and Becoming involves negating one's present state. Humanity's inherent nega-

tivity is the source for its development, where those contradictions which result in crisis and which are resolved lead to higher levels of Being (p. 9).

Finally, Bahm's (1970) study of polarity, dialectic, and organicity is the most thorough and extensive ever undertaken. For our present purposes, we will only be concerned with his thinking regarding change and permanence. When change is viewed dialectically, it also involves permanence. Thus, a change-permanence polarity is established involving the recurrence of something; that is, something *is*, then *is not*, and then *is* again. The second occurrence is partly like and partly unlike the first occurrence. That is, there are *both similarities and differences*. For example, as the hand on a clock goes around, it is the same in that it is another round, but it is different in being a *different* round. Thus, the more often the same kind of change occurs, the more permanent it is in one sense, and the more different it is in another sense.

Being, then, is characterized by contradiction, conflict, and the negativity of its existing state. Dialectical change is not a mechanical process but an emergent, spiraling, dynamic process. The essential point is that before any change can occur (negation, negation of negation), a thing must paradoxically become what it is first.

This theory reinforces the idea that negativity is an essential part of human existence and change. It is similar to the concept of positive feedback in cybernetics. For example, the therapist may set the dialectics of growth back in motion by giving a paradoxical directive or by prescribing the symptom. This directive has the effect of setting up a therapeutic dilemma; i.e., a pragmatic paradox does not give a person any choice. The therapist is telling the client to remain the same in one sense while implying change in another sense. The directive helps to exaggerate one pole of the dialectical polarity of change-permanence, increasing positive feedback and perhaps promoting awareness of what one is doing, feeling, or thinking.

The pragmatic paradox changes the meaning attributed to the symptom. In general, what was heretofore perceived to be out of one's control is brought under conscious control by the directive—a second-order change. Additionally, a new kind of feedback is added to the system because each time the symptom occurs, it is because the person wanted it to occur. Herein lies the type of change described by Bahm (1970)—something recurring. Each time the symptom occurs, it is *both* something the *same* and something *different*. The symptom is no longer what it was, because it is now under conscious control (not-a); but it is also *not* not-a because its appearance is that of the original symptom (a). The symptom becomes both "not-a but also *not* not-a," and the person is no longer trapped in the first-order solution.

Stanton (1981b) has recently developed a theory to explain how paradoxical interventions work. His theory is similar to our more philosophical theory in that he stresses polarizations or dialectical forces operating in family systems. He uses the concept of "compression" to explain paradox. He has observed that dysfunctional family systems vacillate in cyclical form between an overly close, undifferentiated, fused state to a disintegrating, expansive state with their families of origin. The paradoxical intervention compresses the nuclear and extended families together, producing an explosive counterreaction. However, the therapist blocks the counterreaction and its aftereffects, producing a change in the system. It is not clear whether Stanton would apply this theory to each member of the same family system, although it would seem to be a logical step to do so.

Many psychotherapists have failed to appreciate dialectical insights into personality and psychotherapy (Rychlak, 1973). Perhaps this failure has taken place in Western civilization because we have not come to terms with the coexistence of opposites in ourselves as sources of growth. Many of us lack the synergistic ability to see the opposites in life as meaningfully related. Maslow (1968) was one of the first psychologists to recognize the importance of recognizing and transcending dichotomies. In fact, Maslow felt this was one of the most outstanding qualities of the self-actualized individual. More recently, Riegel (1973) stated that there is a fifth period of cognitive development in which contradictions are appreciated and used as a source of growth. Paradoxical therapists seem to operate at this fifth level of cognitive development.

THE CONTEXT OF PARADOXICAL THERAPY

Dialectical psychology, like humanistic psychology, attempts to understand "the whole." It strives to discover the complex network of connections among things. In keeping with this view, much of the recent critical work in dialectical psychology has examined the relationships among various social, historical, economic, and psychological phenomena. The most sophisticated scheme for examining the dialectics of change has been proposed by Riegel (1975, 1976). He views human development as proceeding simultaneously along four independent dimensions: a) inner-biological; b) individual-psychological; c) cultural-sociological; and d) outer-physical. The first two dimensions refer to "inner" dialectics while the last two refer to "outer" dialectics. According to Riegel, when asynchronization occurs within or between dimensions, a development crisis occurs. Furthermore, a crisis is resolved by synchronizing the dimensions.

Clients seeking therapy are often, perhaps always, experiencing asynchronization between or within dimensions. In short, what we normally refer to as psychopathology or problems in living could actually be developmental problems requiring a "sychronizing reinterpretation" (Riegel, 1976). The therapist's task is to help make this synchronizing reinterpretation. Unfortunately, Riegel never offered any definition of what he meant by this term, nor did he describe any way to facilitate this process. A synchronizing reinterpretation seems to involve at least two components. First, the various dimensions need to be considered. Usually, two or more dimensions are out of synchrony and the dimension which is almost always involved is the cultural-sociological dimension. This means that people do not live in a vacuum, problems do not occur in a vacuum, and treatment should not occur in a vacuum. People live in a social context, and that context is generally their family. In a family system, behavior is not the product of simple cause-effect or bidirectional causality. The behavior of a system is the product of a complex series of transactions. Causality is circular. Because most asynchronization takes place in the context of one's family, it could be argued that marital and family therapies are the most direct forms of intervention. Recent research has demonstrated the effectiveness of the approach (Guerin, 1976; Gurman and Kniskern, 1981) and has shown how treating an individual in a vacuum for a marital problem may produce deterioration in the marriage (Gurman and Kniskern, 1978).

The theory of causality we have been referring to is not new in the family literature. It is based on general systems theory. Systems theory was founded by the biologist Ludwig von Bertalanffy (1968).

He believed systems were more than just the sum of their parts; they were, in fact, "complexes of elements standing in interaction" (1968, p. 33). Von Bertalanffy (1968) believed the family was an open system of behavior because of the input of information from outside the system. As such, the family has all the properties of an open system: wholeness, relationship, and equifinality. Understanding these properties helps us conceptualize the family.

The first property of an open system is *wholeness*. A system is more than just a collection of parts. It is a set of interdependent parts operating as a unit. *Relationship* is the second property. A system cannot be analyzed by examining the parts in isolation. By definition the system can only be understood in terms of the relationships existing among its parts. The parts are defined by each other (e.g., husband—wife). The third property is *equifinality*. This concept refers to the possibility that the same problem may be manifested in many different ways or at different levels. Hence, the problem may be assessed in different ways. It is the content of the problem which changes, not the process. For example, a family may be locked in a power struggle. The members may disagree over work, school, money, children, or sex. The content of their problem is relatively unimportant. It is how and with whom they disagree that is most relevant and this can be determined by observing any disagreement among various parts of the system. The process aspects of the system's behavior would also reveal which dimensions are asynchronized. Assessment and intervention from a dialectic standpoint must be systemic—each of the four dimensions of development must be considered.

The second component deals with the "how" of making synthesizing reinterpretations. According to Riegel (1976), problems occur among and between the dimensions because shifts cannot be made in synchrony. The person gets stuck in a developmental crisis and usually attempts to get unstuck through the application of first-order change solutions. Yet, the system requires a second-order solution, because it must move to a qualitatively different level of functioning. A developmental crisis means there is a difficulty moving to a different stage in the family life cycle. Old strategies have become obsolete; new strategies are required. Haley (1973) and Watzlawick et al. (1967, 1974) have both presented numerous examples of the application of paradoxical methods in making second-order shifts in the life cycle. Weeks and Wright (1979) have developed a dialectical theory for the family life cycle and demonstrated how paradoxes are essential in understanding development and in producing change in dysfunctional systems of behavior. This theory is based on the assumption that family life cycle or developmental crises are resolved through second-order change solutions. In most cases the family can make these changes on its own. When family members fail to find second-order solutions and seek help, the therapist can use paradoxes to help synchronize the dimensions of development.

SYMPTOMS

Every theory of psychotherapy gives special attention to behaviors called "symptoms." Each theory defines what is meant by "a symptom" and offers a treatment for "symptoms." Most theories of psychopathology and psychotherapy have described symptoms in strictly negative terms. The symptom has traditionally been construed as that behavior which is alien, bizarre, uncontrollable, and representative of an externalized weakness. The symptom has been construed as an enemy to its bearer and to the psychotherapist. Thus, the task of the client and the therapist has been to resist, defeat, or "cure" the symptom.

Paradoxical psychotherapy considers the symptom to be a friend. In treating a symptom as a friend, one would embrace and cooperate with it. One would join the symptom rather than flee from it, and learn from it in the same way one learns from carrying on a dialogue with a friend. Before examining the symptom from the viewpoint of paradoxical psychotherapy, we will review the symptom in terms of the three major paradigms of psychology in order to establish a historical context.

In the psychoanalytic paradigm, symptoms represent unconscious conflicts. According to Rychlak (1973), the analytic therapist is really asking, "What two antithetical intentions does this symptom symbolize?" (p. 65). The development of symptoms was described by Freud in terms of a three-stage model (Rychlak, 1973). In stage I, an id wish is opposed by the ego (counterwish). It could involve a son's lustful but repressed feelings for his mother (unresolved oedipal complex).

Then a primal repression takes place which results in fixation. With the advent of the genital stage there is an increase in libidinal energy, which revitalizes the id's previously repressed wishes. The repressed thoughts can no longer be effectively countered by the ego. In order to deal with the two conflicting wishes, another form of expression is found. The wishes are converted into bodily or neurotic symptoms. Freud stated, "a symptom is a sign of and a substitute for instinctual satisfaction which has remained in abeyance; it is a consequence of the process of repression" (1959). The symptom is treated by "working through" the repressed material, using analytic techniques such as free association, dream analysis, transference, etc. (Havens, 1973).

The second major paradigm of psychology to develop was behaviorism. The behaviorist views the symptom as a maladaptive learned response. Unlike the psychoanalytic construction of symptoms, behavioral theory posits no meaning or function for the symptom. The symptom has no reference to unconscious conflicts; nor does it symbolize something else. The behaviorists view symptoms in four ways (Calhoun, 1977). First, the symptom may be a behavior deficit or excess. It may also signify an inappropriate relationship between a stimulus and a response (inappropriate stimulus control) such that a response (symptom) occurs without the appropriate stimulus, or a stimulus fails to elicit the appropriate response. Finally, a behavior (symptom) could be reinforced by an inadequate reinforcing system —one which produces behavior different from that of the statistically average person. Behavioral treatment focuses directly on the symptom. A number of behavioral strategies might be used to facilitate the removal of the symptom. Behaviorists clearly view the symptom as an enemy and strive to extinguish it.

The third major paradigm to emerge was the existential-humanistic. This paradigm is less unified, coherent, and systematic than the behavioral or perhaps the analytic paradigms. It is, therefore, more difficult, if not impossible, to generalize about the way symptoms are viewed. Existential-humanistic psychologists have been less concerned with symptoms and more concerned with the way in which clients prevent or block themselves from actualizing themselves in terms of self-acceptance, honesty, and finding meaning in life.

Rogers is perhaps the most representative of the humanistic school of psychology. According to him (1951), the major existential symptom is anxiety. An individual will become threatened when his self-concept does not match or is incongruent with the objective data. The anxiety is the response (the symptom) resulting from the perceived threat. The individual then attempts to deny or distort the incongruence by using defense mechanisms. Existential psychologists have been more accepting of the symptom as some form of communication about the person. Binswanger, for example, sees the symptom as a form of communication about the individual's existential situation (1958, p. 213). Further, the symptom is an escape or "way out" of a life situation for an individual (1963, p. 462).

Of all the existential psychologists, Frankl has been the most accepting of symptoms. In fact, he used the symptom as a friend through his technique of "paradoxical intention." He theorized that neuroses were caused by feedback mechanisms whereby anticipatory anxiety was responded to symptomatically. He stated, "a given symptom is responded to by a phobia, the phobia triggers the symptom, and the symptom, in turn, reinforces the phobia" (1959, p. 130). The only way to cut the vicious circle was to apply paradoxical intention. Existential psychologists, unlike humanistic psychologists, have also been more inclined to see the symptom as part of a social nexus. Boss (1963) noted that "no psychopathological symptom will ever be fully and adequately understood unless it is conceived of as a disturbance in the texture of social relationships of which a given human existence fundamentally consists, and that all psychiatric diagnoses are basically only sociological statements" (p. 56).

The most interesting aspect of this brief review is that symptoms are being construed in increasingly friendly ways. Many existential-humanistic psychologists see symptoms in the same way that paradoxical therapists see symptoms. Perhaps this change has occurred because psychotherapists have realized that the ascription of a negative label tends to perpetuate the behavior through the self-fulfilling prophecy (Rosenthal, 1973). The label also influences how the client behaves, as well as other people's perception of and reactions to the label-bearer. In addition, while the label may pertain to only one aspect of the client's behavior, labels usually generalize to the individual as a whole. Thus, a child who is blind is said to be a "blind child." His assets are then ignored or distorted in light of this generalization. Negative labels generalize not only to the whole of the individual, but in many cases to the system in which the individual lives. If an individual is labeled as schizophrenic, then it is almost automatically assumed that he has a "schizophrenogenic" mother and that a certain type of pathogenic parental interaction exists.

In the paradox paradigm, the symptom is seen as the vehicle of change, since its function has been one of precluding change in the family system. The symptom is that which makes change possible. In short, the symptom is prescribed using a paradoxical approach. The client may be told to continue or exaggerate the symptom. There are, of course, many variations in how the symptom may be used as a means of change, which are discussed later in this book.

Aside from Watzlawick et al. (1974), another of the earliest paradoxical therapists to develop a theory of symptoms was Milton Erickson (Haley, 1967), as noted in the previous chapter. Erickson viewed the symptom as being the way the patient chooses to communicate with the therapist. Therefore, Erickson would accept the symptom but define the symptom in such a way that change could occur. Further, Erickson was not concerned with the "roots" of the symptom in the past. He did not try to explain the dynamics of the symptom to the patient. Moreover, Erickson departed from the analytic idea of symptom substitution. He found that if a symptom was removed, the patient would not substitute another symptom; in fact, removal of one symptom often led to the recovery from still other symptoms. Indeed, Erickson would often set up or define a therapeutic situation such that one symptom could be used to cure another symptom. In addition, the symptom was not seen as a psychological entity but as a way to deal with other people, including oneself. Thus, Erikson adopted a systems approach. The symptom had roots in the person's social network. Erickson's ideas, especially his ideas about how symptoms should be viewed, have been immensely influential in the development of a paradoxical psychotherapy.

THE DIALECTICS OF SYMPTOMS

Symptoms need to be understood dialectically in terms of bipolarity, opposition, or contradiction (Rychlak, 1976). From the preceding review, it is clear that symptoms may be viewed either negatively or positively, as friends or enemies. It was shown in the previous section how symptoms have primarily been viewed in negative terms. The major implication of dialectics for labeling is that the assessor change the emphasis from finding and perhaps inventing "pathology" or weaknesses in clients to focusing on strengths. When a client is labeled in only negative terms, which often happens in psychiatric or psychological reports, we have a biased view of human nature. A dialectical view of symptomatology means that our priorities become rebalanced. One must ask oneself, "What are this client's assets as well as his liabilities?" and, "How have the symptoms been adaptive for the client?"

Learning to find and emphasize the positive is only the first step in a paradoxical approach. The second step is learning to reframe or relabel symptoms in positive terms. Relabeling can be one means of producing positive therapeutic outcome. A positive label given to some disturbing behavior gives a person a sense of control over that behavior, in addition to an expectational set for positive change. Using one of Landfield's (1975) examples, a client who is confused and feeling even more helpless because of his confusion might be told that his confusion is a breakdown in preparation for new growth. This statement would have the effect of helping the client accept his confusion so that he is freed to work on his specific problem. He would also expect to change in some positive way.

According to Feldman (1976), relabeling is derived from the paradox paradigm. Weeks (1977) has argued that the paradox paradigm can be grounded in a dialectical theory of change. Thus, a dialectical theory of change also underlies relabeling. The only difference between relabeling and paradoxical therapy (or paradoxical injunctions) is that the former is implicit and the latter is explicit. In other words, a paradoxical directive may involve telling a client quite explicitly to do more of the same or remain unchanged. Relabeling carries the same message, but it is implicit. This is the case because any so-called undesirable behavior given a positive label must be desirable. For example, relabeling confusion as preparation for growth gives the client permission to be confused. In either case, there is the implication that the reinforcement of what the client wants to change is a vehicle of change.

SYMPTOMS DERIVED FROM AN UNDIFFERENTIATED FAMILY SYSTEM

L'Abate (1976) developed a theory of family functioning and dys-functioning which provided one way of conceptualizing the symptom dialectically within a family system. A major aspect of his theory was the postulate of self-differentiation, or how one is defined vis-à-vis other members of the family. Dysfunctionality or symptomatology oc-curs in the context of an undifferentiated family system, that is, one which is characterized by digitality—sameness or oppositeness, sym-biosis or autism. Sameness in a family system means that everyone is expected to be just like everyone else. Oppositeness refers to family members' being opposite from others such that if one member of the family says or does something, another member will say or do just the opposite. Symbiosis and autism are more extreme forms of attach-ment or distance because the self lacks sufficient resources to define itself.

The type of thinking present in an undifferentiated family is digital (Wilden, 1972). Digital thinking is "either-or" thinking. Thus, in an undifferentiated family, members will be viewed either as "with us" (sameness) or "against us" (oppositeness). For example, in the Smith family all the male members might be expected to become doctors. If one member decides he does not want to be a doctor, the family sys-tem, as well as the individual himself, would tend to define him as "not a doctor" instead of any of the other things he might be. It is likely the family member would engage in behaviors which prove to his family and himself that he is not going to be just like them. In such a system, there can be no negotiation or compromise. Undifferentiated family members lack clearly defined, autonomous selves. They can-not accept personal responsibility, nor can they act independently. Unlike differentiated family members, they cannot be both similar and different from members of their family, and, thus, fully integrated both as individuals and as members of a family unit.

In an undifferentiated family system, the function of the "symp-tom" is to keep the system unchanged by maintaining the polarization present in the system or furthering the system's either/or logic. Polari-zation may occur, with members assuming stances at the same end of the continuum (e.g., sameness or oppositeness), or members may assume stances at opposite ends of the continuum, i.e., members are opposite from others who are hooked on sameness. The symptom may take any one of many forms. It may appear as a specific individual symptom, such as a phobia, or it may appear as an issue within the family related to sex, money, household responsibilities, etc. As long as the family focuses on someone's symptoms or an external issue, no one needs to change, since it is others who must change. In a system such as this, each member helps the other avoid dealing with himself or herself through some specific symptom or a polarizing issue.

It is no mystery that such a coalition is difficult to break therapeutically. Stanton (1981b) has reviewed the strategic (systems/paradoxical) view of dysfunctions:

> The strategic view of dysfunctions can be summarized as follows: 1) "symptoms" can be viewed simply as particular types of behavior functioning as homeostatic mechanisms which regulate family transactions (Jackson, 1957, 1965); 2) problems in the identified patient cannot be considered apart from the *context* in which they occur and the *functions* which they serve; 3) an individual cannot be expected to change unless his family system changes (Haley, 1962); 4) "insight" per se is not a necessary prerequisite for change. Such a view is radically different from and discontinuous with individually- or intrapsychically-oriented cause-and-effect explanations of dysfunctional behavior (p. 365).

Andolfi (1980) has also pointed out the paradox of change for families. He emphasized the "hidden agenda" of the family that asks for help. The family requests change while at the same time conveying messages such as: a) Help us stay the same; b) help us (me) get rid of the symptom without changing anything else; c) help us with the identified patient but leave the rest of us alone. The paradox is to remove the symptom from the family without changing the family from which the symptom derives.

BEYOND PARADOX; DIALECTICAL SCHEMATA

This chapter has been based on the assumption that paradoxical psychotherapists are able to conceptualize and treat problems dialectically. The mere idea of dialectical thinking is new to most psychologists. The concept of dialectical thinking first appeared in 1973 in a paper called "Dialectic operations: The final period of cognitive development" authored by Klaus Riegel. Riegel's paper generated a great deal of debate among developmental psychologists, especially with regard to Piaget's work.

Theoretical papers on dialectics flourished but none of them attempted to explicate the cognitive-psychological organization of dialectical operations. If the paradoxical therapist is thinking dialectically, as Weeks (1977) has argued, then a detailed analysis of dialectical operations will help to clarify and guide paradoxical intervention. Basseches (1980) conducted an empirical investigation of dialectical thinking, leading to support for a theoretical set of dialectical schemata. Through the coding of 27 interviews he found that college professors use more dialectical schemata than seniors, who in turn use more of these schemata than freshmen.

Basseches defined dialectical thinking as thinking which looks for and recognizes instances of dialectic. Dialectic was generally defined in terms of an emphasis on change, wholeness, and internal relations. His 24 dialectical schemata were derived from this conception of dialectical thinking. The dialectical schemata describe steps in dialectic analysis, the dialectic of epistemology, and the movement of one's thought.

The 24 schemata were divided into four categories shown below:

A. *Motion-oriented schemata*

> 1) Thesis-antithesis-synthesis movement in thought
>
> 2) Affirmation of the primacy of motion
>
> 3) Recognition and description of thesis-antithesis-synthesis movement
>
> 4) Recognition of correlativity of a thing and its other
>
> 5) Recognition of ongoing interaction as a source of movement
>
> 6) Affirmation of the practical or active character of knowledge
>
> 7) Avoidance or exposure of objectification, hypostatization, and reification

8) Understanding events or situations as moments (of development) of a process

B. *Form-oriented schemata*

9) Location of an element of phenomenon with the whole(s) of which it is a part

10) Description of a whole (system, form) in structural, functional, or equilibrational terms

11) Assumption of contextual relativism

C. *Relationship-oriented schemata*

12) Assertion of the existence of relations, the limits of separation and the value of relatedness

13) Criticism of multiplicity, subjectivism, and pluralism

14) Description of a two-way reciprocal relationship

15) Assertion of internal relations

D. *Meta-formal schemata*

16) Location (for description of the process of emergence) of contradictions or sources of disequilibrium within a system (form) or between a system (form) and external forces or elements which are antithetical to the system's (form's) structure.

17) Understanding the resolution of disequilibrium or contradiction in terms of a notion of transformation in developmental direction

18) Relating value to a) movement in developmental direction and/or b) stability through developmental movement

19) Evaluative comparison of forms (systems)

20) Attention to problems of coordinating systems (forms) in relation

21) Description of open self-transforming systems

22) Description of qualitative change as a result of quantitative change within a form

23) Criticism of formalism based on the interdependence of form and content

24) Multiplication of perspectives as a concreteness-preserving approach to inclusiveness. *

The first category describes motion-oriented schemata. These schemata deal with the process of change—how change occurs. Our discussion of the paradoxical theory of change and dialectics represents some of the ideas within this category. The second category is form-oriented schemata. These schemata emphasize wholes or context. Our discussion of the contextualization of problems or symptoms reflects the application of this category. The third category is relationship-oriented schemata. These schemata direct us toward the interactive and constituitive nature of relationships. The term constitutive relationship refers to the fact that the relationship plays a role in making the members of the relationship what they are, while the term interactive refers to the reciprocal influence they exert on each other. This category relates to the dynamics or transactions within a system. This category has not been explicated in our discussion, just as the transaction between and among family members has been poorly researched (Kantor and Lehr, 1975). The fourth category consists of meta-formal schemata. This category is difficult to grasp because it was designed to integrate the "relationships among forms and transformations through forms, as well as the process of form construction" (Basseches, 1980, p. 407)—in other words, the change of one form into another rather than change within a form. A change through forms is asserted to be a developmental transformation associated with greater inclusiveness, differentiation, and integration. This description of the meta-formal level is equivalent to the idea of second-order change and is reflected in our discussion of the synchronization of dimensions in helping systems move beyond developmental crisis.

---

*From "Dialectical schemata: A framework for the empirical study of the development of dialectical thinking" by M. Basseches, *Human Development*, 1980, *23*, 400-421. Copyright 1980 by S. Karger, A. G. Basel. Reprinted by permission.

Our application of these dialectical schemata is obviously primitive. We have taken a first step but the real benefit may be derived when these schemata are applied to the study of systems both theoretically/ clinically and empirically. The dialectical schemata provide a philosophical and pragmatic framework for studying systems which seems to be congruent with the paradoxical approach to therapy. The hope for the future is that these schemata will take us beyond our current view of systems and the paradoxes needed to change their forms.

3

The dialectics
of psychopathology

In the previous chapter a dialectical framework was used in examining the nature of "symptoms" and the need for a contextual approach to psychopathology and therapy. The purpose of this chapter is to expand those ideas and formulate a model of pathology based not on negatives, but on positives. In general, psychopathology has been viewed in terms of negative antecedents. There has been little, if any, attempt to postulate a positive basis for pathology. The basis of pathology is an important question and one that can be usefully explored within a dialectical framework. Discovering a positive antecedent to pathology may help therapists conceptualize and intervene in more appropriate ways. This investigation begins with a historical analysis of psychopathology. The scheme employed for conceptualizing psychopathology closely follows the three levels of organization proposed by Dewey and Bentley (1949). This evolutionary scheme consists of three major phases: a) action; b) interaction; and c) transaction.

Self-action: Where things are viewed as acting under their own powers.
Interaction: Where thing is balanced against thing in causal connection.
Transaction: Where systems of description and naming are

employed to deal with aspects and phases of action, without final attribution to "elements" or other presumptively detachable or independent "entities," "essences," or "realities," and without isolation of presumptively detachable "relations" from such detachable "elements" (p. 108).

Historically, pathology was first viewed as being mythically determined; that is, its "cause" was attributed to abstract origins like the "gods" or supernatural phenomena. In other words, the pathological behavior erupted entirely on its own without any apparent external provocation. It appeared by its own power. Next pathology was seen to be related to some definite contextual factors such as the environment or other people. An external element of causation was called into play. This conception gave rise to such well-known terms as "psychobiological" and "social" in the area of abnormal psychology. While pathological behavior was regarded as occurring in relation to other systems, each system was considered independently, and the causes of behavior were believed to be *unidirectional*.

Finally, we have a conception of psychopathology which depicts behavior to be the functional outcome of historial, intentional, and contextual exchanges, which must be considered within the context of their being observed and evaluated by an "outsider." That is, the observer's biases, interests, and psychodynamics must be considered as part of the system of causative behavior and as part of the explanation of the behavior of others. All parts of this system are interdependent; one behavior affects and is affected by all other parts of the system. This final conception is transactional because it does not describe unidirectional behavior, but *multidirectional* behavior.

Each of these conceptions of psychopathology relates not only to notions of action, interaction, and transaction, but also to three additional psychological ideas, namely, a) innateness, b) inability, and c) protectiveness. Each of these ideas and its relatedness to the conception of psychopathology we have discussed will now be drawn out in greater detail, bearing in mind the fact that, although there is considerable overlap among the ideas presented here, history is a continuous rather than a discrete process. Older ideas become incorporated into newer ideas. Inasmuch as this is the case, each idea represents a paradigmatic change in viewing psychopathology.

ACTION—PATHOLOGY AS INNATENESS

The most primitive conceptions of pathology included two causes
—spiritual causes and inner causes. The spiritual origins of pathological behavior derived from demons, goblins, gods, goddesses, supernatural influences, etc. Inner causes were either psychological or
physiological and included such etiological factors as pride, jealousy,
shame, body humors, and the brain (Clark, 1973). The most primitive of these two conceptions might be termed magico-religious or
supernatural. In this view, pathology was explained by abstract, inde-
finable, and unspecified origins. This view predates written history. It
stemmed from primitive man's animistic view of the universe—a view
which held that natural events, both in nature and man, had human
motivations. Thus, if a primitive man became ill (mentally or physically), he would attribute the cause to one of his enemies or some malevolent invisible god. Inner causes were later recognized as causes of
mental illness. One of the earliest accounts of this notion is from Egypt
around 1900 B.C. It was held that the displacement or "starvation" of
the uterus caused morbid states in women.

The turning point in the history of psychopathology was the Classi-
cal era. For the first time, mental illness was conceived without its
causes being attributed to demons. This period gave rise to primitive
organic and psychological conceptions of pathology, some of which
have carried over into modern psychiatry.

Much of modern psychiatry also falls within the framework of "action." The objective-descriptive school of psychiatry emphasizes symptoms and treats mental illness as a physical illness with the natural
course of a disease. Psychoanalysis emphasizes the importance of
conflict and dissociations, unconscious motivation, wishes and fanta-
sies, and childhood events (Havens, 1973). Hence, psychopathology is intrinsic to the individual, either biologically or psychologically.

The modes of therapy for the conceptions of pathology presented
above confirm and reflect the idea of pathology as innateness. The
earliest forms of treatment for madness included techniques ranging
over a wide spectrum, including trephining, incantations, therapy by
amulet, even numbers, charms, herbs, leeches, laying-on-of-hands,
faith-healing, exorcism, and all forms of physical punishment. The
"therapist" was usually a medicine man, magician, or priest who was

believed to possess supernatural powers. Therapy in the later phase
—the Greek period—took the form of incantations which Plato described as "beautiful logic" and also included proper diet and rest. In
the latest part of this phase, modern psychiatry developed procedures
such as drug therapy, psychosurgery, electroshock, and psychoanalysis.

In summary, the action model, or innateness model, attributes
pathology to abstract, imagined, or hypothesized internal states that
essentially predetermine the individual to act crazy.

INTERACTION—PATHOLOGY AS INTERACTIONAL INABILITY

The next major view of pathology grew from an emerging human-
ism and advances in psychological theory. In the previous view,
pathology was equated to "sickness" or "possession," which meant
the individual was not responsible for his or her behavior. He or she
simply could not act otherwise. The current interactional view has as
an underlying assumption the idea of "free will," personal responsibility, or at the very least the assumption that people can act otherwise
under certain conditions. Pathological behavior is conceived as the
inability to behave in a "better" or "healthier" way as a result of historical and contextual factors. To be more specific, this view is commonly
referred to in four major ways—the moral, behavioral, existential,
and social models of psychiatry.

According to Maher (1966), adherence to a moral model leads one
to question the act of labeling a person to be mentally ill. Labeling a
person turns him into an impersonal "thing," diverts attention away
from his needs and values, and robs him of his sense of personal responsibility. In this model pathology is represented as problems in living. The main proponent of this model is Thomas Szasz.

The behavioral model holds that pathology is the result of a learning process. One is unable to act in a healthier way because he has
been conditioned not to do so by other people. This model is based
on a large body of experimental literature and is not specific to any
one psychologist. The definition of pathological behavior in this
model is usually based on some statistical norm.

The existential school of psychiatry emphasizes the role of feelings and emotions resulting from man's lived experience in the world. It emphasizes man's feelings of meaninglessness, isolation, loneliness, and aloneness in an absurd world. It also emphasizes how the "other" may rob us of our freedom.

Finally, social psychiatry focuses on the role of societal factors in the individual's life history. It focuses on both the individual and society. Pathology lies in both individual and social processes.

While these models and schools make different assumptions about the nature of man, it is clear they all view pathology at the interactional level; that is, two independent systems come into contact—one affecting the other. The direction of influence is generally seen as unidirectional; e.g., a mother influences her child to act in crazy ways, or social processes influence an individual to behave in deviant ways.

The treatment procedures following from these models and schools are well-known and include individual and group therapy. The dominant therapeutic situation is one in which the patient is treated in a one-to-one encounter or with persons who are strangers. The patient's relational network, his significant others, are generally not included in treatment and, in fact, often become viewed as enemies. In short, the patient is treated in a *vacuum*.

A DIALECTICAL THEORY OF PSYCHOPATHOLOGY

The transactional view holds that psychopathology occurs in a context, and that context is the family. Psychopathology is a multi-person event. The behavior of each individual influences others and is in turn influenced by others in a circular rather than a linear fashion. These ideas are commonplace in theories of family therapy. These theories are usually called systems theories rather than transactional theories (Foley, 1974).

Dialectics stresses not only the importance of context in studying pathology but the place of opposites in understanding how problems emerge. Watzlawick et al. (1974) applied dialectic theory in explaining the nature of problems. According to them, if *a* represents a problem, then for most people *not-a* represents a solution. For example, if an individual is depressed, then the solution is to cheer the person up. The solution is seen as the opposite of the problem. The individual caught in this situation is in a double-bind—not the kind of double-bind that is usually described, but what we call a meta double-bind. In a double-bind one is trapped between two unacceptable alternatives which can be stated explicitly. In a meta double-bind the individual is bound to a frame of reference in which the solution cannot be described because it lies outside the frame of reference being used.

In this situation, the individual is bound to one frame of reference because the rules of problem solution are linear and immutable. The individual believes the solution is more or less of same behavior, a change in quantity not quality. The situation is more difficult if this rule is shared by all the members of the person's social network, including therapists. In fact, the therapist has as much power as anyone to lock a system into this rule forever.

The purpose of the rule of problem solution is obvious. It guides the individual and others in dealing with problems. Like other rules, it serves to protect the individual. Unfortunately, a rule which binds a person to one frame of reference does not work. It was pointed out earlier how second-order solutions were needed to make life-cycle changes. The application of a first-order solution would not allow development to proceed normally. In a family system, the rule of problem solution is designed to help regulate the system in its growth. Once gained, it has a protective function.

Selvini Palazzoli et al. (1978a) have observed that pathological systems adhere rigidly to solutions which maintain their homeostatis. These systems of behavior appear powerless to change themselves. They have theorized that *the power is only in the rules of the game which cannot be changed by the people involved in it* (p. 6). Their position is the same as ours, only stated differently. Their statements also point out how individuals trapped in the game act under the illusion of power. They believe they have the power to find the solution in the present frame of reference. Selvini Palazzoli et al. also suggest that families may actually be powerless as long as they are bound to one game or frame of reference.

This theory of problem solution or pathology is highly abstract.

Their basic premise is that individuals use a fixed linear rule of problem solution which has a protective function. If this theory is to be successful then it must be concretized.

One way of elaborating this theory is to extend a model of family pathology based on Karpman's (1968) drama triangle. In the drama triangle family members become bound to the three roles of Persecutor, Rescuer, and Victim. These roles may shift rapidly for varying periods of time, i.e., the Victim becomes a Rescuer or Persecutor. This triangle demonstrates how the rules (roles) have the power and how there is no escape.

When family members become ensnared in the drama triangle, there is only one set of rules to play by. They cannot change the rules of the game. When they attempt to solve the problem of being locked in these roles, they find themselves shifting or changing roles within the triangle. The victim may, for example, feel the solution to being in a one-down position is to do *not-a* or become a Persecutor. While the triangle has many destructive properties, it is itself homeostatic. The members of the triangle are locked together, which preserves the system. In the case of a three-person family, the identified patient (child) may act as a safety valve for the parents' hostility toward each other. If the game were to change, the parents might separate. Hence, the triangle insures survival of the system. Let us look closely at these roles.

Rescuer

The role of Rescuer seems to be a particularly feminine role; however, it is not limited strictly to that sex. In this role selflessness, generosity, and cooperation are emphasized. The Rescuer is one who helps others at her own expense. The process of rescuing may be injurious not only to oneself but to the person rescued as well. For example, a father may continually save his son from conflicts with the law. This will only serve to reinforce his son's behavior by keeping him in the role of Victim. The son's payoff may be that this is the only way he can obtain attention from his parents. Thus, rescuing serves to keep one in a "one-up, I'm O.K." position and places the person rescued in a "one-down, I'm not O.K." position.

Persecutor

According to Steiner (1974), the role of Persecutor emerges from a Rescuer-Victim transaction. The new roles are those of Persecutor-Victim. This change in roles may occur as a result of two processes. First, a person (Rescuer) may attempt to help someone (Victim) who is not helping himself. This attempt usually results in the Rescuer's failure to give help (rescue), which in turn produces anger or frustration. This anger will manifest itself toward the Victim in a persecuting stance. Secondly, each time a Victim is rescued by a Rescuer, he is being placed in a one-down, powerless position. Over time, being forced into this kind of position may result in anger, thus leading the Victim to take a Persecutor position with regard to his would-be Rescuer.

The training ground for the Persecutor role is the nuclear family. In the nuclear family, it is the father who commonly displays this role and transmits it to his children through modeling. He determines what is "right" and "wrong," "good" and "bad," and "correct" and "incorrect," and then exercises his power as judge by deciding what punishment is appropriate when his "law" is violated. Silverman (1975) discussed a particular personality type, the victimizer, whose persecuting stance is determined by a need for control and also a need for constant justification of his own actions so that he can represent his actions to be "good" and "correct."

Victim

The role of Victim is played by a person who cooperates or colludes with a Persecutor and/or Rescuer. By refusing or failing to overcome his own situation, he chooses a one-down position. This selection may occur because the Victim is relatively powerless as compared to the Persecutor or Rescuer. Oftentimes the Victim in a family is the child. Victimization may also occur because it is sometimes easy and inviting to let others take control. One does not have to make decisions or accept personal responsibility when controlled externally.

The Victim is not as powerless as one might imagine. There may be a great deal of power in powerlessness. The Victim may acquire the attention, effort, and even the money of many Rescuers. The Victim may manipulate the system in ways that bring all these payoffs and may eventually gain enough power to assume the role of Persecutor.

Most clinical research on the Victim role has been centered around the concept of scapegoating. This research may be used to support our thesis that pathology from a transactional viewpoint is a means of protection, survival, and sameness. Specifically, pathology as protectiveness serves to maintain the nuclear family intact either actually or in the eyes of the family.

The Scapegoat (Victim) as Family Protector

Scapegoating is a concept commonly found in texts on family theory and therapy. It has been argued that by assuming the role of "sick," "crazy," or scapegoat, the identified patient is protecting the family system from having to deal with itself (Ackerman, 1968; Haley, 1963; Vogel and Bell, 1961). Furthermore, Vogel and Bell (1961) have asserted that the role of the scapegoat is to stabilize tensions in the family and to help it to maintain its solidarity. The scapegoat may also serve other similar functions.

First, scapegoating may mask marital discord. The tension between the parents may be redirected toward or discharged to a child without the parents realizing that the problem is theirs. Secondly, the scapegoat may be used by the parents for their acting-out of stored hostility and covert dependence. On a deeper level, scapegoating may interlock with the unresolved conflicts of separation and maturation the parents experienced with their families of origin. Finally, the cooperative scapegoat may have the covert approval of the family as a "good" and loyal family member. In any event, scapegoating is an attempt to "balance" the system.

Haley (1963) also discussed the protective functions of scapegoating between the mates. He maintained that scapegoating between mates was the primary obstacle standing in the way of couple's changing, and that partners scapegoat in such a way as to protect one another. Although each partner might make wild attacks on the other, it is understood that some issues are not to be used in scapegoating. His example is illustrative.

A wife who was the manager in a marriage would insult her husband for his drinking, lack of consideration, bad behavior, and general boorishness. Alone with the therapist one day she said the real problem was the fact that her husband was just a "big baby" and she was tired of mothering him. When the therapist asked why she had not brought this up in a session with her husband present the woman was shocked at the idea of hurting his feelings in that way (Haley, 1963, p. 133).

Ackerman (1968) conceptualized the triangle in the family even before Karpman's formulation. He stated, "We observe certain constellations of family interactions which we have epitomized as a pattern of family interdependence roles, those of destroyer or persecutor, the victim of the scapegoating attack, and the 'family healer' or the 'family doctor' " (p. 628). He also recognized a pattern of attack, defense, and counterattack, a shifting in roles. Vogel and Bell (1961) elaborated on the reasons for the change in roles. They held that role reversals may be a way to rationalize scapegoating. For example, mothers of bedwetters saw themselves as Victims because of the inconvenience involved.

In summary, the clinical and theoretical literature supports the thesis that scapegoating protects the family. In a sense, the Victim becomes the Rescuer of the family. The Victim is overtly the weakest and covertly the strongest member of the family. But the Victim simply reflects the distribution of power within the family. The scapegoating process represents a power struggle of intense proportions.

The Power of Powerlessness

The Victim in the drama triangle plays a powerless or helpless role. The Victim's powerlessnes is overt. The powerlessness of the Rescuer and Persecutor are not obvious. They appear to be strong, because they have the ability to help or hurt another person. Yet, they too are like the Victim in the sense that they are bound together in a pathogenic triangle. They are helpless to behave in more constructive ways. They are unable to fulfill their needs for growth and change. By considering the different levels of their behavior, it is possible to understand how such a complex system operates paradoxically.

   This analysis will involve an examination of the Karpman or drama triangle in terms of the paradox of the power of powerlessness and exchange theory. Power can be viewed as the possession of resources that others lack. Foa and Foa's (1974) resource exchange theory offers a comprehensive approach for defining some of the lesser discussed resources and also for defining power in terms of resource possession. Foa and Foa view all behavior to be an exchange of resources; the resources of love and status are two of the resources that are sought and exchanged in transactions. By viewing power as the possession of a resource that another person needs or wants (e.g., love), a clearer picture of the meaning of power emerges. Before proceeding further, let us summarize some of the basic ideas of Foa and Foa (1974):

1) There are six resources exchanged in interpersonal transactions based upon the needs of the exchangers, the institution of exchange (e.g., family), and the properties of the resource. The six resources are love, status, services, information, money, and goods. All transactions involve the exchange of one or several of these resources.

2) Resources have a property known as particularism. Particularism refers to how important the person is who gives the resources. For example, love is the most particularistic resource, and money is the least particularistic resource. Therefore, the person who gives us love is of vital importance, but the person who gives us money, e.g., the bank teller, does not make much difference.

3) Love is the most particularistic resource, status and service are next, then information and goods, and last is money. The more particularistic a resource is, the more it does not follow the laws of common sense or economics. For example, if a person takes away love from another, the taker does not become more powerful or richer in love. Instead, taking love away from another is the same as taking away love from self, and giving love to another is the same as giving love to self. The person who takes love away becomes less powerful in the resource of love. Conversely, the person who gives love becomes more powerful in the resource of love.

4) The extent to which a person *actually* has or *perceives* himself to have a particular resource can determine his or her feelings of power or powerlessness.

The last two ideas of Foa and Foa are basic to our thesis and need to be expanded. If power equals the possession of resources that can be given and taken away from others and self, then how can a person powerless in resources be powerful? A person who actually has or sees himself as having little in the way of a given resource (e.g., status) has less to lose than a person who is rich or perceives himself to be rich. The more powerless a person feels, the less the threat of loss, which can confer a desperate or quasi-power to this person. For example, a severely depressed person typically suffers from low self-esteem. According to resource theory, the depressive feels that s/he possesses little, if any, status and love. If the depression becomes severe (e.g., to the point that the person is suicidal), then the depressive by virtue of having or perceiving self to have low status and love can reason that there is nothing left to lose and commit suicide. This nothing-left-to-lose attitude can lead to a feeling of desperateness or quasi-power. In this instance, the depressive uses feelings of powerlessness to become powerful enough to take his/her life, although s/he is unaware of the power of this powerlessness.

Paradox of the Power of Powerlessness in Karpman's Triangle

The Karpman (1968) triangle provides an excellent example of the paradox of the power of the powerless in terms of resource theory. Love and status are the resources being negotiated in the triangle, and it appears that the Victim is powerless, whereas the Rescuer and Persecutor are powerful. Our model shows the deception behind the appearance of the Persecutor's and Rescuer's being more powerful.

It is essential to remember that love and status are particularistic resources which follow paradoxical laws of exchange. Thus, taking these resources from another does not make one richer in them but actually diminishes them. In the process of degrading the Victim, the Persecutor takes status away from self. The Rescuer knows rescuing the Victim will only serve to keep the Victim in the role. The Res-

RESCUER 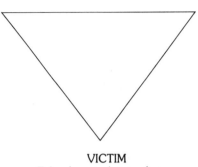 PERSECUTOR
Takes love from   Takes status from
Victim which in   Victim which in
turn takes from   turn takes from
self.   self.

VICTIM
Takes love and status from
self which in turn takes love
and status from Persecutor
and Rescuer.

Figure 1
Allocation of Power in Karpman's Rescue Triangle

cuer is motivated to help the Victim anyway in order to win the love of the Victim as well as others. The Rescuer's manipulative attempts to "save" the Victim and extract love for self fail because the Rescuer is only taking love for self. The more the Rescuer attempts to take from the Victim, the more bankrupt they become.

The role of the Victim is most unique. The Victim colludes with the others in taking resources from self. In taking these resources away from self, the Victim is like a funnel which drains these resources from the Rescuer and Persecutor. The Victim's willingness to take these resources away from self gives this member quasi-power in the system. The Victim can covertly take from others, who have little to give. The Victim acts even more helpless. In turn, the Rescuer and Persecutor escalate their behavior. Any member of the triangle may escalate behavior, which triggers a chain reaction in the negotiation of resources in the system.

The Karpman triangle is a system bankrupt in resources, with each member fighting to gain love or status illegitimately. It is a vicious system which feeds on itself as long as the Victim is willing to take from self and others. For example, when the Persecutor and Rescuer attempt to take from or give more to the Victim, s/he simply retaliates by taking more from him/herself, i.e., by being a better Victim.

Exposing the Power of the Victim

We have asserted that the Victim has a great deal of quasi-power by virtue of being able to manipulatively take love away from the Rescuer and status from the Persecutor. We view the Victim as key to therapeutic intervention in this pathological system. The primary task of the therapist is to expose the power of the Victim and help the Victim to use his/her power in different ways.

Two paradoxical techniques may be used to expose the power behind the powerlessness of the Victim. First, we suggest reframing the Victim's powerlessness by congratulating him/her on how much power s/he has in being able to take away love and status from other members in the triangle. This approach could also include confronting the Victim directly on his behavior, e.g., acknowledging that he must enjoy this feeling of power, and also asking the Victim to demonstrate how he could be a better Victim; i.e., carrying his behaviors to an extreme (prescribing). Further, the other members of the triangle could be asked to discuss what happens when the Victim enacts this role or gets worse. Reframing the Victim's feelings of powerlessness in terms of power and having the behaviors carried to the extreme have proven to be effective interventions, in our clinical experience.

The second paradoxical technique involves giving injunctions to members of the triangle to escalate their respective behaviors (after Haley, 1976; Watzlawick, Weakland, and Fisch, 1974). The purpose of this technique is to expose the behaviors of each member by making the covert overt. Some examples of paradoxical injunctions for making the behavior of each member overt are:

To Rescuer: When you feel unloved, I want you to do something for (the Victim).

To Persecutor: When you feel lacking in self-confidence, etc., I want you to invent ways of blaming others for your shortcomings or mistakes.

To Victim: When you feel helpless or powerless, I want you to pretend to be even more helpless and get people to take care of you just like you were a child.

Example of Injunctions Using a Paradoxical Letter

A young married couple revealed all the aspects of the power of powerlessness. Their marriage followed the classic pattern of the husband being the Parent and the wife the Child in Berne's (1972) terminology. The husband originally rescued his wife from her family of origin where she was the Victim. However, he reported that he was tired of having to take care of her and had shifted to the Persecutor role through blaming her. The wife's typical pattern was either to placate her husband or to use distracting behavior in order to assert her power. For example, she would go on shopping sprees and buy expensive antiques, knowing that her husband would be furious with her. Whenever the husband felt he was losing control in the marriage, he would start an argument with his wife. He had a strong investment in always being right, as well as being in control. Each seemed powerless or unable to break out of this pattern. A paradoxical letter was written to this couple containing the following injunctions:

> The next time you are feeling powerless, make a major purchase on your own, or start an argument with your mate. At all costs you should not tell each other when you are feeling powerless or out of control, but you should do as we have suggested. In fact, if one of you asks the other, "Do you feel powerless or out of control in the marriage?", you should deny it.

This letter had the effect of stopping the wife from buying things and making her husband angry, and the husband said that he would reflect before starting a fight. Both husband and wife reported having fewer fights. Moreover, after a period of three weeks, the wife said that she had become more assertive with her husband and with other people. The polarization of this couple into Persecutor and Victim had shifted considerably as a result of the injunctions contained in the paradoxical letter.

CONCLUSION

The purpose of this chapter has been to develop a view of psychopathology which is consistent with the paradoxical approach to problems and this treatment. A historical analysis helped to explain much current thinking about problems—thinking which is still primarily linear and interactional. Our theory is based on a dialectical approach to problems and their treatment. From a dialectical viewpoint, problems are the result of not being able to resolve a thesis-antithesis dilemma because of fixed rules of problem solution which bind the individual to one view of reality. The drama triangle was used to flesh out this theory and provide some indirect clinical support. The task of future theoreticians is to develop other models of family pathology which stem from this theory.

4

When to work paradoxically

The paradoxical psychotherapy literature abounds with case summaries but virtually nothing has been written about when a therapist can or should intervene paradoxically. The guidelines presented in this chapter are based on our experience and the experience of others we consider effective paradoxical therapists. Our ideas are also extracted from case studies and theories.

The *when* of paradoxical intervention refers to the types of patients, problems, and situations amenable to this approach. It could be argued from the outset that paradoxical techniques can be used in almost every case, in the same way that it could be argued that behavior therapy is best for each case. The flexibility of this approach is well documented in Jay Haley's (1973) book, *Uncommon Therapy: The Psychiatric Techniques of Milton H. Erickson, M.D.* Erickson demonstrated that he could successfully treat a wide variety of disorders through the use of hypnotic paradox. However, paradoxical methods are probably more appropriate for certain types of cases. Our discussion is directed toward those clients, problems, and situations where paradoxical methods should be considered the treatment of choice. There are nonetheless many cases where the therapist may choose to intervene paradoxically in order to work more efficiently or effectively.

Before examining the types of cases appropriate for paradoxical treatment, we would like to focus attention on the therapist. Regardless of how appropriate a case might be for paradoxical treatment, the therapist must first and foremost be able to think circularly or paradoxically about the case. This type of thinking process has been described in the first three chapters. Among other things, the therapist must: a) see the symptom as the vehicle of change; b) see the symptom in functionally positive terms (e.g., care, protection, closeness, stability, etc.); and c) understand how the frame of reference perpetuates the problem. When paradoxical techniques are used without being able to conceptualize the problem paradoxically, the chances of success are limited. Paradoxical thinking is a special process grounded in communications/systems theory.

One of the fundamental principles of psychopathology is that diagnosis and treatment should go hand in hand. This principle stems from traditional, medically oriented diagnosis, which leads to traditional therapies. We do not advocate or support the use of traditional diagnostic categories. Therapists who practice paradoxically generally find little value in using diagnostic categories. Instead, we find it essential to grasp the pattern of a problem paradoxically. We strive to describe the problem, not to explain it through the use of a label. However, most of us were trained to think in terms of diagnostic categories. For this reason, we share a basis of communicating, despite the fact that it is simplistic.

Stanton (1981b, pp. 368-369) has reviewed the literature on paradoxical intervention and found that this approach has been used successfully in a wide variety of cases. These include: adolescent problems, aging, alcoholism, anorexia and eating disorders, anxiety, asthma, behavior problems and delinquency, childhood emotional problems, crying, depression, dizziness, drug abuse and addiction, encopresis, enuresis, fire-setting, homosexuality, hysterical blindness, identity crisis, leaving home, marital problems, obesity, obsessive-compulsive behavior, obsessive thoughts, chronic pain, paranoia, phobias, postpartum depression and psychosis, premature ejaculation, public speaking anxiety, schizophrenia, school problems and truancy, sexual problems, sleep disturbances, stammering, suicidal gestures, excessive sweating, temper tantrums, thumb-sucking, tinnitus, vomiting and stomachaches, and work problems. Of course, there are

numerous cases of couples and families being treated paradoxically where diagnostic categories have no relevance. This information
still gives us little data about when to intervene paradoxically. Like
Erickson's work, it suggests that the approach has wide applicability.

IMPORTANCE OF HISTORY

There are a couple of practical ways of assessing a client or family
for paradoxical treatment. The first is to obtain a history of previous
therapy from the client. We believe "therapist-killers" and "therapy-
addicts" are appropriate candidates for paradoxical treatment. Therapist-killers are individuals who have had a number of therapists,
none of whom has been successful. Therapist-killers seem to delight
in telling stories about how ineffective their previous therapists were or
how they were mistreated by them. Therapy-addicts seem to live for
their weekly therapy session. They have ups and downs in their therapy, but in the long run show no improvement. Both therapist-killers
and therapy-addicts are highly resistant clients. They may claim they
want help, but they always manage to sabotage it.

For these individuals therapy has become part of the problem
rather than part of the solution. They may project or externalize their
responsibility for change onto the therapist. From a systemic point of
view the therapist may be joining the system in such a way that the
problem is maintained. For example, a therapist who is not trained in
systems theory might ally consistently with the parent of an acting-out
adolescent. The therapist might use more of the same strategies used
by the parents in trying to control the child. Therapist-killers and
therapy-addicts, whether individuals or systems, must be joined with
in a special way. Basically the therapist must declare his/her impotence with the clients.

We do not always have the luxury of a therapy history with some
clients at the beginning of therapy. Some clients will not be honest
about previous treatment. They may not even reveal the fact that they
have been in therapy. If they have been in treatment they may say it
was a good or growing experience without having solved any problems, simply to justify the time, effort, or money expended. Clients
who have received treatment may have medical records which take

weeks to obtain and arrive incomplete or so vague as to be useless. Ultimately, the therapist must decide whether the client is an appropriate candidate for paradoxical treatment.

RESISTANCE AND CHRONICITY

There appear to be two interrelated continuums on which to judge the applicability of paradoxical techniques: 1) the dimension of resistance, ranging from very cooperative to difficult or impossible; 2) the dimension of pathology, ranging from mildly disturbed (e.g., transient and neurotic disorders) to severely disturbed (e.g., psychotic disorders). The literature and our experience suggest that paradoxical techniques are most useful at the resistant/severely disturbed poles of the continua (see Selvini Palazzoli et al., 1978a; Rosen, 1953; Stanton, 1981b). However, we have observed that paradoxical techniques tend to produce more rapid change at the cooperative/mildly disturbed poles of the continua. In addition, problems which are chronic, hence sometimes labeled severe, are appropriate.

When we use the term severely disturbed, we are not specifically referring to diagnostic categories. We agree with Weakland et al.'s (1974) position regarding severity of symptoms. They asserted that long-term problems are no more severe than other types of problems, but that they have been handled poorly over and over again. According to them, difficult (severe and chronic) problems are those which have strong positive feedback loops and are reinforced in a social context. Paradoxical intervention is appropriate under these conditions since it explodes the feedback loops which maintain the problems. In summary, paradoxical intervention is most useful in resistant, chronic, and severe problem cases.

ASSESSING RESISTANCE

In order to assess the new client's willingness to change, homework tasks are assigned. The first tasks assigned are direct and simple. They involve engaging in specific behaviors at home which are helpful in solving the problem (see Haley, 1976). If the client does the task as assigned, there is little necessity for paradoxical intervention. However, if the client forgets, resists, changes, or distorts the assignments several times, it is clear he is resisting and requires a different approach. In these resistant cases paradoxical methods prove to be the most efficient and effective. Paradoxical homework tasks or indirect tasks are assigned rather than direct tasks. This guideline for when to intervene paradoxically does not imply that paradoxical techniques should not or cannot be used in cases where the client is cooperative. In cooperative cases one simply has a wider choice of approaches or techniques which may be used effectively. The use of paradoxical techniques with an easy or cooperative case may be no more effective than the use of other techniques; however, paradoxical techniques may be more efficient in reducing the total amount of time required to solve a particular problem.

PARADOXICAL INTERVENTION WITH FAMILIES

It is difficult to describe when to intervene paradoxically with a family because there is no diagnostic classification for families. The aforementioned guidelines apply to families, but it is also useful to delineate, as specifically as possible, times when paradoxical intervention is appropriate.

In general, it seems appropriate to intervene paradoxically when a family and/or any of its subsystsms is in a developmental crisis. Family therapists have become aware that families undergo certain discrete changes over time, although they have not been able to specify what changes are functional or dysfunctional at different stages of the life cycle. While attempting to provide a systematic way of organizing the hypnotic and psychotherapeutic work of Milton Erickson, Haley (1973) formulated a clinical framework for the family life cycle. Erickson and Haley argued that families experience distress when they are unable to shift from one stage to another stage in the family life cycle; i.e., when asynchronization occurs. Interestingly, the therapeutic approach advocated by Haley (1973) is basically paradoxical. Paradoxical psychotherapy may be used to bring about the second-order change necessary when shifting from one stage of the life cycle to the next (Hughes, Berger, and Wright, 1978). Watzlawick et al., (1974) realized life-cycle changes were of the second-order when they stated, "the transition of a teenager from a child to a young adult is one of the several periods of change in families which require corresponding changes in their interactional rules, i.e., a second-order change" (p. 142). However, they failed to elaborate on this essential point in terms of using paradoxical therapy when dealing with life-cycle transitions.

Accounts of how paradoxical psychotherapy has been used to facilitate life-cycle changes or resolve developmental crises have been presented by Watzlawick et al. (1974), Haley (1973), Hughes et al., (1978) and Weeks and Wright (1979). In one of our cases a young couple experienced difficulty over becoming parents. Linda and Scott began therapy complaining that his frequent temper outbursts and her anxiety over being a good mother to their ten-month-old baby were hurting their relationship. At this time, Scott was having one to two outbursts weekly (with as many as four some weeks); Linda was very fearful of these outbursts. We assigned Scott the task of having a blow-up and Linda the task of experiencing anxiety over not doing a task well. During the course of therapy (two and a half months) Scott had only one outburst and, according to Linda, it did not measure up to previous outbursts. Linda stated that she remained pretty much free of her intense anxiety states. Furthermore, early in therapy we discussed an alternating pattern of Victim-Persecutor-Rescuer in Linda and Scott's relationship. Linda played a Victim, setting Scott up to persecute or rescue her (or both). We assigned their roles to them. The intentional enactment of these roles helped them in controlling their arguments—making them constructive rather than destructive.

Fisher, Anderson, and Jones (1981) have presented some specific ideas about the use of certain types of interventions in patients, mostly families, with specified characteristics. They have identified three types of paradoxical interventions. The first type of intervention, *reframing,* was defined to mean giving the symptom another meaning. This is the same definition used by Watzlawick et al. (1974) and is fully described in a later chapter. Fisher et al. stated that reframing should be used when the following family characteristics are observed: a) moderate resistance; b) non-oppositional; c) ability to reflect; d) non-action-oriented; e) able to handle frustration and uncertainty; f) little or no severe impulsive or acting-out behavior; g) no pressing external problems; h) a rigid family structure; and i) repeated but not severe crisis.

The second method of intervention identified was *escalation* or *crisis induction*. This method was broadly defined in two ways. The first was simply symptom prescription, i.e., telling the client to do more of the same. The second method involves increasing the frequency or intensity of a crisis situation. Instead of trying to prevent the crisis, the therapist pushes the family toward the unresolved situation in an effort to make the covert aspects of the problem more overt and unite the system. The method of escalation should be used when the family has the following characteristics: a) vague style; b) excessive verbal manipulation; c) oppositional; d) power struggle; e) marked resistance; f) need to move slowly; g) potential for acting-out; h) excessively rigid; i) blocked with no area of compromise; and j) adults are competitive with therapists.

The third type of intervention Fisher et al. discussed was called *redirection*. Redirection refers to changing some aspect of the symptom's occurrence. It specifically relates to changing the circumstances under which the symptom occurs without necessarily changing the symptom itself. They give the following characteristics for the use of redirection: a) individual setting; b) presenting problem with a young child; c) specific symptoms; d) repetitive symptoms; e) educational and guidance settings; f) family can respond to direction without sabotage; g) non-oppositional; and h) overly compliant.

The work of Fisher et al. (1981) is extremely important. They are beginning to link specific methods with family characteristics. This kind of work must be done extensively in insuring the proper use of paradoxical methods. It should be noted that most of their work applies to families and not individuals. In addition to the characteristics they list, we have observed a number of familial patterns where we believe some type of paradoxical intervention is appropriate. Unlike Fisher et al. (1981), we do not attempt to suggest what kind of paradoxical interventions are appropriate, although their guidelines are generally confirmed in our clinical observations.

PATTERNS OF FAMILY TRANSACTION

Families exhibit a number of dysfunctional transactions where paradoxical intervention appears especially appropriate. Some of these patterns are described and exemplified in the next few pages.

1) *Expressive Fighting and Bickering*

Fighting may be short-term and intensive or long-term and low level. In either case the members of a system find that they relate to one another overtly by fighting. This pattern is based on a reactive marital relationship of sameness-oppositeness (L'Abate, 1976). The members constantly oppose one another regardless of the issue. A therapist who tries to deal with this kind of family straightforwardly will find him/herself at odds with the family. The therapist must join with this type of family paradoxically.

> A family entered counseling because of the extremely defiant attitude of their youngest daughter, who was 15. Mother and father were in their early forties and had three other children, one son, age 18, who lived at home, and another older son and daughter, who were married and lived away from home.
>
> Excessive fighting and bickering occurred each time the daughter was expected to comply with the rules and expectations of her parents. It seemed that mother and daughter were intensely involved in a power struggle, which usually escalated until father became involved. Since father had had two coronaries, mother and daughter would temporarily stop fighting, which by this time usually reached proportions of a physical brawl. Mother was in charge of discipline. It seemed that mother and father had agreed that mother would assume the heavier, more responsible role while father would be the nicer, more passive parent. Since this agreement placed mother in the role of disciplinarian, she and daughter were in a continuous struggle over all issues.

2) *Unwillingness to Cooperate with Each Other and Complete Assignments*

These families are more passive and subtle than the families who fight overtly. They may comply with each other verbally but defeat one another nonverbally. In fact, this pattern can also be traced back to the marital dyad, where one spouse, usually the wife, is verbally more articulate and explosive, defeating her husband actively through her continuous complaints and diatribes. The husband, on the other hand, usually defeats her nonverbally. Unable to articulate his feelings verbally, he acts out by drinking, watching TV, leaving home, etc.

In both the foregoing patterns, present most often in families of rebellious teenagers, verbal agreements are not honored and most transactions are left incomplete, since no one takes personal responsibility, as could be said of most self-defeating patterns. These families usually distort or forget homework assignments.

> A family came to counseling because of their 16-year-old son's nonverbal aggressive behavior. According to the other family members, the adolescent's aggressive behavior and unwillingness to comply were unbearable. When confronted with this problem or any other issue, he pretended to be sleepy. Because of a poor relationship with the parents, an older brother and sister had left home before completion of high school.
>
> Mother and father came from very different backgrounds, which had caused confusion over the way in which the children should be disciplined and what their expectations were to be. Mother attempted to be the enforcer, but felt she got no support until she exploded in rages. Although father was concerned, he did not offer much support to his wife because he either left town on work-related business or avoided her by not listening or engaging in another activity whenever his son's behavior needed to be taken care of. Since mother was the most verbal in the family, she defeated both father and son by either exploding or completing statements for them. They, in turn, by not cooperating and conversing with her, also refused to take any personal responsibility for dealing with family issues.

3) Continuation of Same Patterns in Spite of All Types of Intervention

There are families who are rigidly resistant to any type of intervention. No matter what, they will continue their behavior *regardless* of interventions. In most of these cases, the therapist may feel like hitting his/her head against a stone wall. The family will not budge.

> The identified patient was a 15-year-old boy whose violent antisocial behavior brought this family to counseling. This was a

blended family consisting of mother, her two children, ages 15 and 16, and a stepfather. Although the stepfather and mother had been married for three and a half years, the mother complained that the problem could not be altered because the stepfather would not discipline either the son or daughter. When this family was first seen, they had previously been in therapy for one year, but said they saw no evidence of change.

This was a first marriage for stepfather, who was so quiet that no one listened to his "mumbling." Stepfather explained that since he had never had any children, he really did not know how to parent. When stepfather did attempt to move closer to the son, the move was interpreted by the mother as their being too independent and no longer needing her. Mother, therefore, would become overly critical of the son for not assuming responsibility for his work at home, which broke up the stepfather-son relationship. Son would then become furious with everyone, and the stepfather would start feeling incompetent again. Son and daughter "acted out" their frustrations by destroying property at school and at home and by fighting with those in authority.

In spite of numerous straightforward interventions to strengthen generational boundaries so that mother and stepfather would be supportive of each other, mother and siblings remained bound in an enmeshed relationship.

4) *Divide and Conquer*

This fourth pattern is especially visible in families with teenagers, who are masters at separating the parents from each other, making hay out of whatever polarization may have been present in the marriage (Stierlin, 1974). Children, especially adolescents, test their parents' limits and, hence, their own limits, as they develop. In dysfunctional families the limit-testing behavior often becomes extreme. The child's behavior may be used to keep the parents apart or serve as a buffer between them.

This family of four came for family counseling because of the "acting-out" of their oldest son, age 15. Father was a truck driver and mother a shampoo girl. There was one younger sibling, a

brother, age 10, who was in the fourth grade. The identified patient was a large, handsome youth who towered over his father.
He was neatly dressed and appropriately groomed. According
to this family, the youth was doing such things as leaving home
without permission in the family car, but only going a few miles
away. He was also consistently lying about his behavior and taking things that would be rather conspicuous by their absence. He
would also place beer and other undesirable items in his room
where they would easily be found.

5) *Disqualifications*

Families may use a wide range of disqualifying communications,
ranging from self-contradictions, inconsistencies, and subject switch-
es, to the use of metaphor and cryptic statements (Watzlawick et al.,
1967). Haley (1959) has provided an excellent discussion of how
family members may disqualify statements. According to him, the
speaker may disqualify the source of the message, the message itself,
the receiver, or the context. It has also been observed that more
dysfunctional families use more disqualification. In addition, the
ultimate disqualification of the therapist may be the family suddenly
dropping out of therapy without proviso.

This family was first seen in counseling because of the extreme
antisocial behavior of their 16-year-old daughter, who had been
suspended permanently from school for persistent drug use and
disrespect to teachers. There was one other younger daughter at
home, age 15, who engaged in equally destructive behavior,
but was never caught. Father held an administrative level position and mother was a housewife. She reported that her husband wanted her to find work away from home; however, she
could not do so because of the trouble with her older daughter.
The mother reported also that they all felt very insecure and
scared about being in counseling, because they had been in
counseling before and no one had ever helped. The mother, in
particular, doubted that they would continue in therapy from the
very outset.
Excessively critical comments of the daughter's behavior were
verbalized by mother, who commented that she received no

support from the father. Although father tended to be withdrawn and quiet, he was extremely critical of the way in which mother handled the problems with the older daughter. Father reprimanded the daughter in the counseling session, whenever mother reported that she received no support from him. Daughter was extremely critical of her mother and other authority figures but was easier on father and her younger sister.

In this family each member talked about what they needed to do, but it was quite evident that no action had been taken. For instance, no punishment was administered when rules were broken, there was no movement on the mother's side to find work, and father and mother made no effort to show their daughters that they were supportive of each other. This family was intolerant of themselves as well as of others.

CONTRAINDICATIONS FOR PARADOXICAL INTERVENTION

The existing literature offers almost no contraindicatons for the use of paradoxical techniques. The techniques are still so new and exciting that therapists have been focusing on successes and not failures. At this point our experience suggests that paradoxical interventions are contraindicated in four types of cases.

The first contraindication is when the client is not actively involved in the therapeutic process or has little ego involvement. A condition for a paradox as well as a double-bind to work is that there exist a relationship. Individuals who are carried into therapy by courts or family members may neither resist nor cooperate with a therapist.

The second type of individual who does not seem to respond is the sociopath. A task given to a sociopath may be changed to fit his own needs. Tasks given to be learning experiences do not register.

Thirdly, paranoids may sense the "deceit" involved in an intervention, if not carefully formulated and delivered, causing them to become more suspicious. This situation could produce deterioration in the client and a split in the therapeutic relationship. On the other hand, there are successful case reports of intervention with paranoid schizophrenics (see Rosen, 1953).

Fourthly, the clearest contraindication is for destructive behavior, especially homicidal and suicidal behavior. Needless to say, a therapist would not prescribe suicidal behavior. However, suicidal behavior has been treated in a paradoxical manner by Farrelly (Farrelly and Brandsma, 1974). Farrelly provokes an affective response, usually anger, in suicidal patients by doing such things as criticizing their proposed methods of killing themselves and making absurd suggestions about the right way to kill oneself (e.g., sawing off one's arms with a hacksaw, using a vise to hold the arms). The paradoxical literature contains no cases of paradoxical intervention with suicidal or homicidal clients (Weeks and L'Abate, 1978). However, one can prescribe depression to help control the suicidal behavior.

Rohrbaugh et al. (1977) have stated that paradoxical treatment is probably inappropriate in situations of crisis or instability. Problems such as acute decompensation, acute grief reactions, and loss of employment should not be treated paradoxically.

Fisher et al. (1981) identified four family patterns where paradoxical interventions are contraindicated. They stated paradox is not appropriate in chaotic families. These families are characterized by loose and vague structures. They do not present with a clear problem or repetitive pattern of disturbing behavior. Childlike families are also contraindicated. In these families, the adult members are immature. The parents in these families are searching for a parent figure in the therapist.

Thirdly, impulsive families who express hostile behavior openly are inappropriate. These families may act on the paradox in a destructive manner. Finally, they observed that families which project responsibility onto others and accept the interventions with little opposition or negative behaviors are poor candidates. In summary, they believe paradox should not be used when the family is not resistant or when there is a lack of structure and a potential for severe acting-out.

CONCLUSION

Paradoxical interventions have been successfully applied in many different types of cases. Paradoxical psychotherapy is a very flexible approach. A therapist may choose to work paradoxically with an "easy" case in order to work more quickly or efficiently. However, there are probably cases where this approach would be the only effective treatment. This chapter attempts to provide some guidelines for when paradoxical treatment would be the treatment of choice. In fact, we are still years away from being able to state which type of therapy is most appropriate for most problems. Psychotherapy research has, of course, shown that certain problems respond to specific treatments, mostly in the behavior therapy field. However, there are so few controlled group studies on paradoxical intention/therapy that a scientific answer to the question of "when" cannot be given. Hence, the guidelines offered in this chapter are based on our clinical experience, experience of our colleagues, and clinical case reports.

5

How to work paradoxically

Very little has been written about how to intervene paradoxically. Case studies seem to suggest that such interventions appear as if by magic. If paradoxical psychotherapy is a scientific and replicable mode of therapy, then the therapist should be able to discuss the process of intervention articulately. It could be that one of the reasons why paradoxical therapists have not described how they work is that the "logic" used by the paradoxical therapist is circular rather than linear. Our language is basically linear and causal, e.g., If—then. Thinking and articulating about circular processes are not easy tasks. Using paradox requires a shift to a multicausal system of thinking. The therapist must think dialectically rather than demonstratively (Weeks, 1977).

Only a few therapists, all of them family therapists, have attempted to describe how they proceed in working paradoxically. Even those who have made such an attempt still leave therapists wondering about many aspects of the process. They all speak to therapists who are assumed to be knowledgeable in systems theory. Their descriptions omit many of the nuts and bolts for this kind of approach as they offer general guidelines for family interventions. This chapter will first review how others proceed in working paradoxically and then offer recommendations of a more specific nature which may be applied to individuals, couples, or families.

WORKING METHODS OF HALEY, MADANES, AND SELVINI PALAZZOLI

The first therapist to offer guidelines on how to work paradoxically was Haley (1976, p. 72-74). He outlined eight stages of paradoxical treatment:

1) The therapeutic relationship must be defined as one that will help bring about a change. This contract may be implicit.

2) The problem must be clearly defined.

3) The goal(s) of treatment should be established.

4) The therapist offers a plan or strategy. The therapist attempts to "sell" the family on his approach to the problem.

5) The person in the family who has been acting as the authority on the problem must be tactfully disqualified. Haley reasoned that the person acting as the authority is somehow reinforcing the problem and must change if the identified patient is to change.

6) The therapist gives a paradoxical task or directive.

7) The responses to the directive are tracked and the symptomatic behavior is encouraged.

8) The therapist accepts no credit for improvements. Credit is given to the family. In fact, the therapist appears puzzled when improvement does occur because the therapist is either prescribing the symptom or predicting a relapse.

It was not until 1980 that two other paradoxical therapists attempted to outline their methods. Madanes (1980, 1981) described six steps which can be followed to paradoxically intervene in a family:

1) Defining the problem and setting goals.

2) Conceptualizing the problem. The problem child was seen as a protector of the parents or familial system.

3) Devising a directive or strategy that the parents use to help the child. The directive given to the parents should include one of three types of prescriptions for the child. The first type of pre-

scription was that the parents request that the child have the problem. The child may be instructed to exaggerate, schedule, or voluntarily enact the symptom with the parents' help and full involvement. The second type of prescription involved the parents' request that the child pretend to have a problem. The child was instructed to pretend to have a symptom s/he previously displayed. The parents were also to pretend that the symptom was real and act accordingly. The third type of prescription consisted of the parents' request that the child pretend to help the parent. This strategy placed the parent in an overtly inferior position and the child in an overtly superior position in a playful way.

4) Having the family enact or engage the directive in the session before carrying it out at home.

5) Following up on the directive by getting a full report in the next session and then prescribing the same directive.

6) Giving the parents credit for the child's improvement.

Other symptoms were then dealt with using the same set of procedures. Madanes further recommended that these strategies be used with loving and helpful families and not with families with a history of abuse or violence since the directives could become punishing.

The other group of paradoxical therapists to explicate their methodology was the well-known group of Italian family therapists, Selvini Palazzoli, Boscolo, Cecchin, and Prata (1980). Their influential book, *Paradox and Counterparadox* (1978a) described a number of specific interventions but did not provide an adequate theoretical foundation for their work. Recognizing this weakness, they established three principles to assist the observer in understanding their interventions. They call these principles hypothesizing, circularity, and neutrality.

Hypothesizing refers to the therapists' formulations about how families function. Hypothesizing begins with the family's first telephone contact with the therapists and continues throughout the entire therapeutic process. The team formulates hypotheses based on direct observation of the family and on the feedback and responses provided by the prescriptions and tasks given by the therapists. The team views hypotheses not as true or false, but as useful or not useful. They believe the hypotheses must track relational patterns or be systemic in nature. The team tests their hypotheses through observation. Each intervention is seen as an experiment in which a hypothesis is being tested.

The second principle is *circularity*. Circularity involves obtaining information from every member of the family system. It involves having one member comment (meta-communicate) about the relationship between two other members of the family. Selvini Palazzoli et al. believe this "triadic modality of investigation" renders more information about systems, especially differences in a system. In accord with the principle of circularity, they specify a number of strategies. Like other family theorists, they stress the importance of defining the problems in specific interactive behaviors in specific circumstances. They do not ask about feelings or make interpretations. They also look for differences in behavior. How does one member respond differently from another? They are not interested in motivations. In fact, they will have each member of the family rank others on specific behaviors or specific interactions (e.g., who appears most upset). The team also investigates changes in behavior following specific events in the family, such as someone being sick, and they will ask the family to respond to hypothetical circumstances (e.g., "If one of your children had to remain at home, who would be most pleased?").

The third principle of *neutrality* is based on the epistemological assumption that a system can best be understood through the examination of everyone's perception of differences. This principle is used to obtain information about differences and change within the family. It dictates that the therapist be perceived as a neutral figure. The therapist should not take sides with a member of the family. By asking each member to state his/her views, the therapist appears to ally with everyone at some time or another. Consequently, the family will be confused about where the therapist stands.

The principles described by Selvini Palazzoli et al. (1980) are the basis for their interventions. They have speculated that the conduct of an interview based on these principles might be enough to effect change through a "negentropic effect." In other words, the feedback generated through such an interview might be enough to change a family.

GENERAL GUIDELINES OF PARADOXICAL INTERVENTION

The first step in intervening paradoxically is the same as for any other approach to psychotherapy. This step is diagnosis, assessment, or an analysis of the problem. Yet, the language used to describe our first step is misleading. Diagnosis usually refers to the linear process of deciding what kind of label to attach to a person. Assessment often carries the same connotation. Our first step is to *understand the problem concretely*. After an initial analysis has been made, the therapist continues to reassess the problem and new problems throughout the therapeutic process. Rather than attempt to offer a definition of what we mean by assessment, the term will be operationalized through a description of our method. In order to minimize confusion, the term assessment will be used instead of diagnosis.

Initial Contact

Most clients call to make an appointment rather than walk in off the street. The initial telephone contact should not be seen simply as a means of setting up an appointment but as a way to begin collecting information about the problem or to begin assessing the client or family. The initial contact may give the therapist information about who is most concerned about a problem simply by who makes the call. In many cases it will not be the client or identified patient who makes the call but another family member or relative. The caller is usually highly motivated and will probably respond to linear interventions or comply more readily to paradoxical interventions. Callers who make special demands on the therapist from the outset, involving such issues as scheduling, payment, or bringing in family members, are likely to be resistant in therapy. These individuals, as well as those members who do in fact resist coming for treatment, should be considered for paradoxical treatment.

The therapist should attempt over the phone to find out the basic problem and who lives in the family. If the person is not living alone, it is useful to have everyone who is involved with the problem or has intimate knowledge of the problem come in for the first session. The caller's reaction to this request may range from complete cooperation to a flat refusal. These reactions can be noted as feedback about how the caller views the problem and the family.

In many cases the caller will see the utility of having a spouse or other family members come in for treatment but will say they would not come. This problem can be dealt with in several ways. The therapist needs to be firm in insisting that it is important for others to come. Should the therapist relent readily, s/he allows the family an out. The therapist should ask why the other person(s) would not consider coming. A discussion of the reasons given by the caller sometimes helps the person realize they are unfounded. Should there be actual resistance from others, one way to frame their visit to the office is to say that it is to get everyone's perspective on the problem or get their help in helping the caller (client). Getting the resistant member in for just one session to help someone else is usually enough to effect a gentle reframing in the session, which serves to actively involve that person.

The initial telephone contact may prove futile in getting others to come for the session. In those cases, the first session may need to be devoted, in part, to working on ways to get others involved. This may include further discussion of others' resistances but it usually has more to do with the resistance of the person who is in the office. If his/her resistance to getting others to come in can be worked through, then there is usually a better chance of getting the participation of others.

The therapist may wish to call other family members directly. This maneuver is sometimes just enough to motivate the client to take action. The client would rather explain the initiation of treatment than allow a stranger to do it.

A paradoxical technique useful in breaking through the client's resistance to getting others to come to the session is to be pessimistic about the outcome of individual treatment. There are many cases where pessimism is justified. A woman who calls to set up an individual session for a marital problem is the classic case. The therapist is justified in saying that seeing her individually will be relatively ineffective as well as possibly contributing to further deterioration in the marriage (Gurman and Kniskern, 1978). Giving this kind of information is nothing more than preparing for informed consent.

In some cases family members will refuse to come for therapy even when it is necessary for them to be involved. The therapist may decide to work with one or more family members in such a way that the other person must be involved. In other words, a therapist may work systemically through just one individual. This way of working is probably less effective than having everyone present and more time is required to reach the goal. This approach involves conceptualizing problems systemically and then working to change the behavior of the client in such a way that others will be forced to respond differently. It is best to prescribe homework intended to change the interaction between individuals.

> In one case a wife came for treatment without her husband. She complained that she could never finish a job she started at home. She said she would do it halfway and stop because her husband would distract her. He did seem to help her avoid doing her housework. She was instructed to stay in bed on the odd days of the week reading magazines, eating chocolates, and eating only TV dinners, in order to save up enough energy to complete just one small task the next day. She was to tell her husband what she was to do and he was to not make any demands of her on her days in bed. He liked this prescription initially but later realized he did not want a wife who was so helpless. The wife became motivated to do her housework while her husband supported her by staying out of her way or helping her. Two weeks later she took a job because the husband no longer felt he would lose her should she become more independent. However, he started to see other problems in the relationship and came in for treatment.

THE INITIAL SESSIONS

In the initial sessions the task of the therapist is to assess the nature of the problem in order to develop an approach and plan of treatment. Weakland et al. (1974) have stated that the first step in preparing to intervene paradoxically is to define the problem in concrete terms. In fact, this step appears to be uniformly followed by those who practice paradoxical psychotherapy (Weeks and L'Abate, 1978). Paradoxical psychotherapy is symptom-focused. Dealing with underlying reasons and motivations is not essential for change to occur.

Defining the Problem

The problem should first be clearly and concretely defined as it presently exists. The emphasis should be on the who, what, where, and when of the problem, not the why. Questions that are useful in obtaining information include: Who is involved in the problem? Where does the behavior occur? How frequently does it occur? What happens when you experience this problem? Inquiries about feeling states are not made. Problems are repetitive patterns of behavior. These patterns must be explicated for the therapist. This involves examining the sequence of events leading up to the problem and/or the vicious chain of events in the problem. In defining problems within systems, the therapist must discover the problem-initiating feedback. The circularity of events, which is accepted as a given, compels us to assume that everyone is involved with a problem in some way if we are dealing with a multi-person system.

Secondly, it is essential to determine how the problem is being maintained or find its problem-maintaining feedbacks. Problems may develop a functional autonomy. This means it is more important to understand the problem as it presently exists than how it started. There are several areas which should be probed in problem maintenance. The first is to investigate the principle of the problem-maintaining solution we discussed earlier, i.e., how the client's solution to the problem may be the obstacle to its resolution. The most common pattern is for clients to do more of the same in trying to solve a problem. An example would be the depressive who constantly tries to cheer up and feels that any depression is bad and will lead to more depression. In such a case, the harder the person tries to fight the depression, the more helplessness s/he will experience. The second task is to determine how others, usually significant others, contribute to the problem's perpetuation.

Whatever the presenting problem, it is useful to have significant others present their perspectives. Family or systemic assessment is more useful than individual assessment. The therapist's basic question is: How do other people help maintain the problem or (prevent) the client from finding a solution? This question is never put to the family directly. Once again the task of the therapist is to look for interactional or transactional patterns that would maintain the problem.

If it is clear to the family that they are somehow involved in the problem or if the problem is between two or more members of the family, then the therapist should assign a diagnostic task during the session. Haley (1976) has called this idea the interactional stage of the interview. Rather than have family members talk about a problem, the therapist has them enact it. Thus, in a family with a teenager out of control, a therapist could have the parents talk together for five minutes in finding a solution. This task would give the therapist information about how the parents fail to unite and provide leverage for changing the parents. For more information about the specifics of conducting the family interview, the reader should consult the first chapter of Haley's *Problem-Solving Therapy* (1976).

The family will probably not be aware of its role in the development or maintenance of the problem. In these cases Selvini Palazzoli et al.'s (1980) method of getting everyone in the family to comment on the problem is assigned. As the information is revealed, the therapist can use it to link the problem to the family in a slow and gentle manner. Confronting the family members directly on their role in the problem would simply make them defensive. The therapist must stay within the family's frame of reference initially but ask how others can help with the problem. The therapist must alter the family member's perception of the problem in such a way that they believe they can be helpful. Family members may deny they caused a problem but they will almost never reject the idea of wanting to help solve it.

Individually oriented therapists will probably find it difficult to see how others support the client's problems until they become more familiar with systems theory and gain more experience. The patterns are often subtle and the situation is further complicated when one spouse is likable and appears to behave appropriately. As a result, we assume that others are usually involved in the maintenance of the problem and persist in our observations.

History of Problem

The final step in assessment is to obtain a history of the problem. This involves inquiring about any changes in the problem over time as well as obtaining a picture of how the problem began. The emphasis continues to be on *what* was happening at the time the problem started rather than on why. The same kind of analysis that is done for the problem that exists in the present is done for the problem when it began.

Part of obtaining a history of the problem is finding out what happened to make a client seek therapy when s/he did. The client should be asked, "Why did you seek treatment at this particular time?" In many cases clients will seek treatment following a crisis or after deciding the problem is hopeless. Information about the reason for seeking treatment can provide the therapist with data on what triggers the problem and how the person has dealt with it in the immediate past. In other cases the person will enter therapy because someone else, usually a significant other, recommended treatment or forced the client into therapy. If the therapist does not ask this question, s/he may not obtain any of these facts because the client may assume they are unimportant. This question usually yields valuable data regarding the use of paradoxical strategies and pinpoints the motivation for treatment. If the motivation for treatment resides in another, then his/her presence in treatment is indicated. As Haley (1976) has pointed out, the person with the greatest motivation for change can be a powerful ally for the therapist in producing systemic change.

Attempted Solutions

After obtaining a clear definition and history of the problem, the next task is to explore what solutions have been attempted to resolve the problem already (Weakland et al., 1974). Has the client been in therapy? What happened? What has the client done to treat himself? People do try to solve their own problems. If they consult a therapist it is because they have failed in their attempts. Knowing what a client has already tried helps the therapist understand the client's attitude toward the problem and tells the therapist what has not worked. This information serves as the basis for formulating different solutions while minimizing the potential for future failures.

Setting Goals

The next step in the assessment process is deciding on the goals of treatment. The goals need to be concrete or behavioral. The client is requested to discuss how s/he would like things to be at the end of treatment. This step serves a number of purposes. First, the goal of treatment is usually to eliminate behaviors the person defines as symptoms. By asking for goals the therapist gains more understanding about the symptoms and what the person expects from their elimination. In some cases, the goal of treatment and the complaints of the client do not match. When incongruence occurs, the therapist must help the client see this fact and probe further into what the client wants.

Watzlawick et al. (1974) have pointed out that goal-setting allows for the evaluation of progress and serves as an end-point to therapy. Goal-setting also places responsibility on the client rather than on the therapist. The helping relationship is defined as one where the therapist helps another achieve goals. The goals a client presents may in the therapist's judgment be overly ambitious, insignificant, or irrelevant. The therapist is obligated to help the client set realistic goals. The therapist can help the client test the reality of his goals from the outset by reflecting, providing feedback, and confronting. Even though the goals are ultimately established by the client, every therapist implicitly agrees on the appropriateness of goals and decides whether s/he can help the client achieve those goals. Having a clear-cut set of goals also helps place the therapy within a time framework. More experienced therapists know roughly how long it should take to solve certain problems. A time-limited contract can then be obtained from the client. A closed rather than open contract is useful for two reasons. First, the person has an expectation that change will occur and occur within a certain period of time. Second, the drop-out problem is partially resolved because the person has a realistic set about what to expect and has hopefully committed himself to the period of time required.

Difficulty arises when the client is unable or unwilling to specify goals. There are several reasons why a client may not readily state goals for treatment. One reason is previous therapy in which treatment goals were neve expected by the therapist or expected as part of the treatment process. Unfortunately, many humanistic therapists have been willing to accept the client's statement that they wanted to "grow"as the goal of treatment. Goals such as growth, happiness, or understanding self better are not directly observable. The client must set goals which are observable in order to know whether those goals have been achieved. It is often the therapist's task to help the client(s) translate global, unobservable goals into concrete, behavioral goals. If the client does not establish goals, the therapeutic process may be the beginning of a game without end.

A second reason that specific treatment goals may not be set is lack of skill and/or motivation on the therapist's part. A therapist must know how to help the client establish concrete or behavioral goals. This skill can be learned by reading some of the behaviorally oriented textbooks on psychotherapy and through consultation and role-playing with a supervisor. Setting goals is in many cases not easy. It requires the perseverance of the therapist. The therapist must be committed to this concept if s/he is to ask the client to set goals.

A third reason goals may not be set is because the individual or family is too upset when treatment first begins. In other words, the focus of the first meeting may be to help resolve some immediate crisis. Setting short- or long-term goals under such conditions is inadvisable. Only after the immediate crisis has been resolved can the client begin to think in terms of other changes or goals.

We have observed couples and families who present themselves for treatment in a state of chaos. In fact, the family may have been living in a state of chaos for some time. It is difficult, if not impossible, to get these families to state goals. Rather than increase the family's sense of chaos by trying to get them to focus on concrete goals, the best initial strategy seems to be that of reducing the family's level of chaos. We have found that relabeling and prescribing chaotic behavior is sometimes an effective way to reduce this behavior. In brief, the chaotic behavior is labeled in a positive way; e.g., "Out of chaos comes change and growth." "You must really love each other to work so hard to keep each other busy." "You really care about each other to fight so much." Then the therapist prescribes the chaos. Hopefully, the relabeling will have convinced the family at some level that its chaos serves a useful function.

Clients may refuse to set goals because they do not really want to make any changes or are ambivalent about making changes. There are three basic strategies for dealing with this problem. 1) The therapist may proceed with treatment, setting goals as s/he goes and checking them out with the client. The therapist's supervisor or treatment team can be invaluable during this difficult period of clarification. Any tasks assigned would ideally have the effect of helping the client solve some immediate problems and produce insight into further changes needed. The client may then begin to ask for help with specific problems and/or set specific goals spontaneously. If the client does not become more concrete, the therapist may from time to time return to the issue of goals. 2) In those cases where there appears to be no progress and the client refuses to set goals, we recommend that the therapist ask the client to focus on the smallest possible change that would be helpful, even if it is a trivial matter. 3) If the client cannot state and then make a small change, the final move is for the therapist to declare his impotence (Selvini Palazzoli et al., 1978a). In other words, the therapist declares himself to be helpless, without blaming the client. This technique is described in the next chapter as a restraining strategy.

Another problem sometimes encountered, especially with more disturbed clients, is the presentation of grandiose goals. Even in less disturbed clients we sometimes witness the presentation of idealistic and unrealistic goals. The tactic for dealing with this problem has been discussed by Watzlawick et al. (1974). When the client refuses to give up unrealistic goals, the therapist joins with the client and pushes the ambitions to the extreme. The client is essentially told that the ambitions are too limited and not challenging enough for someone with such remarkable abilities. The symptom of being unable to set realistic goals is exaggerated. Invariably the client will react with some expression of surprise, amusement, or shock and then make a more realistic statement.

> In one case a woman who had been an inpatient in a large hospital repeatedly said she wanted to use her time to crusade against the mistreatment mental patients received and write a book about her experiences. The therapist, who was seen as an extension of the hospital, encouraged the patient to become a public advocate. He discussed how she could begin to expose the system, with an increasing emphasis on the personal sacrifice she would have to make. The patient decided her advocacy would require too much time and effort so she dropped the issue.
> The therapist also encouraged her to write her book by sug-

gesting she make it a personal account of her experiences. The therapist felt it would actually be helpful for her to examine her feelings about her hospitalizations as well as give her something constructive to do. She wrote a massive amount of notes. She learned a great deal about herself during the process and when she finished she destroyed them as a symbolic way of letting go of her past.

Finally, how does the therapist deal with a client setting unrealistically low goals? We have found that exaggeration may also be useful in challenging clients to make more realistic appraisals of their ability.

In one case a man did not feel he would be able to work for several months. This 32-year-old client, who had been hospitalized for simple schizophrenia, claimed that he was simply unable to work. He felt he would be able to do only the most menial task if he did work, although he had special vocational skills. He had set a date for himself of when he thought he might start working after he entered therapy. He also mentioned that in his spare time he might like to write a book. The therapist suggested that he might write a book on how to find a job. To write this book he would have to develop job hunting techniques and learn how to do well in job interviews. He was encouraged to go to as many interviews as possible to collect data for his book. He was not told to actually look for a job. For several weeks the client looked through the paper and went to what interviews he could find. He announced just a few weeks later that he had accepted a job ahead of his schedule. In this particular case the idea of going to a job interview to find a job was anxiety-provoking for the client. Reframing the task of finding a job or going to interviews as gathering information for a book allowed him to interview under low anxiety conditions.

The goals of treatment set in the initial session need to be monitored throughout treatment. They may need to be reassessed as the client changes. New goals may need to be established. The reason for setting goals is actually twofold: 1) The therapist and client, as we have stated, have a way of assessing progress; and 2) the therapist uses the goals to guide the interventions. Each intervention should be related to the eventual attainment of the goal. This step brings us to the *how* of paradoxical intervention. It takes us beyond the initial session to the whole process of paradoxical treatment. It should be noted that our initial approach is similar to that of behavioral therapists. Our functional analysis involves finding the circular sequence of behavior that maintains the problem.

FORMULATING, DELIVERING, AND TRACKING PARADOXICAL INTERVENTIONS

Formulating a paradoxical intervention is not an easy task. The intervention must be carefully timed, precisely formulated, and convincingly delivered. In the next chapter we will review a number of specific paradoxical strategies and suggest the conditions under which they would be appropriate. Our discussion at this point will be on the more general or global issues surrounding paradoxical interventions.

Each therapy session is viewed as the beginning of making a behavioral change. The emphasis is clearly on doing rather than insight. In fact, it appears that some clients use insight-oriented therapy to avoid making changes. Insight may help clients better understand themselves and their relationships to others, but this fact does not mean they will change their behavior. The fact that couples change more rapidly in problem-solving therapy than in insight therapy has recently been demonstrated empirically by Slipp and Kressel (1978).

There are opposing views about how a paradoxical therapist should proceed during the therapy hour. One view is that from the outset of therapy the therapist must decide whether to work paradoxically or nonparadoxically. If the decision is made to work paradoxically, it has been asserted that all strategies within the session must be paradoxical and all the tasks must be paradoxical. The proponents of this view tend to work with more disturbed individuals, couples, or families, and the clients tend to be less educated. We have also encountered cases where it was necessary to keep a firm and consistent paradoxical stance. These cases were among our most dysfunctional.

Our view is that the strategy used at any particular time should be determined by the individual client(s) and the specific problem being treated at that moment. In short, a combination of paradoxical and nonparadoxical procedures appears to us to be most useful. The methods used derive from a problem-solving paradigm. The emphasis is on getting the client(s) to do things rather than develop insight. The two most significant procedures used are teaching clients new skills and giving clients homework tasks.

Teaching a client skills is essential when the elimination of the problem behavior will create a behavioral vacuum. It is easy to forget that clients do not have all the skills they need to function adequately. A couple that fights chronically may not be able to communicate in any other way. The therapist must attack the problem on two fronts. The fighting should be reduced to a normal level, while the couple is trained in communication skills. There are also cases where clients do have the skills they need to replace the symptom. The therapist needs to ascertain whether clients possess these skills by obtaining an adequate history and noting the use of those skills in various interactions. Spouses who report constant fighting and the fact that they have never felt they knew how to talk to each other would surely be candidates for skills training. However, spouses who report that they once talked to each other and felt understood probably do not require skills training.

The second strategy is giving homework or tasks to do outside the session. Homework tasks are structured experiences which allow clients to practice skills learned in the session, discover more about themselves, or change existing patterns of behavior. Homework tasks may be linear or paradoxical. Linear tasks generally produce slow changes in behavior by increasing or decreasing certain behaviors. An example of a linear task would be to make three "I feel" statements each day to one's spouse.

A large percentage of our tasks are paradoxical. These tasks are designed to explode patterns of behavior. Paradoxical tasks are usually behavioral prescriptions to be carried out at home. They include reading paradoxical messages outside the session as well as carrying out assignments given in the session.

When we talk about formulating, delivering, and tracking a paradoxical intervention, we are in effect referring to the process of setting up a homework assignment. Whatever happens in the session has little therapeutic import in itself. Thus, the purpose of the session is to set the stage for the next week's assignment. If the client requires some skills training, this should begin in the session and be extended in the homework assignment.

Delivery of Task

If a paradoxical intervention is required, the therapist should wait until s/he has sufficient information and assign the task at the *end* of the session. The therapist uses the session to collect data about the problem. As the session proceeds, the therapist formulates hypotheses about the problem in terms of how it is sustained and how to change it. A paradoxical homework task should always be assigned at the *end* of a session, even if the session must be terminated early. There are several reasons for this rule.

A task may be assigned prematurely. A therapist who assigns a task early in the session probably does not have enough information to give a directive. The therapist may also discover that with more information a better task could have been developed. The client's agenda for the session could also have been that the more important issue would have been discussed later in the hour.

A task assigned early might not deal with the most important issue unless the therapist decides to change the task. Changing tasks is not recommended since it could lead the client to lose confidence in the therapist and give the client more reason to object to undesirable tasks.

The most important reason for giving the directive at the end of the session is that a paradoxical directive creates a double-bind. By definition, the person placed in a double-bind is not permitted to comment on it. In order to prevent the client from commenting on the bind or undoing the task, the therapist must give the task and quickly terminate the session.

The paradoxical task should be given as clearly as possible and the therapist should check to see whether the directive has been understood, unless the task's purpose is to confuse the client(s). In most cases questions about the task should not be answered. After receiving a task, clients may appear shocked, angry, depressed, placated, and often times perplexed. The therapist should not get hooked on those feelings since they are a part of the client's game of escaping from the bind. The therapist may mention that the task will be discussed in the next session and that a detailed account of how the task worked is expected.

Paradoxical tasks may be given with a *motivation or rationale* for doing them. The rationale for an assignment depends upon whether the therapist actually wants the client to follow through on the task or resist it. In delivering a task which the therapist wants the client to fight, the therapist wants to maximize the client's level of resistance. Several methods may be used to increase resistance. The therapist may present the task in an authoritarian manner or from a one-up position. Clients who need to one-up the therapist can win only by resisting the task. Rohrbaugh et al. (1977) have suggested using the non-dominant representational modality of the client in presenting these types of tasks. For example, if the client operates in the kinesthetic modality the task could be presented in the auditory modality. The therapist may want to be challenging, even judgmental, e.g., "I don't think you will be able to _____." Finally, the therapist may exploit the client's sense of pessimism. Telling clients to enact their worst thoughts or that things are going to change slowly or are hopeless is almost always perceived to be a challenge.

The therapist may want the client to do or try to do the task. In these cases the level of resistance needs to be minimal. The therapist will need to motivate the client in whatever way possible or provide a rationale before the task is given. Many clients will already have sufficient motivation to carry out the task. Others will comply because "you are the doctor." Some clients will respond to straightforward encouragement about the importance of doing the task. The level of resistance also seems to vary with the immediate level of psychological hurt and discomfort. Sometimes clients do attempt to avoid dealing with the hurtfulness of a problem. Clarification and discussion usually produce a deeper concern and awareness of the destructive elements of the problem, especially when the long-range consequences of the problem are examined. One of our favorite ploys is to ask the client to predict what things will be like one year from now if the problem continues. One man, for example, had been postponing the final decree of his divorce for over two years. He could not resolve his ambivalence about returning to his wife, nor could he realistically perceive whether she would have him return. He had felt so pressured to make a decision that he had already entered the hospital once for exhaustion. He was asked to predict what would happen if things were to continue unchanged. He immediately said that he would "lose his health." This insight helped give him more motivation to carry through on resolving the situation and doing the homework.

The rationales used in giving assignments is limited only by the therapist's creativity. Rohrbaugh et al. (1977) have developed an interesting rationale for prescriptive paradoxes. They tell the client that learning to control a symptom is a two-way street. One must therefore learn how to turn a symptom on or enact a dysfunctional pattern or sequence of behavior before one can stop it. They also schedule symptoms (e.g., be depressed 15 minutes each morning) and offer as their rationale that it is better to take charge of when the symptom occurs than for it to occur spontaneously.

We often stress the importance of learning from symptomatic behavior. The task is assigned and the client is instructed to become a spectator of his own behavior. The client is told to observe how s/he initiates his/her symptomatic behavior, how s/he perpetuates it, and how others react. The client is told that by engaging in the behavior consciously s/he will learn from it.

> In one case, a young woman would start a fight with her husband when she was feeling a need for affection from him. Through a discussion of their fights, we discovered that she would stop herself from letting her partner know when she felt she needed his affection and support. She was instructed to start a fight the next time she felt empty, unloved, and unsupported; under no circumstances was she to tell him how she felt. She was also instructed to try to find some way to stop the argument once it started. The "learning from the symptom" rationale was given to the client.
>
> She had an occasion to use this task later the same day it was prescribed. She reported learning several things about herself. She saw a clear connection between her feelings of needing or wanting affection and starting a fight. She also realized that she launched a rapid fire attack on her partner so that he could not possibly respond in a supportive way. Most importantly, she felt

ashamed of her behavior, seeing that it hurt her partner and herself. The task led to the wife giving herself permission to express her needs and wants. The husband also learned more about himself. He saw how he withdrew from his wife's anger and did not know how to express his hurt or anger. Work was initiated to help the husband and wife express hurt and anger more directly.

Tasks may be assigned which have some special appeal to the client. A task with a good chance of succeeding must somehow fit the client's style or interest. These tasks take advantage of a client's special interests or abilities. It has sometimes been useful to appeal to the client's ability to act. In a few cases we have used clients' poetic ability or writing ability to help them formalize and communicate reactions to a task or reactions to others. Clients have been asked to draw schematics, make flow charts, develop contracts, and devise formulas related to their problem.

A practical issue is when a person should do a task during the day or week. The task should fit the circumstance and the client's schedule. In some cases clients have been instructed to do their task early in the morning or just after going to bed, depending upon when the symptom spontaneously occurred and when the client has time to do the task. Generally speaking, the task should be assigned so that it is not permitted to occur spontaneously.

Tracking the Intervention

A task is assigned in order to help achieve a particular goal. Part of giving a task is being able to predict what kind of change(s) will take place. Experienced paradoxical therapists are usually able to discuss the kinds of change a task will produce and make plans for the next assignment. This method can be called tracking an intervention.

The task assigned needs to be carefully recorded. At the beginning of the next session, the client is asked to report on the task. It is important to obtain everyone's reactions if we are dealing with a multiperson system. Since the task is designed to meet a specific goal and the therapist has predicted to him/herself how it will turn out, s/he is able to evaluate the effectiveness of the task.

Sometimes a task will not produce any change or it will produce an unexpected change. In a few cases the therapist will discover that a week is not enough time for the task to take effect. In fact, Selvini Palazzoli et al. (1980) have advocated meeting on a monthly basis since they believe it takes that long for their paradoxical tasks to produce all the effects. We have found that most tasks work or at least begin to take effect within a one-week interval. There have been a few cases in which the task had a clear-cut delayed reaction. The issue of how long the interval between paradoxical sessions should be is still unsettled. Our experience certainly does not correspond to that of Selvini Palazzoli et al. (1980). One way to explain this difference is that they work with very disturbed families, while we have worked with more functional families. In addition, we have done more work with individuals and couples. It could be hypothesized that the sessions need to be spread out more in direct proportion to the number of clients being treated and the severity of the problem. Selvini Palazzoli has, in fact, pointed out that if the interventions "hit the mark," the changes in feedback loops take a while to produce an observable change. These changes should be clear to the therapist before making further interventions, hence requiring longer intervals between sessions.

When a task does not produce the desired changes, the paradoxical therapist accepts responsibility for the failure. The client is not seen as a culprit. An ineffective task indicates that the therapist erred somewhere in the previous steps. To remedy this situation the therapist must review the problem again and remain cognizant of the most recent failure. Information about why a task failed is usually critical in formulating the next task.

Assuming a task has succeeded, the therapist and client are ready to proceed. An experienced paradoxical therapist can begin a session with several possible tasks for the next week and change or modify them as necessary. A beginning therapist will discover that it is difficult to formulate a paradoxical task during a session. The concentration and familiarity with the approach required to formulate a task are usually too much for a beginner to deal with in the session.

There are two ways to deal with this problem. One solution is to go to the session with several potential tasks. This solution will work only if the therapist has a good supervisor or support team. It is usually beyond the limits of a beginning paradoxical therapist to develop strategies prior to a session. A second solution is to take a break following the session in which to formulate a task and then deliver it to the client verbally or send the clients home and mail them a letter containing the message or task. We will discuss the numerous advantages of taking the last option in a later chapter.

A question we are frequently asked about giving paradoxical messages and homework assignments is how we keep a straight face when telling clients to carry out seemingly absurd tasks. On the surface many tasks do appear absurd to the point of being humorous. The therapist may feel like laughing as the directive is being given. If the therapist understands the intent of the task and believes it will work, the problem of delivering the task disappears. The assignment then becomes just another assignment. There do seem to be some emotions reflected in giving certain types of directives. We tend to appear very serious and solemn in restraining behavior, predicting relapses, and declaring impotence. Prescriptions to do more of the same seem to be conveyed with some degree of nonverbal disqualification or humor. This issue deserves careful videotape analysis. As yet, nothing has been written on this topic.

PRINCIPLES OF PARADOXICAL INTERVENTION

The paradoxical therapist must learn to think a certain way if treatment is to be successful. Otherwise there will be no real understanding of how the paradox will affect the problem or how to follow up on an intervention. Working paradoxically involves conceptualizing problems systemically and paradoxically. Systemic conceptualization of problems is ecological, dialectical, and reciprocal. From an ecological point of view, problems (behaviors) do not exist in a vacuum. Hence, it is essential to grasp the social nexus in which the problem exists and involve that network whenever possible. The symptom is part of a system of behavior and serves a function for that system. The symptom affects the system and is in turn affected by it. There is a relationship between the symptom and the system which is reciprocal or circular and precludes simple cause-effect thinking about problems. The problem permeates the system as a sequence or pattern of behavior. It is not an isolated entity.

From a dialectical point of view, problems may represent difficulties in creating new roles of behavior for new situations. Systems are in a constant state of change, requiring new rules for governing themselves. From the dialectical perspective, a problem can occur when one believes the solution to a difficulty is the implementation of that difficulty's opposite polarity. An "either/or" view of reality is a trap which denies us the ability to move to different frames of reference, to multiple alternatives. Reality cannot be hypostatized, for it changes as we do. Finally, dialectical thinking means looking at both the positive and the negative aspects of symptoms in terms of their antecedents and consequences. It must be recognized that symptoms serve a positive function.

The therapist must also think paradoxically. At the theoretical level this means seeing problems in terms of the double-bind described earlier. At the practical level, it means devising therapeutic double-binds as methods of treatment. After the problem has been interpreted within the systemic/paradoxical perspective, the therapist is ready to act.

There are five basic principles in paradoxical therapy. These principles may be applied within or across sessions to individuals, couples, and families. The methods of intervention mentioned in this section are described in the next chapter.

The first principle uses the symptom as an ally:

> *Principle One:* New symptoms are positively relabeled, reframed, or connoted.

The second principle applies to all symptoms which occur within a social context. If the symptom does not serve any social function, go to the next step. This principle is critical in treating couples and families:

> *Principle Two:* The symptom is linked to the other members of the system.

Selvini Palazzoli et al. (1978a) have combined these first two principles through the use of positive connotation. Positive connotation simultaneously gives the symptom a positive function and puts all the members of the system, including the identified patient, on the same level. The symptom may be linked to the rest of the system by involving all the members in the paradoxical task. This procedure is discussed in the next chapter under the headings of interactional and transactional paradoxes.

Symptoms are traditionally viewed as behaviors which are beyond voluntary control or which control the behavior of a system. The third principle involves changing the direction of control:

Principle Three: Reverse the symptom's vector.

In terms of the individual, this principle means that the symptom is to be consciously enacted. The intentional enactment of the symptom places the individual in charge of the symptom. In addition, it is usually advantageous to change the magnitude of the symptom. The symptom is enacted in such a way that it is amplified. If the symptom is reversed within a system of interaction, it is essential to involve others in this process. There are two basic ways to achieve this goal. The first is to have other system members help the symptom bearer have the symptom. For example, the father may remind mother that it is her time to feel depressed and take charge of the children so she can do her task. The second strategy is to have the other members play a paradoxical role. Assume the symptom is a daughter's acting-out and taking charge in a single-parent family. The daughter is told to exaggerate her taking charge of the mother. At the same time, the mother is told to assume the paradoxical role of the child. She is instructed to give up her position of authority and to pretend to be a helpless child.

The fourth principle deals with the temporal aspects of the symptom:

Principle Four: Prescribe and sequence paradoxical interventions over time in order to bind off the reappearance of the symptom.

The symptomatic behavior must be paradoxically prescribed. One or more methods may be used over time in order to block the reappearance of the symptom. A single intervention is usually not enough to produce the desired outcome. The therapist should develop an overall strategy. In many cases the following sequence of paradoxical interventions will prove effective: 1) positive relabeling, reframing, or connotation; 2) symptom prescription; 3) predicting a relapse; 4) prescribing a relapse.

Principle Five: The paradoxical prescription must force the client(s) to act on the task in some way.

There are several ways to insure the client's active involvement. The first is to prescribe the task in a ritualized fashion (Selvini Palazzoli et al., 1978). Ritualized prescriptions must be carried out at specific and regular times. The therapist may also prescribe a number of behaviors in a fixed sequence. A second way to force behavior is to paradoxically prescribe that, whenever *x* occurs, the client is to have the symptom. In other words, the paradoxical task is made contingent on some event known to occur. Finally, the paradoxical message can be put in writing and the client(s) told to read the message on some regular basis. This method forces the clients to think about their situation or act it out in a prescribed fashion.

CONCLUSION

In this chapter we have offered both general guidelines and principles for paradoxical intervention. The reader must remember that these guidelines are highly flexible. However, we believe it is important to closely follow the principles outlined here until the therapist has become experienced in this approach.

The five principles of paradoxical interventions provide a general outline. In the next chapter, each method of intervention referred to in the principles is fully described. The therapist must synthesize the principles and the method of intervention in a creative and flexible manner. Learning to practice this type of therapy requires considerable cognitive effort. The therapist may need to read and reread the principles and methods of intervention several times in order to see the various combinations of strategies.

6

Organizing paradoxical techniques

Watzlawick et al. (1974) discussed ways of reframing problems. They used the term "reframing" as a class to refer to different paradoxical techniques and presented ten different ways to reframe problems. In each case of reframing, the problem is lifted from an old frame of reference and placed in a new one which helps change the system so that the problem can be resolved. As an organizational system their ten ways of reframing fails. While it is true that all the techniques allow the problem to be reframed, the techniques which are described seem to share little in common with each other.

Andolfi (1980) has also attempted to organize paradoxes. According to him, there are two ways to reframe problems: 1) prescribing the symptom; and 2) prescribing the rules. Prescribing the rules simply refers to prescribing the disturbed behavior and is used to enlist the cooperation of a system.

Another group of therapists to present an organized view of paradoxes were Rohrbaugh, Tennen, Press, White, Raskin, and Pickering (1977), in an APA symposium. Tennen presented the organizational structure by identifying three basic techniques: prescribing, restraining, and positioning. These techniques are described in detail later in the next chapter.

Sluzki (1978) also attempted to provide a how-to manual of paradoxical techniques. For each technique he provided a rule, rationale, and description. He said, for example:

> If A and B concur in defining A as victim and B as victimizer, *then* find a way of reversing the roles/labels and state the reversal forcefully (p. 377).

> If A and B describe a sequence of events that leads to conflict or to the emergence of symptoms, *then* search for the events or steps that precede what has been described as the first step in the sequence. If you cannot specify it, nonetheless state its existence. If it has been detected, and is accepted by A and B as possible, then repeat the cycle (i.e., search for a still previous step, or at least assert its existence) (p. 378).

> If A has a symptom that fluctuates within the day or the week, *then* instruct A to select times in which the symptom improves to tell B that it is worse (p. 381).

The problem of defining paradoxical interventions is a difficult one. The definitions either seem so broad and abstract as to be meaningless or not broad enough to include all the techniques asserted to be paradoxical in nature. Therefore, we lack underlying dimension(s) or a continuum on which to classify, type, or organize the techniques. We do not have a solution to this problem. In order to be as inclusive as possible, our working definition of a paradoxical technique is one that produces a second-order change. The benefit of adopting this definition that is not clear and precise is that it allows us to synthesize the literature of paradoxical techniques.

There are two ways in which all the paradoxical techniques may be classified. The first way has to do with the level of the intervention. This refers to whom the intervention is directed. The second way is according to whether compliance- or defiance-based paradoxes are used.

LEVELS OF PARADOXICAL INTERVENTION

The level of intervention refers to the fact that paradoxes may be directed to individuals, couples, or families. The basic distinction is that of individual or systemic paradoxical intervention. In the family therapy literature, this question has been raised as: Should the focus of intervention be directed toward the individual or should it be directed toward the family relationships? For the paradoxical therapist the question is the same: Should the paradox be individual or systemic? The answer to this question is not an either/or proposition. The level of the intervention depends upon the therapist's theoretical orientation, the number of clients present, and the therapist's knowledge of how to work at different levels. Many family therapists use both types of interventions, while others use mostly systemic intervention (e.g., Selvini Palazzoli et al., 1978a). A review of the paradoxical literature shows that much of the early paradoxical work was individually oriented.

There appear to be at least three categories of paradoxical intervention within the individual vs. systemic class (see Table 1). The first category of paradoxical intervention (Category I) is strictly individual. The paradoxical message is directed toward only one person, as in individual therapy, or toward one member of a family. The second category of paradoxical intervention (Category II) is directed toward all the members of a system, but as individuals. Each member is given a paradoxical message or task, and each is clear about what his task is to be. Category II paradoxes focus on dyadic interactions. In order to be effective the individual paradoxical messages must also be inter-

Table 1

Individual vs. Systemic Paradoxes

Category	Descriptive Name	Focus of Message
I	Individual	Paradox directed toward one individual
II	Interactional	Interlocking paradoxes directed toward two or more members
III	Transactional (or Systemic)	One paradox directed toward a system of behavior which focuses on a single dynamic or pattern of behavior within the system

locking, just as the behavior of dyads is interlocking. The third category of paradoxical intervention (Category III) is directed toward the relationship between or among the members of a system.

Category I paradoxes are the most prevalent in the literature. Some of the Category I paradoxical tasks may be carried out alone while others require the involvement of other people. There are many excellent descriptions of Category I paradoxes available in *Uncommon Therapy*. For example, in one of Erickson's cases (Haley, 1973) a young man suffered a driving phobia. He was unable to drive on certain city streets and could not leave the city limits without vomiting and fainting. Erickson instructed him to drive to the edge of town in the middle of the night wearing his best clothes. He was to stop and leave his car for 15 minutes to lie in a ditch next to the road. The man was to repeat this behavior after driving every two car lengths. The man quickly became so angry at the task and Erickson that he drove on without any problem.

Category II paradoxes are more complex. They require that the therapist give two or more interlocking paradoxes to the members of the family. These paradoxes usually prescribe the pattern of interlocking behavior in a system. For example, the therapist might say to the couple, "Mary, the next time you feel unloved, start a fight with John. John, the next time you feel you are getting too intimate through your fighting with Mary, get out of the fight by being logical or rational or by leaving the room."

Category III paradoxes are extremely complex and require a thorough understanding of the family relationship system. This category of paradoxical intervention requires that the therapist "collapse" his Category II paradox by focusing on a single dynamic and avoiding naming names in giving the paradox. This means the paradox is directed toward the plural "you." For example, a couple complaining about their differences could be told, "So, you don't have anything in common. Maybe you should split up." Collapsing a Category II paradox may take the form of prescribing that the members act in certain ways when they experience a certain feeling or when a certain event occurs. It could also involve giving the family a single descriptive message or relabeling a system's behavior. These paradoxes place all the members of the system on the same level of focusing on one sequence of behavior.

The following message demonstrates a Category III paradox: "We have some suggestions about how to improve the ways you already fit together. The next time you are feeling powerless, make a major purchase on your own, or start an argument with your mate. At all costs you should not tell your mate when you feel powerless or out of control. In fact, if one of you asks the other whether you feel powerless or out of control, you should deny it." Note that in this paradox the issue of powerlessness is the central dynamic, and reference is made to "you," the couple, not the individuals.

Another Category III paradox reframes the behavior of the family in positive terms and is descriptive rather than prescriptive. For example, "This family must really care about each other to come here for help," or "This is a strong family to be able to admit that (it needs help, etc.)." Category III interventions may also keep the family guessing. The paradox may be true of only one of several members of the system. For example, the statement "The more this family changes the more it stays the same" suggests that at least one person in the system has changed and someone else has not. This statement creates a puzzle for the whole family. It creates confusion and tends to destabilize the system. The intent of this paradox is to pull everyone together and facilitate communication by getting them guessing who has changed and who has not.

The therapist's first decision is whether to intervene at the individual, dyadic, or transactional level. The second decision s/he must make is based on the type of problem and the amount of resistance present. This brings us to the next class of paradoxes—compliance- and defiance-based paradoxes. After the therapist has decided which categories of paradoxes to use, s/he is then ready to select the most appropriate technique for intervening.

COMPLIANCE- AND DEFIANCE-BASED PARADOXES

Rohrbaugh et al. (1977, 1981) divided paradoxical interventions into two categories depending upon whether the purpose of the intervention was to have the client carry out the paradox or reject the paradox.

Tennen (1977, 1981) described the *compliance-based* paradox as one in which change will occur when a client tries to obey a paradoxical prescription. He stated that compliance-based strategies may work in two different ways. Either the client will find it impossible to comply with the prescription or the prescription will create an aversive or punishing situation for the client.

Suppose a client is told to enact the symptomatic behavior. One effect this type of intervention has is to bring under voluntary control behavior which has heretofore been out of control. This type of intervention seems to be effective in treating obsessions, anxiety attacks, and other symptoms where the client is actively fighting the symptoms. When the client enacts the symptom consciously, the symptom is no longer a spontaneous or uncontrollable behavior.

The second way a compliance-based paradox works is by creating an ordeal. For example, one extremely distressed woman was afraid she would harm her children by stabbing them with knives from the kitchen. She would only think about this late at night or when she awoke during the night. She slept poorly so she spent much of her night in these obsessive homicidal thoughts. This client was instructed to set her clock for 2:00 a.m., go outside when the alarm rang, lock herself out of the house (this part was actually the client's idea), and obsess over these thoughts on her front porch. It was midwinter in the northeast, which meant she confronted an ordeal with the weather. After just two weeks she was sleeping soundly and her thoughts of harming her children had disappeared. In addition, there was no evidence of child abuse or symptom substitution. She did become aware of, and angry with, her husband's lack of support.

Defiance-based strategies are based on the assumption that the client will defy or oppose carrying out the paradoxical directive. The therapist actually wants the client to not carry out the prescription, thus allowing the client to change. In other words, by predicting that something will happen, the therapist helps to make it *not* happen.

An example of this type of strategy is to predict that something will happen which the therapist knows the client will oppose or fight vigorously. This strategy has frequently been used with couples who fight with one another. They are instructed to fight more on the basis that: a) even if they tried they couldn's stop; b) they like fighting too much; c) they're really artists and shouldn't stop; d) this is the way they prove their love to each other and so on. The rationale used should be one as unacceptable as possible to the clients in order to give them more reason to defy and defeat the therapist.

Another strategy is to instruct clients to go slow, in short, to restrict the client's view of his own self-determination. Telling a couple they're not ready to give up fighting completely so they should have at least X number of fights the following week is an example of restraining change. What the therapist is really doing through a defiance-based intervention is getting the clients to fight with him rather than with each other.

> In one especially resistant case a couple entered therapy in order to become more intimate. They had a long history of communicating by blame only. After several attempts to get this couple working together in a more intimate way, it was clear they would not. Straightforward interventions had at best a transient effect. The couple was sent a lengthy paradoxical letter listing reasons why they would find a more intimate relationship too difficult to achieve and suggesting that they work on developing a parallel marriage. The couple responded to the letter with hurt and anger. They said they were more willing than ever to work together. Each spouse said they had to be personally responsible for making change happen. They were angry because they felt the letter was "too strong" and they said they didn't want the therapist to "write them off." The letter had the effect of breaking the impasse over their ambivalence toward personal and marital change. This letter is included later in the next chapter to illustrate the technique of restraining.

Tennen (1977) noted that compliance-based interventions place an emphasis on the *intra*personal or *intra*psychic. They deal with the client's struggle to eliminate the problem by doing more of the same. Defiance-based paradoxes emphasize the interpersonal domain. They reflect the client's need to oppose, defeat, or be one-up on the therapist. In general, Watzlawick et al. (1974) have done more work with compliance-based paradoxes, while Haley (1976) has done more work with defiance-based paradoxes.

Rohrbaugh et al. (1977) asserted that the social-psychological theory of reactance developed by J. W. Brehm (1966, 1973) and S.

Brehm (1976) offers the best framework for understanding when to use each of these two categories of paradox. Psychological reactance is the need to maintain or preserve one's freedom. The loss of freedom can be either self-imposed or imposed by others. One could feel depressed, for example, either because one is making negative statements about oneself, or because of a number of losses created by self and others. The degree of reactance in a client is a function of three variables which may be manipulated by the therapist. These variables include: a) the importance of the free behavior to the individual; b) the number of freedoms threatened; and c) the magnitude of threat.

Rohrbaugh et al. (1977) emphasized two parameters of the Brehms' theory in deciding whether to use a compliance- or defiance-based strategy. The first is the *reactance potential* of the individual(s). Some individuals seem to constantly need to defy others. L'Abate (1976) has called those types of individuals oppositional and Millon (1969) called them negativistic. Highly reactant clients play a game of opposites with their therapist. They manage to say or do the opposite of what the therapist suggests. They also fail to carry out tasks or homework assignments and reject efforts to see or do things differently. The second parameter of importance is the client's *perceived freedom* of his symptom or symptomatology. An unfree symptom would be one that is perceived to be out of the patient's control. In short, an unfree symptom occurs spontaneously.

According to Rohrbaugh et al. (1977), when the symptom is unfree and the reactance potential is low, the compliance-based strategy is indicated. If the reactance potential is high and the target behavior is free, then a defiance-based strategy is recommended. The defiance-based strategy also applies to situations where others generally see the target behavior(s) as a problem but the symptom-bearer does not feel his behavior is out of control. Instructing an acting-out teenager to be even more disruptive would be one example. In a case such as this one, the teenager might believe he can control himself but others would disagree.

Paradoxical interventions are not indicated when reactance potential is low and the target behavior is perceived to be free. In this case, a more traditional or direct approach to therapy is appropriate. If a paradox is used, they recommend a compliance-based paradox to make the symptom an ordeal. For example, a woman could not decide whether she liked her breasts because she thought they were too small. She was instructed to think for 15 minutes each day about how small and ugly her breasts were. A week later she decided her breasts "weren't too bad after all."

Finally, the most difficult pattern with which to deal is when there is high reactance and an unfree target behavior. Rohrbaugh et al. (1977) suggested a couple of ways to deal with this pattern. One way would be to elicit compliance. This could involve soft selling the intervention (e.g., "I only have one suggestion, but I can't know whether it would work for you. This problem really has me baffled and feeling helpless"). A second approach could consist of providing a number of alternatives or an illusion of choice (e.g., "You can do it today or tomorrow"). A third approach is based on Watzlawick et al.'s (1974) strategy called Devil's Pact. The client is urged to agree to a plan before it is heard regardless of how unreasonable it might be. A fourth option would be to target free collateral behaviors using a compliance-based strategy. Getting a client to enact his symptoms in certain places or in limited ways exemplifies this idea. In other words, the symptom itself is not attacked, but where it occurs is modified by having the client enact the symptom only in specified places.

The level of reactance exhibited by the client can be modified by a skillful therapist. A therapist may change his style and manner of delivering directions. The therapist may act authoritarian, controlling, and powerful to increase reactance potential or he may approach the client gently and take a one-down stance to lower reactance potential. The use of language also appears to be extremely important. If the therapist joins with the client's linguistic style and use of metaphors, and presents the paradox in the client's dominant representational system, he is more likely to obtain compliance. If the therapist does the reverse, he is more likely to elicit reactance and increases the chance that a defiance-based paradox will be effective.

Grinder and Bandler (1976) have suggested a way of manipulating the client's resistance by using his/her linguistic style. They have stated that people organize and communicate their experiences in terms of three representational systems: visual, kinesthetic, and auditory (see Table 2). They maintain that people tend to use one repre-

Table 2

Identifying Representational Systems

Meaning	Kinesthetic	Visual	Auditory
I (don't) understand you.	What you are saying feels (doesn't feel) right to me.	I see (don't see) what you are saying.	I hear (don't hear) you clearly.
I want to communicate something to you.	I want you to be in touch with something.	I want to show you something (a picture of something).	I want you to listen carefully to what I say to you.
Describe more of your present experience to me.	Put me in touch with what you are feeling at this point in time.	Show me a clear picture of what you see at this point in time.	Tell me in more detail what you are saying at this point in time.
I like my experience of you and me at this point in time.	This feels really good to me. I feel good about what we are doing.	This looks really bright and clear to me.	This sounds really good to me.
Do you understand what I am saying?	Does what I am putting you in touch with feel right to you?	Do you see what I am showing you?	Does what I am saying to you sound right to you?

NOTE: From *The Structure of Magic. Vol. II.* Palo Alto: Science and Behavior Books, 1976. Reprinted with permission of Science and Behavior Books. Copyright 1976 by John Grinder & Richard Bandler.

sentational system more than the others. When the therapist and client speak the same language or use the same representational system, greater trust and cooperation is induced (low reactance). The opposite happens when there is a mismatch between the representational systems of therapist and client. A therapist may assess a client's dominant representational system by listening to the kinds of verbs used and manipulate his sytem depending on the degree of reactance he wants to induce.

7

A compilation of paradoxical techniques

The purpose of this chapter is to describe different ways of intervening paradoxically. Most of the existing literature on paradoxical psychotherapy has been case study reports presenting one or two techniques in specific situations (see Weeks and L'Abate, 1978). It is difficult to see how some of these interventions are related, except in the case of symptom prescriptions, which are relatively common. This chapter attempts to organize sets of paradoxical techniques and is designed to serve as a "mental template" for paradoxical intervention.

The main emphasis in this review of techniques is on their clinical application. In order to work paradoxically the therapist must first have a thorough knowledge of different techniques. A wide array of paradoxical techniques have been catalogued in this chapter. This compilation allows the therapist to sort through interventions until the appropriate technique is located. Next, the therapist must know the mechanics of interventions, the specific formats for interventions. These formats can be described in some cases and illustrated in the others. Finally, a compilation helps give the therapist a rationale for interventions. Certain paradoxical techniques are more effective than others in given situations. Knowing that a specific technique is likely to produce a given outcome allows the therapist to make some predictions about whether the goals of treatment will be fulfilled.

The systemization of paradoxical techniques is a difficult, if not impossible, task. The organization of the techniques is based on several criteria. Techniques which are similar in format are grouped together. For example, when the therapist wants the client to exaggerate or enact the symptom, we say a prescription has been made. Some techniques are grouped by the intent or goal of the therapist. If the therapist wants to prevent a relapse, then a restraining technique is postulated. Other techniques are organized around resistance. The therapist may or may not want the client to actually carry out a directive. The confusion over a definition of paradox may stem from the fact that all the principles underlying paradoxical therapy have not yet been explicated. A therapy in search of theory stumbles along in an unscientific way. It is as much an art as a science. The purpose of this chapter is to delineate guidelines for paradoxical interventions and describe the interventions grounded in those guidelines.

The paradoxical techniques reviewed in this section have been grouped together and each group may be used to achieve specific goals or unravel a particular bind in which a client is trapped.

The compilation of techniques presented in the following pages is by no means exhaustive. It is a beginning effort to distill and organize the various paradoxical techniques reported in the literature in addition to those developed in our own clinical work.

REFRAMING

Watzlawick et al. (1974) defined reframing as changing " . . . the conceptual and/or emotional setting or viewpoint in relation to which a situation is experienced and to place it in another frame which fits the 'facts' of the same concrete situation especially well or even better, and thereby change its entire meaning" (p. 95). In short, the meaning attributed to the situation is changed. Watzlawick et al. (1974) transformed this concept into clinical practice by the use of basically prescriptive paradoxes (see Watzlawick et al., 1974, Chapter 10).

Grunebaum and Chasin (1978) have suggested that the term reframing be used to refer to a change in the model in which behavior is viewed. Reframing would then refer to shifts from the moral to the medical model or from the individual to the family model. Moreover, they assert that reframing automatically leads to a change in the way a person is labeled. Relabeling, then, refers to a change in the way a person is labeled without a change in the frame of reference. Their attempt to differentiate between these two terms may be most useful in shifting the frame of reference for pathology from the individual to the system. In essence, the problems of the identified patient are diffused to the family system. If it is useful to view psychopathology as a trans-actional phenomena, as we have argued, then the therapist's first task is to reframe the identified patient's problem as a contextual one. In fact, the most common use of the concepts of reframing and relabel-ing have been to frame problems in a family context.

The use of reframing to achieve a systemic definition of a problem has been best described by Selvini Palazzoli et al. (1978a). They call this procedure *positive connotation*. The purpose of positive conno-tation is to avoid drawing lines in the family such that the identified pa-tient is "bad" and everyone else is good. They maintain that the con-notation " . . . puts all the members of the group on the same level, thus avoiding involvement in any alliance or divisions into subgroups, which are the daily bread of such systems' malfunctions" (p. 56).

Positive connotation allows the therapists to access the systemic model. Selvini Palazzoli et al. (1978a) assume that the purpose of pathology is ultimately "the stability and cohesion of the group." The connotation is designed to emphasize the homeostatic goal of the family as a whole. It defines the relationships among the family mem-bers in a positive way, while shifting the context of therapy to the sys-temic level. The connotation also creates a paradoxical situation for the family. Why does a family that wants to preserve itself need a "pa-tient" to achieve its goals which the therapist has connotated as good?

In one of the cases presented by Selvini Palazzoli et al. (1978a), a ten-year-old boy developed psychotic symptoms following the death of his grandfather. The message given to this boy and his family at the end of their first session demonstrates both positive connotation and symptom prescription. The male therapist said, "We are closing this first session with a message to you, Ernesto. You're doing a good thing. We understand that you considered your grandfather to be the central pillar of your family . . . he kept it together, maintaining a certain balance. . . . Without your grandfather's presence, you were afraid something would change, so you thought of assuming his role, perhaps because of this fear that the balance in the family would change. . . . For now you should continue this role that you've assumed spontaneously. You shouldn't change anything until the next session . . " (p. 81). In this case it is clear the connotation is designed to help the family see that it is searching for stability through the use of Ernesto. The framing of Ernesto's behavior also has the effect of changing his label from a "bad" child to a "good" child.

Peggy Papp (1977) demonstrates the use of positive connotation in one of her full-length case presentations. She told a woman that she should continue to act helpless and incompetent because that gave her husband a chance to show how strong, caring, and protective he could be. She further warned of the negative consequences that might occur should she attempt to change.

RELABELING

Relabeling refers to changing the label attached to a person or problem without necessarily changing the frame of reference in the sense of moving from the individual to the dyadic or systemic level. Relabeling in the paradoxical literature almost always means changing a bad label to a good label. The emphasis has been on the positive, adaptive, or normal.

In recent years there has been a great deal of controversy over the effects of labeling clients as "sick," "mentally ill," or even as "patient." It has become apparent that it is much easier to attach a label of any kind, especially a negative label, than it is to remove the label. Labeling has a tendency to determine the person's behavior through the self-fulfilling prophesy. It also tends to determine other people's perception of, and reaction to, the label bearer. Psychologists and other professionals are not as immune to this process as many would like to believe (Rosenthal, 1966). In fact, in their training, psychotherapists are encouraged to label individuals with a variety of negative labels. Therapists do, however, have a choice in how behavior is labeled. They are not locked into a rigid nosological system, even though some psychologists and psychiatrists behave as if they were.

Relabeling is a creative and complex therapeutic technique. It produces change for several different reasons. One of the effects of relabeling a behavior is to change the client's phenomenological perspective. The new label provides the client with a new way of thinking and feeling about the behavior. When the label is directed toward a system of behavior, it changes not only the identified patient's perception of the problem but also the system's view of the symptom bearer. In addition to changing how a problem is perceived, a new label may imply that the symptom is the vehicle of change. It may give the client an expectational set that change is imminent. Landfield's (1975) example of labeling confusion as a preparation for new growth is an excellent illustration. The client's confusion is relabeled as a step in the process toward new growth. This statement leads the client to expect something good will happen next, as well as, perhaps more importantly, relieving the usual tension associated with confused states.

Relabeling a symptom almost always gives the client a greater sense of self-control. Sometimes clients are more upset by feeling out of control than by the symptom itself. The new label changes the direction of control. The symptom no longer controls the client; the client controls the symptom. In Landfield's example, the client would no longer feel the confusion was forever in change, but would see that it is good, useful, or necessary for change to occur.

Theoretically, relabeling exemplifies the linguistic principle that language is not reality—the map is not the territory (Bandler and Grinder, 1975). Words do not represent or symbolize an immutable reality. Selvini Palazzoli et al. (1978a) see this principle as releasing individuals from *linguistic tyranny*: We act as if we are locked into a certain kind of reality because of our language. They emphasize the fact that language is linear rather than circular. Therefore, we tend to define behavior in terms of simple cause-effect, rather than systemic-circular, processes. The interactive and transactive nature of living systems is therefore ignored. In addition, language emphasizes the digital—good vs. bad, black vs. white, normal vs. abnormal. It also keeps us on the level of content. In short, language is poorly designed to help us talk about relationships. These points are consistent with Kelly's (1955) position that there are many different and workable ways to construe reality.

Relabeling may occur at a variety of levels and in at least two ways. Relabeling may occur at the individual, dyadic, and systemic levels, as we pointed out in our earlier section, and the labels may be positive or negative. Giving a previously defined undesirable behavior a positive label makes it desirable, and giving a previously defined desirable behavior a negative label would mean that it is either carried to the extreme or that the behavior is poorly or inappropriately expressed. Most of the work on relabeling in the paradoxical literature has emphasized the change of negative labels to positive labels. There are, however, therapeutically useful ways of attaching more pathological labels and relabeling the "good" as "bad."

Landfield (1975) emphasized the use of positive labels for apparently individually isolated symptomatic behavior. He offered several examples of how behavior usually viewed negatively could be seen positively. These included rigidity as a steadfast purpose, immaturity as aggressive exploration, and hostility as involvement. Weeks (1977) offered a number of examples which once again require the therapist to be creative and break from the usual set of accepting, assigning, and perpetuating negative labels. His examples included:

> reclusive—exploring one's own consciousness; withdrawing —taking care of oneself; passive—ability to accept things as they are; social—carefully selecting one's acquaintances; submissive —seeking authority and direction to find oneself; insensitive— protecting oneself from hurt; seductive—wanting to attract other people and be liked; wandering—exploring all possibilities; oversensitive—tuned in to other people, very alive and aware; controlling—structuring one's environment; impulsive —able to let go, be spontaneous; oppositional—searching for one's own way of doing things; self-deprecating—admitting one's own faults to oneself; crying—ability to express emotion, especially hurt (p. 286).

The new labels given in these examples are all positive in connotation and involve some element of truth. The labels are intended to open up new possibilities for the client by establishing a powerful contradiction. At the individual level, conversions from the negative to the positive have been very popular.

Relabeling at the dyadic or marital level has been reported frequently by paradoxically oriented therapists and family therapists. As early as 1963, Haley had identified relabeling as a general therapeutic strategy for couples. He stated, "in general, whenever it can be done, the therapist defines (labels) the couple as attempting to bring about an amiable closeness but going about it wrongly, being misunderstood, or being driven by forces beyond their control" (p. 139). Milton Erickson (Haley, 1973) was a master at relabeling couples' problems. In one of his cases a newly married man with a playboy reputation became impotent on his wedding night. His bride felt disappointed, bitter, and rejected. Erickson relabeled his impotence as a compliment. He told the couple that the husband was so overwhelmed by the beauty of his new bride that he felt incompetent and he was incompetent.

Relabeling a couple's behavior follows the same principles extracted from Selvini Palazzoli et al.'s (1978a) work. The couple's symptoms are redefined in such a way as to suggest they are striving for stability and cohesion. We will present a number of cases in later chapters of our approach to this problem. Our examples tend to emphasize the couple's symptoms as an expression of love, care, or protection.

L'Abate (1975) pointed out how positive behavior or motivation could be given a negative connotation. A prime example is how mates may be told that they love and protect each other so much that they go to all lengths to avoid conflict, confrontation, and thus, intimacy. Intimacy is bascially viewed as the ability to share hurt (L'Abate, 1977b, 1979). The fact that the couple's problem resulted from their love and protection of one another implies that love and protection are negative labels. Yet, they are not negative labels in the couple's perception. The paradox for the couple is that their particular expression of love and protection is destructive. To escape from this paradoxical situation the couple must learn to fight fairly and share hurt. We have found this particular strategy useful in dealing with systems of behavior where pathology has positive antecedents.

Andolfi (1979) uses the term redefinition to refer to both reframing and relabeling. In one of his cases he begins the first session by relabeling the symptomatic behavior of a young girl who mutilates her face by saying, "This is the first creative product of your curriculum vitae! It seems that in this sea of conformity the only creative thing you see or feel is what you have written on your face" (p. 71). This redefinition was intended to help the client find her creative potential and feel less conventional.

Stanton (1981b) has discussed the use of relabeling with drug-dependent families. He and his co-workers have labeled extremely destructive behavior as having a good motivation. Their term for this process is *ascribing noble intentions*.

Grunebaum and Chasin (1978) have shown how the use of more pathological labels may be therapeutically useful. In two of their couple cases, the husbands had been depressed and their wives had become angry and frustrated with them. The wives had defined their husbands' behavior as bad or irresponsible. Following the attachment of the diagnosis of manic-depression, each couple showed improvement. While the therapists do not speculate why this procedure worked, it could be hypothesized that the diagnosis reduced the anger of the wives, making them more amenable to treatment. The change in labels in this case also changes the frame of reference from the moral to the medical model. Attaching a pathological label may be of use if it makes the client more amenable to change and if the label implies the possibility of a "cure."

In another case, Grunebaum and Chasin (1978) described a man who had been labeled by psychologists as suffering from "atypical development." His parents and sibling had considered him to be basically normal and had pushed him to do things beyond his limitations. Their efforts had disturbed him to such an extent that he was psychotic when admitted to a hospital. After a diagnosis of mental retardation and psychosis was made, the family lowered their expectations and helped the client find a situation more appropriate to his limitations. In this case the pathological label helped the family respond more appropriately to the client.

Relabeling may also be used at the systemic or familial level. The technique is essentially the same as for the dyadic level. The most common form of relabeling at the systemic level is to point out the positive aspects of the identified patient's behavior or to normalize the behavior. In anorectic families, Minuchin deemphasizes the idea of anorexia as an isolated phenomena to emphasize how the anorectic wants to be special or is stubborn (Minuchin, Rosman, and Baker, 1978). In general, the label connects the identified patient's newly defined behavior to the family.

We would like to point out one important use of relabeling in the early phase of therapy at the systemic level. Families seek therapy because they experience difficulties they have failed to resolve. They come for help to eliminate a problem. Their motivation for seeking therapy is negatively motivated and results, we believe, in a high dropout rate. The family enters the first session with a sense of failure. They have a problem they have been unable to resolve. Entering therapy is often seen as an admission of failure or self-defeat. Family members usually feel angry and split off from one another. The problem tends to alienate them from one another rather than unite them in the way people feel united in success. It is useful in the first session to relabel the family's motivation for therapy (L'Abate, 1975). This relabeling can be achieved by pointing out that only a strong family could admit problems or weaknesses. The fact that the family came in together "proves" that the family members care about one another.

Relabeling is a challenging art. The therapist is challenged to think dialectically—to see the good in the bad and the bad in the good. This kind of thinking requires practice. It requires a genuine commitment from the therapist that the new label is not a trick but will have meaning for the client(s). It is sometimes surprising to see how clients readily accept the truthfulness of new labels even when they appear far-fetched.

While it is possible to discuss reframing and relabeling as two separate techniques, we recognize that they are, in fact, overlapping. Unlike Grunebaum and Chasin (1978), we believe relabeling may lead to reframing, just as reframing may lead to relabeling. For example, an anorectic child is viewed by the parents as sick, which means the parents have nothing to do with the etiology or treatment of the problem. If the child can be successfully relabeled to be stubborn, then the parents do become involved. Parents know they are expected to deal with stubborn behavior so an interactional agenda is sold to the family. The problem is no longer individual, but systemic— hence, reframed.

Prescriptions

The most common form of a therapeutic or pragmatic paradox is symptom prescription. According to Rohrbaugh et al. (1977), the underlying message or paradoxical situation created by prescriptive interventions is: a) In order to lose your symptom, keep it and/or exaggerate it; and b) will your uncontrollable symptom to occur voluntarily. There are literally hundreds of cases in the literature of symptom prescription at the individual, dyadic, and familial levels.

Using the work of Milton Erickson as his model, Zeig (1980b) listed three principles in symptom prescription. These are: a) using the client's frame of reference; b) using the client's behavior, motivation, or cognitions to make small changes; and c) allowing the client to use his/her resources in discovering a solution. In short, the therapist elicits the solution from the client.

The mechanics of symptom prescription are not as simple as they appear. Zeig (1980b) pointed out that a symptom is a communication which can be divided into several components. Thus, there exists a symptom complex of which any part may be used in prescribing the symptom. The elements of the symptom complex are:

a) Cognitive—The client's thoughts when the symptom occurs.

b) Affective—The client's feelings when the symptom occurs.

c) Behaviors—The client's behaviors when the symptom occurs.

d) Contextual—The context in which the client experiences the symptom.

e) Relational—The effect the symptom has on others.

f) Attitudinal—The client's attitude toward the symptom.

g) Symbolic—An object which represents the symptom.

In making a prescription the therapist may select just one element of the complex to prescribe. For example, the cognitive element of depression could be prescribed by saying, "Whenever you are depressed, pay close attention to what you are saying to and about yourself. Learn from your depression. Make a list of all these thoughts and bring them to the next session." The decision to use one element over another cannot be specified. The therapist can use this schema in attempting to match the client's ways of thinking, feeling, etc., about the problem.

In an earlier section of this chapter we discussed compliance- and defiance-based paradoxes. Ways of eliciting the client's cooperation to do tasks were also discussed. Zeig (1980a) has added five more techniques which maximize the chances of the client attempting to carry out a prescription. The first technique is *to provide a rationale for the paradox*. This technique is very common and has been discussed already. The second technique is *to use indirection*. The symptom is prescribed in an ambigious way such as, "Don't do anything about your problem this week so we can see how really bad it is!" Indirection may be used with any of the elements of the symptom complex. The third technique is *to prescribe the symptom in such a way that the client can reject some of the directions*. This technique works well with contextually oriented tasks. The therapist may specify several context conditions for the occurrence of the symptom. The client can then discharge any resistance by not doing part of the task. *Utilizing the client's curiosity* is Zeig's fourth technique. The client is told that a special task will be given when the time, place, etc. are right. The last technique is *to effect a small change in the symptom*. Making a small change in a symptom must be viewed phenomenologically; i.e., the therapist considers how important certain aspects of the symptom are to the client. As the client describes the symptom, the therapist assesses which of the elements are over- and underemphasized. The client may, for example, focus on the feelings attached to the symptom while never mentioning the thoughts attached to the symptom. Since resistance can be lowered by promoting what the client perceives to be a small peripheral change, the cognitive aspects of the symptom could be prescribed. The use of these techniques is also useful in making a variety of other paradoxical interventions.

There are literally dozens of cases in the literature of symptom prescription at the individual, dyadic, and transactional level. These cases demonstrate the technique of symptom prescription, as well as the kinds of problems, client's relationships, and special techniques used in making this kind of intervention.

Much of the early work in the area of individual symptom prescription was done by the logotherapists. They called the technique *paradoxical intention*. Paradoxical intention, a technique devised by Victor Frankl (1967), has been used successfully in the treatment of phobias, obsessive-compulsive disorders, and anxiety states (Gerz, 1962; Solyom et al., 1972). The technique is similar to that of prescribing the symptom. The therapist instructs the client to train himself to experience the symptom to an extreme degree as frequently as possible. The symptom has run its course when the client recognizes its absurdity and gains sufficient self-detachment to laugh at the symptom.

Frankl (1975) described the viciously circular nature of symptoms which brings forth a fear of recurrence or anticipatory anxiety. The anxiety provokes the symptom, whose recurrence reinforces the anxiety or fear. The technique of paradoxical intention is aimed at the phobic's flight from his fear and the obsessive's tendency to fight his fears. In short, the client is instructed to give up the mechanisms of resistance he has developed to avoid giving in to his fear and to face his fears head on.

Frankl (1975) reported the case of a woman who had suffered from severe claustrophobia for 15 years. She feared riding in all modes of transportation and entering buildings. She would become anxious and would fear that she would suffocate and die upon entry into a closed, confined space. As part of her desensitization treatment, she was encouraged to let the symptoms become as severe as possible and to seek out places where her symptom had previously occurred. Within a week, she was able to enter innumerable places symptom-free, first with her husband and then by herself, that she had previously entered only under considerable duress.

Symptom prescription has also been used in the treatment of a number of other resistant individual problems. Lamb (1980) described a case involving a college student who suffered from severe test anxiety attacks and fainting. These symptoms first occurred after an unspeakable incident with her ex-boyfriend. She had been medically evaluated and treated by specialists at two prestigious medical centers but with no results. The student first consulted Lamb, her instructor, about taking her test in a private session; otherwise, she felt she would pass out in class. Lamb described a similar problem of her own to this student. The therapist suffered from grand mal seizures and described some of her worst seizures in graphic detail. Her seizures were so severe that, were the problem not so serious, the situations would have been humorous (e.g., throwing strawberries all over the inside of her mother's car during a seizure). The therapist declared that she was a far better "passer-outer" than this student could ever hope to be and challenged her to a contest. She told the student to go home and practice passing out. If on the day of the exam she could demonstrate more flair than the instructor in passing out, she would be awarded an A on the exam. On the day of the exam, the student was rechallenged. During the exam, as soon as Lamb noticed the student hyperventilating, she mimed that she should try harder to pass out. The student laughed and continued working. She had not fainted since the first meeting nor could she pass out now in any situation.

One other case relevant to this discussion involved a day hospital client who was obsessed with the facts that he might die at any moment and that he was suitable for only manual labor. This therapist suggested a number of menial job possibilities to the client but the client found a reason to reject each one. It was then suggested that he consider becoming an embalmer or mortician. He smiled and said he would find that a disagreeable occupation. Finally, it was suggested he become a professional grave digger so that if he did die on the job all he need do was fall inside the grave. The client laughed and said that while the job did have its good points he was not that close to death. Every time this client was confronted with the immediacy of his death or his lack of job skills, he resisted the therapist. Unfortunately, this client was seen only once by this therapist (Weeks). The psychiatrist treating him continued to use this strategy and in a matter of weeks the client, though still unemployed, had significantly reduced his references to death and dying.

Watzlawick et al. (1974) presented two interesting variations of symptom prescription with individuals They called one method "advertising instead of concealing." This technique is used with behaviors that are usually inhibiting or embarrassing, such as public speaking. The client is instructed to advertise the symptom. A client who blushes might be told to force blushing to a bright red, or a nervous speaker might be instructed in ways to appear more nervous. Another form of symptom prescription is used to help make the covert, overt. This procedure also operates on the principle that small changes can produce great effects. If a client fears making mistakes, s/he is told to go ahead and make one small mistake in the problem situation.

Prescriptions at the dyadic and familial level have become more popular as family therapy has developed. In order to make prescriptions at these levels the therapist must carefully assess the sequences of behavior, remembering that causality in relationships is not linear, but circular. The prescription is then delivered to the system. It is important to set up systemic prescriptions so that they cannot be undone or commented upon. The bind must be an inescapable box requiring a "jump" to a higher level. In some cases it is important to note that a behavior is prescribed but the prescription must be denied if questioned.

A prescription is in effect a double-bind. One aspect of a double-bind is that the bind must not be commented upon. Hence, in a prescription it is sometimes essential to instruct the participants to deny that they are carrying out the prescription. The members may be told that they are to deny that this was their homework assignment. Many couples and families will immediately recognize this bind. They will ask how they are to tell when they are really being serious from when they are doing the assignment.

> One young couple had not negotiated who would do what in the running of the household. The husband constantly requested that his wife do everything related to the running of the family. She would comply but later feel so resentful that she would eventually explode. They were told that the husband should ask his wife to do three things a day that he knew she would not want to do, without telling her these requests were part of an assignment. She was to respond to his requests by first using devious tactics not to comply and then telling him no. He was to continue pressing her until she had said no three times. The rationale given to the couple was that she needed all the practice she could get in saying no. While this statement to her was true, the husband needed to learn how to recognize her no's and respond ap-

propriately. The husband also became immediately concerned that he would need something done that his wife would refuse to do because she would think the request was homework. He would be forced to consider his requests carefully. He felt all his requests were reasonable and underestimated the requests he made of her.

There are other cases in which part of the behavior to be prescribed includes an element of denial. Building denial into the prescription serves two purposes. It helps to make the bind more compelling and it prescribes an important part of the problem behavior.

In one family a 13-year-old boy was requested to clean his room thoroughly once a month. He would invariably do a sloppy job but deny this fact and feel angry and resentful that his mother called him a storyteller. First, the sequence of behavior was prescribed but with an important change. The boy was told to clean his room but leave one part dirty so that when his mother "caught" him he could do it over easily. The mother was told to do a military-style inspection. After her inspection she was to guess what the boy did not do properly. The boy had been told to make her job as difficult as possible by leaving something she would never guess, such as dirt in a corner, or a book out of place. The boy was told that even if his mother guessed the right thing, he was to deny it and tell her it was something else which he was not to do over. By building in the denial aspect to this situation, the therapist is in fact prescribing what happens and averting a power struggle. The boy can win or be one-up if he does a good job of cleaning and leaving something difficult to find.

Paradoxical prescriptions are usually given in the form of tasks or homework assignments. Guidelines for developing these tasks have been presented in Chapter 5. Homework tasks have been used in many ways. Haley (1973) presented a case of Erickson's involving the breaking of an overly-involved mother-son dyad. The son wet his bed almost on a nightly basis. The exasperated mother brought her son to Erickson, who assigned a task to the two of them. The mother was to get up between 4:00 A.M. and 5:00 A.M. each morning to check her son's bed. If it was wet, he had to get up and practice his handwriting with his mother supervising him. If the bed was dry, his mother still had to get up to check. The boy went along with the task because his mother would like it less than he. The boy ended up with a dry bed, beautiful handwriting, an admiring mother, and even increased involvement with his father, who now played ball with him.

Hare-Mustin (1975) used a similar strategy with a four-year-old boy who threw spectacular and frequent temper tantrums. She instructed the boy to continue having his tantrums but only in a special tantrum place at home. The child and his family decided on the specific location. In the following session, the child picked a time of day he would tantrum. By the third session the tantrums had decreased to a bare minimum. Hare-Mustin expressed concern over the rapid change and asked the child to choose a day for a tantrum the following week. The child had no further tantrums.

DeShazer (1975) presented an excellent example of a task used to point out the functions of a symptom in a family's interaction. A family brought in their 14-year-old son, who had a stealing problem. The therapist instructed the father and son as a team to hide five one-dollar bills around the house. If the son resisted stealing the money for one week, he was to be allowed to come in for a previously denied private session with the therapist. Otherwise, the whole family was to come in. The son did come in alone and received instructions to steal two of the bills but to delay his usual dramatic confession until the next family session. At this time the son went through a dramatic display of guilt and sinfulness, gaining the full attention of his family, but this time the father's open complicity was known to all. The father was able to recognize his part in his son's stealing episodes, as were other family members.

DeShazer (1978a) has suggested that the use of prescriptive paradoxes is useful in certain types of relationships. He used Jackson's (1968) typology of relationships. These were: stable satisfactory, unstable satisfactory, stable unsatisfactory, and unstable unsatisfactory. The satisfactory relationships were the ones to respond to prescriptions such as fighting more in order to fight less. The unsatisfactory relationships responded better to a type of paradox we will describe later.

In the last chapter we reviewed several ways Madanes (1980) prescribes behavior in family situations when the child is presented as the identified patient. These included prescriptions to have a problem; to pretend to have a problem; and to pretend to help the parents. The use of pretense has been infrequent among paradoxical therapists. Yet, it appears to be a powerful change technique. The simplest method is to ask the client to have a problem. This request allows the client to gain control over a symptom that was defined as either partially or fully out of control. It gives the client permission to have the symptom through the positive connotation.

An excellent example of "pretense" is demonstrated in the case of "A Modern Little Hans" (Haley, 1976). In order to prevent a child from suffering a relapse over a dog phobia, the therapist encouraged the dog-phobic boy to pretend to be afraid of his new pet.

> In one of our cases, a couple was feeling helpless vis-à-vis the wife's in-laws. Her parents constantly gave them gifts and made subtle demands on them. They were instructed to begin asking for more and more from her parents (see Watzlawick et al., 1974, p. 116-119). Furthermore, they were told that they must also pretend to be very helpless and childish. The latter task was emphasized because this couple was immature. By pretending to be childish, they not only became more aware of their behavior, but were, as instructed, pulled closer together in coaching each other on how to be childish in order to successfully complete this paradox.

Andolfi (1980) has identified another prescription in which *the rules of the system are prescribed*. This is illustrated in one of our cases. A family had an implicit rule not to fight or argue. They were told: "During the next week something will happen to make you angry with each other, and you will want to get these feelings out in the open by fighting. The family rule not to fight is good because if you were to fight it could be disastrous for the family. The next time a fight happens, we want you to avoid it by everyone going to his room. When you get angry you should hide it, and deny you are angry when someone asks you." Notice how this message prescribes the rule not to fight and not to comment on the rule. However, the message implies that people get angry and talk about being angry. The paradox also creates a guessing game of who is angry and not talking about it.

Selvini Palazzoli et al. (1978a) have described a technique which seems identical to Andolfi's (1980) prescription of rules. The main difference is that Selvini Palazzoli et al. (1978a) are more formal and specific in their approach. These therapists described a prescriptive technique called the family ritual. The family ritual is prescribed when the family has developed a myth which is destructive to a family and its members. The family ritual is designed to " . . . change the rules of the game, and therefore the family epistemology, without resorting to explanation, criticisms, or any other verbal interventions" (Selvini Palazzoli et al., 1978a, p. 95). The family ritual is itself highly formalized. Every action is prescribed to the family: time, place, frequency, what is to be said, and the order in which the member speaks. Some family rituals are carried out repeatedly and others only once.

Selvini Palazzoli et al. (1978b) have also described a technique they call the *ritualized prescription* for use with family systems with child identified patients. A ritualized prescription is void of content. It dictates only limited formal aspects of the family's behavior. The ritualized prescription was developed for use with a variety of families; no specific behaviors are prescribed. The format of the ritualized prescription is: On even days of the week—Tuesdays, Thursdays, and Saturdays—beginning from tomorrow onwards until the date of the next session and fixing the time between X o'clock and Y o'clock (making sure that the whole family will be at home during this time), whatever Z does (name of the patient, followed by a list of his symptomatic behavior), father will decide alone, at his absolute discretion, what to do with Z. Mother will have to behave as if she were not there. On odd days of the week—Mondays, Wednesdays, and Fridays—at the same time, whatever Z may do, mother will have full power to decide what course of action to follow regarding Z. Father will have to behave as if he were not there. On Sundays everyone must behave spontaneously. Each parent, on the days assigned to him or her, must record in a diary any infringement by the partner or the prescription according to which he is expected to behave as if he were not there. (In some cases the job of recording the possible mistakes of one of the parents has been entrusted to a child acting as a recorder or to the patient himself, if he is fit for the task.) (p. 5).

This prescription has several goals. First, it prevents the parents from interfering with each other in dealing with the child. Selvini Palazzoli et al. assume that part of the problem has been the parents' inability to work together. Second, the usual transactional patterns or triangles are broken up. The team hopes this prescription will establish a competition between the parents to see who can be most helpful for the child. Third, the task is an information-gathering device for the therapists, especially if the task is not followed as prescribed. Like all tasks, the ritualized prescription is a diagnostic device. The ritualized prescription prescribes the process or the pattern of interaction among family members.

Prescriptions Related to Time

Prescriptions can be developed with regard to time and contingent on certain internal events, such as feeling states and the actions of others.

An important and relatively popular form of prescription is known as *symptom scheduling* (Newton, 1968). The procedure involves setting up a time for the client to enact the symptom, including the length of time that the symptom is invoked. In setting up a symptom schedule, some rationale is usually provided to convince the client to do it. Statements such as "you have to learn how to start it before you can stop it" or "it's going to happen anyway so let's take charge of it a little" could be used. The symptom is then scheduled. The client may be instructed to engage in the symptomatic behavior for a certain period of time each day, perhaps at a specific time.

> A client who was anxious and worried chronically was told to set aside one hour a day to worry. She was told she worried constantly because she had always avoided thinking about troubling matters, and consequently never made any changes. She was further told that she would have to become a competent worrier if she could ever hope to resolve her anxieties. Effective worrying meant she had to think the worst possible thoughts and keep a list of everything that might worry her for her "worry time." Moreover, she was told to worry the full hour even if she felt like stopping early.

Most clients for whom this method is used will find the first couple of days to be painful. They will worry the fully prescribed time. In just a few days clients typically want to stop short and resent the task. They report they are no longer worried and think that "all that worrying" was absurd.

The time of day may also need to be prescribed in scheduling a symptom. The scheduling of the symptom should occur prior to the time of its spontaneous occurrence, provided there is a typical time during which the symptom occurs. Therapists have variously scheduled symptoms first thing in the morning, at bedtime, during the middle of the night, and during the first five to ten minutes of each hour. However, scheduling a symptom at a given time is not always the best strategy. Contingent enactment is also appropriate to feeling states (e.g., feeling anxious, depressed, fearful, inadequate) and thoughts or obsessions. In other words, when a particular feeling arises, the client is instructed to "stay with it" for a given period of time and to exaggerate it as much as possible.

Another variation of this technique is not to prescribe the length of time but to instruct the client to extend the feeling state. One man who felt depressed from time to time was told to pay attention to the moment he started to feel better and then force himself to stay depressed for 15 more minutes before he let himself feel better. The purpose in making this kind of prescription is to show clients how they control their moods. Usually, clients following this prescription realize what they do to place themselves in an undesirable mood because they use those ideas to keep themselves in the mood longer. At the same time they are learning to keep themselves in the mood longer, they are also learning what they can do to control the mood.

When a specific behavior is involved, it is more appropriate to prescribe an increase in the frequency of the behavior, in addition to requiring that the behavior be exaggerated. For example, a beginning therapist thought he had to study and read constantly in order to be a good therapist. When his therapist suggested that he carry all his books to his sessions so he could check things, the idea was recognized as absurd and his obsessive studying stopped.

Descriptive Paradoxes

When something is described, it is also prescribed to have certain attributes. A description of a phenomenon is a statement of how something exists which we believe others must share. A description becomes a prescription for others to accept our way of seeing a phenomenon. The descriptive messages we give to clients are usually written and involve three parts. Two parts of the message are recognized paradoxical techniques while the third part is a technique we developed. Most of our descriptive paradoxes have been used with couples or families and are described in detail in a later chapter.

The message usually consists of three parts: a) a positive connotation; b) a dialectical description of the relationship; c) a cryptic or restraining statement. First, we tell the couple or family how we like the pattern of behavior or symptomatology they have established. We usually say something like: "We like . . ." "We want to congratulate . . ." or "You have a real talent, ability, etc." In short, a negative behavior is relabeled as a positive behavior. The second component of descriptive messages is to describe the nature of the family relationship in dialectical terms. That is, oppositeness, contradiction, or polarization is pointed out in their relationship (e.g., if one spouse or member of the family is up, good or right, the other(s) must be down, bad or wrong). In other words, the polarization present in the system is described and exaggerated. In order to be an effective message, the dynamics of the system must be well understood. Our experience has shown that dysfunctional family systems are characterized by polarization. There are many different types of polarization which may exist in family systems. These polarizations have been best described in the family theories of L'Abate (1976), Stierlin (1974), and Boszormenyi-Nagy and Spark (1973). The third component of the message is a question directed toward the family about the pattern of their behavior. This question usually asks if the family is really happy with the situation described and may ask them to "wonder" about different ways of relating or may suggest different ways of relating. The third message may also restrain change. The client(s) may be told not to change or that it is too risky to change. The following letters exemplify written paradoxical messages:

Dear _____,

I am very impressed with your commitment to your marriage and how much you care for each other. Each of you is very considerate of the other's feelings, and you do not wish to hurt each other.

I think that it's very commendable that you care for each other so much that you try to be like your partner. Each of you can depend on the other to avoid confronting your differences. This has allowed you to achieve a harmonious relationship which would be too risky to change right now. Why tamper with a good thing?

* * *

Dear _____,

It has been accurately acknowledged that Eddie is a special child. In part his uniqueness stems from his growing up more slowly than his agemates; his thumb-sucking reflects his need to be younger than he is. He will have to go through a period of immaturity which includes behaviors such as thumb-sucking before he can gain the maturity of his agemates.

We would like to enlist your assistance in helping Eddie grow as fast as he can. Since thumb-sucking is developmentally important to him, he should be allowed—in fact, encouraged—to suck sufficiently. To insure this, we request that you insist Eddie suck his thumb for a minimum of 10 to 15 minutes in school and at home, whenever you observe him sucking his thumb.

It may happen that Eddie will attempt to be rebellious by refusing to suck his thumb. If this should occur, remind him of his need for adequate sucking.

We thank you for your consideration and ask that you have Eddie read this letter with you, both at home and in school.

The third letter demonstrates the use of a descriptive message, plus the use of symptom prescription. This letter also demonstrates in a subtle way the use of metaphor. There are numerous sexual metaphors in this letter because in this couple each spouse complained of numerous sexual deviations in the other.

Dear _____,

We were really impressed in our session with your fighting routine. It is rare that we see a couple who has worked out their fighting to such perfection. You both pick up on each other's cues in a highly sensitive manner and launch penetrating attacks and counterattacks with the precision of a well-oiled machine.

We are convinced that your constant devotion to fighting is the way you express your love and care for one another. Why else would two people who see good in each other expend so much time and energy, endure such wailing pain, and tolerate such self-sacrifice and self-torture? Your fighting also serves to keep the relationship in perfect balance—not too close and not too distant. Unfortunately, something happened to throw it out of balance—probably you're trying to get too close too fast. Getting too close too fast can be dangerous to a relationship which is so delicately balanced. In order to get things back in harmony you should rely on the tried and true method you have already developed of fighting with each other, even if you have to pretend to fight.

Should you decide, against our judgment, to try to move closer to each other than you can too quickly, we believe there is only one safe way for you to do it at the present time. Nick, whenever you want Doris to move closer to you, you should try to make this happen by playing helpless, disorganized, confused, and impotent. Do not under any circumstances tell Doris what you want directly. Doris, when you see Nick doing this, you should be overly helpful, responsible, organized and solicitous, but you should also not offer any *real* help since you know this is a game. Doris, whenever you have the urge, you should convey it to Nick by doing just the opposite. You should castigate him for any moves toward you until your soul can bear no more.

We realize this letter may not be clear to you and may sound unusual. You both should read and reread it over a period of days in order to begin to understand it.

RESTRAINING

There is a myth in psychotherapy that a therapist should always foster or encourage change. The therapist is expected to be optimistic about the future. Therapists are expected to be supportive. When therapy is not proceeding smoothly, then the therapist works harder. The therapist may even work on the problem more as the client works on it less. This kind of approach may eventually lead to a dependency relationship, with the therapist assuming a rescuing role. Traditionally, when it is clear to everyone that no change is taking place or has occurred, the therapist will confront the client or terminate the treatment with a possible referral.

Restraining is a method used to avoid the kind of problem that has just been described. We use the term broadly to denote the fact that the therapist restrains change. Rohrbaugh et al. (1977) have asserted that the underlying message in a restraining statement is: In order to change, stay the same or give up. There are actually many different ways to restrain change. These restraining methods can be used at different points in the therapeutic process to help facilitate or maintain the changes that have already been facilitated. The use of restraining techniques has probably been underemphasized in the paradoxical literature, especially in the schemas of the paradoxical methods. As we stated earlier, the most frequent, and we believe one of the most effective, sequences of paradoxical methods is positive connotation, a prescription, and finally a restraining message.

The therapist may want to use a restraining strategy early in the therapeutic process in order to avert a problem that seems to be inherent in psychotherapy. Clients seeking therapy voluntarily are assumed to want to change. Why then is change so difficult? Why does the term resistance exist? Change implies a loss of sameness or permanence. It involves psychological risk, danger, and adjustment. Change in one person in a system affects all the others. The client will not be able to predict the future behavior of the system as s/he begins to change. The homeostatic ideal of the system is placed in jeopardy. Permanence is a form of protection for self and others. Is it any wonder that clients are ambivalent about making changes?

Negative Consequences of Change

One procedure to help resolve the client's ambivalence about change is to help polarize and crystalize the consequences of change to motivate the client. This procedure may be used in most cases but is probably more useful with problems of long duration and where resistance appears high. In fact, all the restraining methods are well-suited for high-reactance clients. This procedure can be used after the initial assessment and goal-setting. The client is told that change can have both good and bad effects. Before the therapist can agree to help clients make a change they say they want, the therapist must be sure the cost of change is worth it to the clients. The therapist should prepare for the use of this method by thinking of all the "negative" consequences that could occur if the clients achieved the desired goal. In fact, these "negative" consequences are actually positive or beneficial changes but they are framed in a negative way. If possible, the therapist should consider the "negative" consequences in as many areas of the clients' lives as possible.

A client with a long history of depression sought treatment from us. He had been in treatment off and on over many years but never shown improvement. In an early session the "negative" consequences of change were considered. Prior to the session a list of consequences had been developed and in the session we asked the client to provide us with his own. The following is an outline of our concerns by category.

Negative Consequences of Giving up Depression

1) Community—This man had lived a sheltered and withdrawn life with few friends. His social network consisted of his sick mother, wife, and therapists. *"Negative" consequence*—if he were to give up his depression he would be able to make friends; making friends is stressful and often leads to conflict and rejection.
2) Parents—His father had died years before. His mother, 80 plus, had been depressed since her twenties. *"Negative" consequence*—If he gave up his depression, he might be seen by his mother as disloyal. How could he be happier than she?
3) Marriage—The client's wife was an overpowering, assertive woman who had always been in charge of the household. She was rigid, obsessive, and constantly watched for her husband's next depressive episode. *"Negative" consequence*—If he gave up his depression, he would want to be more assertive and take more responsibility in the marriage. This fact would surely lead to fights and deprive his wife of things to do. What would she do with herself?
4) Self—The client's depressions had forced him to be dependent on others. He defined himself as a "depressed man." *"Negative" consequence*—If he gave up his depression he

would become independent. He would have to discover who he was at a late age.

5) Children—The client had two grown children. He rarely saw them because he refused to travel. He once became depressed on a trip. He felt guilty over his lack of support of his children and was overindulgent in providing financial support, which he could not afford. *"Negative" consequence*— If he gave up his depression he would be able to get closer to his children. He would have to get to know them all over. He would also feel more assertive and might start saying no to their requests for money, which could cause conflict.

With the presentation of each "negative" consequence, the therapist pointed out or invented reasons why the change could have bad effects. The therapist would also say things like: "Are you sure you're ready to tackle this? This looks risky or dangerous to me. This is a lifelong pattern—you should think carefully about giving it up."

This procedure challenges the client to change. It is a provocative device used to increase the reactance *not* to change. If the client does not argue with a "negative" consequence, the negative framing should be exaggerated or amplified. In this particular case, the client said, "If these are the 'bad' things that will happen, then I want them to happen."

* * *

In another case an older couple was attempting to move closer together since their last child had left home. Although they wanted to work out several issues, the main issue was one of intimacy. Each time this couple made a gain they quickly relapsed. The following letter was sent to them which contained: a) a positive connotation; b) a prescription (i.e., form a parallel marriage); and c) five negative consequences of change. The negative consequences in this letter were actually paradoxical predictions of events which might happen if they moved closer together. The couple responded to this letter by redoubling their efforts to work together. They disagreed with the five points listed. The letter was sent after the couple had been told that in order to get closer together they would first need to move apart.

Dear Mark and Betty:

I have given our sessions together a great deal of thought and I have arrived at the following conclusion.

It is clear to me that you both care greatly for the other. You have demonstrated your caring repeatedly and you have shared in successes along the way, only to return to your usual selves later.

What impresses me most about your relationship is how much you have sacrificed for each other. It seems important, if not critical, for you to maintain a certain amount of distance from each other in order to protect the relationship and survive as individuals. I am beginning to wonder whether it is possible for you to be closer to each other. Each time you move closer the end result is bad for the relationship.

Perhaps you should change your goals so that you have a parallel marriage.

I believe the consequences of moving closer together would be:

1) A painful period of re-negotiation. The way you define your marriage would change drastically—perhaps no marriage at all.
2) A period of depression would occur. You would have to ask yourselves why you didn't make these changes earlier, and feel you had lost part of your lives.
3) An intense period of self-examination. You would have to examine your reasons for sacrificing so much for the marriage and then decide what you want for yourselves. You have protected each other from making personal decisions for many years.
4) You would probably begin to have explosive arguments.
5) You would probably feel like the other person had won.

I want you to read this letter to each other every night until our next session, with Mark reading it the first night and then switching. Discuss it for no more than 30 minutes each night. I will discuss the letter with you in our next session if you like, but no earlier.

Inhibiting and Forbidding Change

Inhibiting and forbidding change are two other techniques used to deal with the resistance to change. Inhibiting change basically means going at a slower pace than the client maintains things should be going. To inhibit change we make statements such as: "Don't change any faster than you can." "If you must change, do so slowly and cautiously." "Why should you change such a good thing?" Watzlawick et al. (1974) usually stresses the importance of "going slow" from the outset of treatment. To increase reactance they stress the importance of making small changes.

Forbidding change is the next step in restraining change. There are two common ways of forbidding change. The first is what Watzlawick et al. (1974) called "giving in." The client is told to give in to the symptom and then it is prescribed. We use the following rationale and messages to forbid change: "I want you to give in to (name symptom). I want you to do this so we can find out how often it occurs this next week," or "Your (name symptom) is trying to tell you something important about yourself. I want you to try an experiment. During the next week just give up trying to stop your symptom and notice what is happening to you just before, during and after your (name symptom). I want a full report next week."

The other way to forbid change is more direct. The client is told not to engage in the behavior that the client requests help in changing. This technique has become the hallmark of sex therapy, although few sex therapists claim to be paradoxical therapists. In most cases, the clients are prohibited from having sex (Masters and Johnson, 1970). They are then told they may have sex under prescribed conditions only. The main reason for this injunction is to reduce performance anxiety, which is often the basis of sexual difficulties. Sometimes the mere prohibition not to do something is enough to facilitate the change the client(s) desire. They undergo a miraculous cure but will frequently relapse if a restraining strategy is not continued.

Milton Erickson frequently used prohibition of change. He stated:

> But, you see, that's the way human beings are. Whenever you start depriving anyone of anything, they are going to insist that you give it to them. When I instruct a patient to do something, that patient feels I'm ordering him. They want me to be in the unfortunate position of failing at that. Therefore they've got to keep me in the active task of ordering them. When I stop ordering them at the right moment, then they substitute for me and do things for themselves. But they don't recognize that they are substituting for me (Haley, 1973, p. 70).

Erickson used this technique to elicit responses from recalcitrant clients. He would tell clients not to tell him things until they were ready or he would constantly interrupt a client. He took control of the resistance by prescribing it.

Declaring Hopelessness

The most extreme form of going with the client's resistance to change is declaring change to be impossible. The client is told that nothing can be done to change the symptom. The situation is described as hopeless. This strategy is used as a last resort. If the client has not responded to the use of other change strategies, including other types of restraining, the therapist has little choice. The only way to gain control of the client's refusal or inability to change is to declare the situation hopeless.

Selvini Palazzoli et al. (1978a) have described the use of this method with families. According to them, the therapists must declare their impotence to the family without blaming the family. In short, the therapists state that it is they who are at fault because of their confusion, etc. The therapists may discuss their sense of helplessness and self-blame but never prescribe those feelings to the family. The therapists accept a one-down position and disqualify their role of being the initiators of change. Families generally react to this ploy by making "spontaneous" changes.

The strategy of declaring therapeutic impotence has not been described frequently in the literature. The reason is that it is probably not needed too frequently. We have used this procedure only as a last resort or when the client has presented a thoroughly hopeless picture to us. The strategies of inhibiting, forbidding, and declaring impotence may all be useful with "yes, but" clients. When every suggestion is responded to with "yes, but," the client is actively fighting the therapist. Declaring impotence can be useful with couples and families that fail to change or expect too much from treatment. The two cases which follow show how this procedure can be used.

In one case we treated a young couple who had made some changes initially but had deteriorated and failed to successfully carry out any homework assignments or tasks in the past month.

They were unable to set any goals for themselves because they focused on the past. The couple was confronted with what we had observed and told that we had tried everything we knew to help them. In a depressed tone of voice, we expressed our feeling of helplessness and hopelessness about the situation. We painted a very grim picture of the couple's past, present, and future. Finally, we said it would be a disservice to them if we continued to see them. We told them perhaps someone else could help them and that perhaps they needed a break from therapy.

As we made these statements to the couple, we observed that they both looked angry, especially the wife. In the sessions, the wife was typically very quiet and non-assertive. Her affect was almost always bland. When we finished our monologue, there was a long silence. Then the wife asserted that things were not as bad as we had made them sound, that they had done some of the tasks, and that she didn't want to stop treatment.

In the most hesitating and tentative way possible, we agreed to see them once more if they could make some change on their own during the coming week. They were to call us if they did; otherwise we said this was our last session and wished them success in working out their problems. In fact, we were committed to terminating if they could not make a change during the week. We would, however, have followed up on this case to see if they would have been more amenable to change in the future.

During the middle of the week the wife called to say they were ready for another session. Without going into detail, this couple made dramatic changes in the intervening week. They both came to the session looking much better than they had in weeks. Their mood was clearly hopeful and they responded emotionally to each other with positive affect. In a way completely out of character for the wife, she started the session by expressing how angry she had been with us in the last session. Her affect was congruent and for the first time she was assertive and vocal. She reported that she and her husband had spent hours talking during the past week about the problems they confronted. She said they had used some of the skills we had taught them and followed through on old homework assignments.

This case eventually came to a successful conclusion. The turning point had been our declaration of helplessness. The couple became motivated to change and set goals for themselves.

* * *

A second case demonstrates a variation of this technique. Once again treatment goals were difficult to establish because the clients, a professional couple, could not see any way for everyone involved in the problem to win. They were searching for an ideal solution to a complex problem. Rick and Mary had been living together for two years. Mary was married when she was in her late teens but divorced one year later. She said she played a child role in her marriage. Rick had also married when he was young; he had two children by that marriage, which ended in divorce after 12 years. He formed a second relationship with another woman just after his first wife separated from him and they had an unplanned child. The second relationship was never to be a permanent arrangement and when Rick discovered his partner was pregnant, he began to feel trapped and left her for Mary. This couple sought help because of the "on-off" nature of their relationship. They both said they wanted the relationship to work out for them but they seemed to fight constantly and each repeatedly threatened to leave.

In the first few sessions the couple set up short-term goals and were successful in meeting those goals through homework assignments. Their ability to communicate improved, they stopped mindreading, and most importantly, they discovered they could be separate individuals even within a relationship. Before, they each felt they had to put the relationship first and themselves second.

In the fourth session the couple was instructed to develop a series of long-term goals for themselves and the relationship. During that week the couple experienced a crisis, and for the first time Mary asked Rick to leave the house. In the following session, the couple's real problem emerged. Mary felt the relationship had no future because Rick was still seeing Ann, his previous partner. Rick felt he was trapped in the middle. He had decided he wanted to be a father to his one-year-old son by Ann, but Ann would not let him see his son outside of her house. He claimed that if he told Mary he was going to see his son, she would feel rejected and threatened, and if he didn't tell her she would probably find out since she frequently drove by Ann's house. The couple reported talking about this problem in some way almost every day but never to their satisfaction. They said they had talked to friends and lawyers, and had consulted friends who were psychologists.

The way the couple presented this problem indicated that they felt hopeless and were searching for the one right answer which they knew must exist. The first tactic used was to ask about the smallest change that might help solve the problem. They could not agree on any one change that would be workable for both of them. Observing that this tactic was not working, the therapist began to recast the situation. He pointed out how this situation reminded him of a drama with each member playing a fixed role. Next, he suggested that everyone was in a bind in this play—no one could expect to win. Finally, the therapist indicated that some situations are not changeable, but must be endured in the best way one can. The session was ended with the recommendation that each partner decide whether staying in the relationship was worth it under such impossible conditions. The therapist did not offer any possible solutions and did not offer any encouragement as the couple departed from the session.

The feedback obtained at the beginning of the next session showed major changes had occurred during the week. Rick said he had finally realized there was no simple solution to the problem. He could now stop his search for the ideal solution which he thought must exist. He felt better about some of his previous behavior because he realized he was in an impossible situation. In short, his attitude toward the problem changed. It was no longer awful that things were as they were; it was inconvenient. Rick reported his attitudinal change occurred within the first few hours after the session. He had discussed these views with Mary and she felt the same as Rick. Rick also decided he would tell Mary when he was going to Ann's house to visit his son. Mary discovered she could accept his visitations without feeling unloved or rejected. Moreover, Rick began asserting himself more with Ann. He refused to get hooked by problems she made up to keep him at her house longer. He also told Mary about some of his problems with Ann.

By the end of this session the couple expressed hope for their relationship and Mary said she felt Rick was in fact committed to their relationship. This case shows how it is important for the therapist to avoid getting caught up in the same kind of idealistic solution-seeking sometimes practiced by clients. The therapist must help the client find realistic solutions in some cases by being very "unhelpful."

DeShazer (1978a) has described another type of restraining strategy that is useful with certain types of relationships. He has asserted that his method is useful in dealing with what Jackson (1968) called stable-unsatisfactory and unstable-unsatisfactory relationships. These relationships, according to DeShazer, do not permit the clarification or setting of mutual goals. These couples tend to have mutually exclusive goals or insist that it is the other person who should change. In order to help this system set goals, DeShazer accepts and amplifies the resistance. He deals with the problem by obtaining detailed histories for each problem while stating that this is useful to the therapist and by cautioning the couple not to rush into making any changes until everything has been clarified. DeShazer follows up every "lead" immediately without finishing anything. This process amplifies the confusions and conflicting goals in the system, forcing or redirecting the system toward clarity and unification.

Predicting a Relapse

The last two types of restraining strategies to be discussed are probably the most significant because they need to be used frequently in working paradoxically. Predicting a relapse is essential to most paradoxical work. In general, a paradoxical prescription is given first and if it is successful the symptom suddenly disappears. The next step is to predict a relapse. The client is told that the symptom will suddenly reappear. By predicting a relapse the therapist is placing the client in a therapeutic double-bind. If the symptom does occur again, the therapist predicted it, so it is under his control. If it does not occur again, it is under the clients' control. The symptom has been defined in such a way that it can no longer be perceived as uncontrolled or spontaneous.

What happens when a symptom does reappear? The therapist has a number of choices. Another prescription may be in order. In most cases, its reappearance is less severe and can be dealt with by subsequent predictions of relapse until the symptom gradually disappears. As long as the symptom is defined in such a way that it is under someone's control, it is less disturbing or anxiety-provoking to the client. Consequently, the client has more energy to invest in the situation producing the problem. Many clients also view the relapse prediction to be a challenge. The only way to prove the therapist wrong is to not have the relapse.

In general, whenever a client shows improvement in the paradoxical approach, the therapists should wonder what happened to make the change and respond pessimistically. To insure the power of the predictive paradox, the therapist may even discuss things the client might do to make the relapse happen. The therapist may appear puzzled, perplexed, confused, and concerned when change occurs. He may wonder "when things are going to fall apart," "if the client hasn't changed too soon or too fast," or "how this change will affect others." He may predict that things will probably be the way they were or worse the next week.

> In one case a young couple complained about fighting too frequently—about three "big ones" a week. A fighting prescription was given and the next week the couple reported no fights. The therapist suggested that during the next week the couple would more than likely have six fights—the three they regularly had plus the three they had saved up. They were asked to count the number of fights. They responded to this prediction with laughter and actually said they would prove us wrong. As usual, they did. When a problem has disappeared in such a way, it is best for the therapist to quietly drop the issue and say that the client resolved the problem before it was ever "really worked on."

Prescribing a Relapse

The final form of restraining, relapse prescription, is an extension of relapse prediction. Sometimes it is useful to prescribe a relapse rather than just predict it. In fact, we often use both of these procedures as a two-step process.

First, we prescribe the symptom's reenactment so that it is an ordeal. The behavior is represcribed to an extreme degree, with the rationale that it is sometimes useful to look at and learn from old patterns. If the behavior is made an ordeal for all those involved in the problem, it is less likely to recur. In several cases of treating parentified children, we required that the child begin to act like a parent and the parent act like a child (Johnson, Weeks, and L'Abate, 1979). Both parent and child view this task as an ordeal.

Secondly, prescribing a relapse is useful with families to help bind off the child being used as a way for the parents to deal with a marital issue. Once the parents have started to work together, it is easier to see how they used the child. The relapse prescription helps them to see how they could fall back into the same patterns and to discover ways to prevent this from happening. For example, a child could be instructed to have the symptom whenever the parents look angry with each other but aren't talking. If the child begins to relapse in the future, the parents are forced to consider their part in the problem. To facilitate a relapse prescription, it is helpful to ask the child to pretend to have the symptom (see Haley, 1976, p. 249).

The use of restraining strategies requires careful timing and delivery. The beginning therapist is probably too hesitant in making restraining statements. The general rule is that as soon as change begins to happen a restraining statement should be given to the client. Clinical judgment plays a major role in the timing of these interventions. Likewise, delivery of the restraining statements is crucial. We are often asked, "How do you keep a straight face when you say those things?" A restraining statement has multiple levels of meaning. The underlying message is: To change you must stay the same. The nonverbal message may and probably should help disqualify the verbal message. It is clear that restraining statements cannot be made in aggressive, hostile, caustic, sarcastic, or angry ways. It would be interesting to investigate the nonverbal behavior of therapists during the use of restraining strategies. Unfortunately, this kind of work has not been done. We believe the best approach is to display a nonverbal attitude of concern, warmth, and empathy. Knowing that a restraining statement will, in fact, produce the opposite effect is the best guide in making these kinds of statements to clients.

POSITIONING

Positioning occurs when the therapist accepts and exaggerates the client's position or assertion about self (Rohrbaugh et al., 1977). In many cases the client will be in opposition to other people and/or the therapist. Positioning is the ideal way of dealing with a client who plays the "game of opposites." The game of opposites begins as a verbal game which may be extended to behavior. By verbally joining the client in his game, the therapist forces the client to make a different behavioral response. Thus, the client is encouraged to maintain the opposite stance verbally so that change will occur behaviorally.

> A client came in for her appointment one day claiming that everyone hated her and was out to get her. She said she would be better off without any friends and she should go live in the woods. She was visibly upset and angry. She pounded her fist on the desk as she spoke. The therapist took out a sheet of paper and asked her to tell him what people had been doing to her to show their hate. Together they constructed a list of 24 ways people hated her. After about 15 ways the therapist had to prod the client because she had not provided enough proof to him yet. In fact, he claimed other clients had given him 50 to 100 ways and weren't as upset as she. When the list was complete, the therapist agreed that something was going on. After reading her list back to her aloud, he agreed that living in the woods with no human contact would be the safest thing for her. The client sat quietly staring at the floor. She looked up and said she felt just like a "little kid." She then talked about what was actually troubling her with another woman she knew. The session ended with the client laughing and joking.

INDIRECT AND CRYPTIC PARADOXES

Paradoxes may be given in a straightforward, easy to understand manner. The message conveyed to the client is clear. The client knows exactly what has been requested at a cognitive level. However, paradoxical messages may be given with varying degrees of clarity and directness, varying the client's awareness that s/he is receiving a paradoxical message. In other words, some paradoxes may be cryptic. Cryptic messages are also referred to as indirect messages. They contain vague or ambiguous terms, undefined referents, contradictions, double meanings, and a variety of other linguistic devices which make interpretation difficult.

There are a number of advantages to giving cryptic messages. First, they may be especially useful with clients who are therapy-wise, or perhaps therapists themselves. Second, they are useful with intellectualizers or "computers." Since cryptic messages are unclear, the therapy-wise client or intellectualizing client cannot ignore, oppose, or resist the message. Third, cryptic messages are essential for clients who would be too threatened by a more direct paradox and a straightforward confrontation. Fourth, the more cryptic the message, the more the client has to think about what was said and try to make sense of it. In the process, s/he may explore a number of alternative ways of looking at the situation. Fifth, cryptic messages are directed toward the unconscious. Finally, cryptic messages are not easily recognizable as communications or directives. Thus, when a change results from the use of a cryptic statement, the client's sense of control or power is enhanced while the power and importance of the therapist are diminished.

Milton Erickson was the master of being cryptic or indirect with clients. Erickson has stated that a patient is a person who is afraid to be direct (Beahrs, 1977). Beahrs has stated:

A healthy person is direct—he defines a problem, thinking of alternatives, chooses the one that is most likely to achieve the desired outcome, and does it, facing whatever obstacles are in the course. Somehow a neurotic or any disturbed individual is afraid to do this. Neurotics are very indirect in their manner, schizophrenics even more so, and it is Erickson's profound faith that to reach a disturbed patient you have to deal in his terms. If you directly face patients, they are going to resist for the very same reasons that they resist directness in their life anyway (pp. 57–58).

We have generally used cryptic messages to create a state of confusion. This technique derives from the confusion technique in hypnosis (see Haley, 1967). The hypnotic use of this technique involves giving rapid-fire messages of a confusing nature. In order to escape from the confusing messages, the subject retreats or regresses into a trance state. The technique may be used in a similar way therapeutically. The therapist may say a number of things (psychobabble is useful) and toward the end of his monologue insert a direct or paradoxical statement. The client should be in such a confused state that any statement which makes sense is given special import by the client. A few examples of these types of messages follow. Hopefully, they will be too vague to make much sense, but the couples who received them as part of letters spent a good deal of time working together trying to decipher their meaning because they somehow related to their problem.

> Example 1: Your relationship is very nicely complementary, but since you can only be what the other is not, you cannot really be yourself. . . .
>
> Example 2: It hurts me that you seem to feel that you must either choose to keep a busy schedule or withdraw entirely in order to focus on yourselves and each other. I wonder whether you have dealt with the issue of doing vs being?
>
> Example 3: We are impressed by the way in which you are supporting each other's growth as lovers apart from the marriage and family. Continue to be protective of each other's individuality and growth, and continue to move slowly towards forming a new integrated relationship and facing the task of being married and being parents. . . .
>
> Example 4: We want to congratulate you for being such an extraordinary couple by never misunderstanding each other. You both seem to have an in-depth understanding of each other's feelings. It is obvious that you have devoted much thought to this pursuit. Consequently, we feel your thoughtful understanding will enable you to continue your present degree of sharing feelings. . . .

A final way of being indirect is through the use of metaphor. It may be difficult to see how metaphor could be considered paradoxical. First, recall that we have defined paradoxical methods broadly to include any second-order change technique. Secondly, a metaphor is a word or idea which is used in place of another word or idea. The use of a metaphor allows for transposition from one sensory modality to another (e.g., the tie was loud; it tasted like silk) (Koen, 1965).

This observation is directly related to Bandler and Grinder's (1975; Grinder and Bandler, 1976) idea that people deal with problems in different sensory modalities. They maintain that a problem framed in one modality will facilitate its resolution, while dealing with it in another would leave the person at an impasse. Thus, metaphor may facilitate second-order change by changing the representational framework in which the solution is attempted. A technique which emerges directly from these ideas is to ask the client to conceptualize a problem in all the sensory modalities; e.g., "What does it feel, sound and look like?"

A metaphorical way of dealing with clients confronting difficult and anxiety-producing tasks is to find another situation in which the person is competent. For example, a client was very anxious over starting a new job. The therapist asked the client, a skilled mountain climber, to discuss various aspects of mountain climbing (e.g., what to take, what to wear, where to climb, what to avoid in the terrain, and whom to climb with). The therapist alternated between the skills used in mountain climbing and those she could use in approaching her new job. The intermeshing of these two "apparently" unrelated tasks helped the client transfer her knowledge from one area to another and reduced her anxiety over the new job.

The therapist may manipulate space and objects in the therapy session to symbolize the relationships. Family therapists often have clients move to specific locations in the room to symbolize particular aspects of the relationship. Satir's (1967) use of spatialization is a good example of using spatial relations in a metaphorical way.

Objects may provide another metaphorical way of representing relationships. One young couple had reached an impasse. They were vague about their complaints and maintained emotional distance in their relationship. The partners were sitting on opposite ends of a sofa in a session when the therapist began to place bean bag chairs between them. The couple recognized this concrete metaphor and began to talk about what concerned them in specific terms.

DeShazer (1980) has recently investigated the use of indirect symbolic suggestions. He reported on the successful experimental treatment of three men experiencing erectile dysfunction. These men were treated hypnotherapeutically. In one case an architect was placed in a trance and then a tall building was described to him. DeShazer emphasized having a good foundation and functional wiring and plumbing as he added more and more floors to the "erect, cylindrical building, on a firm foundation—a building that was fully functional." In still another case a retired military officer was given a simple direction that "Now that you are retired from the military, you still should, Mr. B., come to rigid attention now and then." The men in these cases rapidly improved although we are not given adequate follow-up information. While this procedure worked quite well for several men, it did not work for men whose erectile problems were related to marital conflict.

Zeig (1980a) has described how Milton Erickson would use metaphor in symptom prescription. He gave each spouse in a conflictual relationship a symbolic task. One was to climb a mountain while the other visited an arboretum. They then switched tasks. The tasks gave each an opportunity to recognize their typical patterns of behavior. They realized how they had been climbing a "barren mountain" of marital discord for years and decided to divorce.

The use of metaphor in psychotherapy is limited only by the therapists' imagination and creativeness. Erickson's best known metaphor is that of talking about and prescribing a dinner together as a way to deal with sexual problems. The greatest advantage in the use of metaphor is that it allows the client to change "spontaneously" (Haley, 1973, p. 26). There is no need for insight or interpretation.

INSIGHT-PRODUCING PARADOXES

Insight has been recognized as an aim—if not the basic aim—of psychotherapy since Freud. Freud defined insight as intellectual understanding—coming to know the "why" of one's present neurosis. Humanistically oriented therapists such as Rogers have viewed insight as the awareness and acceptance of feelings and attitudes. The way most therapists from Freud up to the present have attempted to produce insight in their clients has been to reflect what the client verbalizes or provide interpretations.

The kind of insight produced from a paradoxical intervention is different from that produced by reflection or interpretation (i.e., by words). Most insights are generated by the therapist's verbalizations and the impact on the client is questionable. We believe most insights are nothing more than cognitions—thoughts about overt behavior. A paradox, on the other hand, can produce a *pragmatic insight*. This kind of insight emerges from the systematic manipulation of the client by the therapist, but it is a self-generated insight. The therapist merely provides a structure for an experience—not the interpretation of that experience. The insight is a perceptual reorganization grounded in the client's immediate experience. Its truth is utterly convincing and inescapable. It is such a powerful insight that the client may slip into a trance state as the insight occurs. It might be noted that using the term pragmatic to describe this type of insight is consistent with William James' (1907) pragmatic theory of truth. For James, truth referred to whether an idea worked, and whether any idea worked depended upon some form of action leading to an experience.

Haley (1976) pointed out that insight is not necessary for change to occur in therapy. The only requisite for change is that the person do the task he is given whether it is a straightforward task or a paradoxical task. Haley is in fact opposed to insight-oriented psychotherapy, and most of his tasks are not specifically designed to produce insight. However, insights are produced many times in spite of the therapist's bias.

A therapist may want to use an insight-producing paradox for several reasons. First, this type of paradox could be used with clients who expect and want insight. Secondly, why not? If the paradox produces the desired behavioral change, then insight is simply a bonus. Insight might help the client become more aware of other feelings and behaviors in facilitating further change.

The basic form of a paradox which produces insight indirectly is often "Whenever you feel, think of, hear, see, etc., I want you to (prescribe some concrete behavior)." As the person does the prescribed behavior, s/he will automatically link that behavior to the feeling, etc. given in the paradox. For example, "Whenever you feel ignored, pick a fight with. . . ." A variant of this structure which is not quite as insight-producing is: "The next time John does _____, I want you to (prescribe the symptom)." This subtype helps to produce insight around the impact another person has on the client. For example, "The next time your wife starts a serious discussion with you, I want you to find something to do to get out of the discussion as quickly as possible." Watzlawick et al. (1974) discussed this type of paradox in terms of making the covert overt. This type of insight-producing paradox could be called the *when-then paradox*.

CONCLUSION

The paradoxes discussed in this section represent many of the techniques found in the literature on paradoxical psychotherapy plus a few we have developed or elaborated. The beginning paradoxical therapist will probably have a tendency to rely on the use of these techniques when making interventions. Using ready-made techniques simplifies the therapist's task. However, the therapist can rely on these techniques too heavily. They can blind the therapist by diverting attention away from the overall treatment strategy. It is the principles and processes of this therapy that one must learn in order to become a paradoxical therapist. The techniques should flow from the principles described in the previous chapter. The therapist may use techniques that others have used or s/he may develop new techniques which seem to emerge in the same magical way that Erickson's interventions appeared. The interventions are creative binds resulting from the interplay of the therapist, the client, and the problem. No two interventions are exactly alike even though the principles guiding their formulation can be scientifically stated and evaluated.

In the next two chapters we will present a variety of ways these paradoxes have been applied with individuals, couples, and families. We have included brief and long-term cases in order to show the variety of ways paradoxical techniques may be used.

8

Recent innovations in the use of paradoxical techniques

This chapter will review two recent developments in the application of paradoxical techniques. The paradoxical treatment of depression and the use of paradoxical strategies with younger children will be considered. Both of these two areas of application are significant because of the number of people potentially affected by the use of the procedures.

THE PARADOXICAL TREATMENT OF DEPRESSION

Most of us feel sad from time to time. In addition, Woodruff et al. (1975) have estimated that 5% of men and 10% of women are clinically depressed at least once in their lives. Given the prevalence of depression, it is remarkable that it has not been treated paradoxically until recently.

Watzlawick et al. (1974) were the first therapists to discuss the possible etiology of depression within a paradoxical framework. They pointed out that when people attempt to cheer up someone who is sad they may turn a temporary state of sadness into a prolonged state of depression. They suggested, for example, that families may develop a rule forbidding sadness. In the event that an individual in the family becomes depressed, she is told to cheer up and thus may in fact be punished for an appropriate emotional response. The sad and depressed individual may internalize other people's responses and try to cheer herself up. The person believes it is "bad" to be depressed and fights to change a normal reaction, increasing the state of depression. Watzlawick et al. (1974) did not discuss how depression could be treated paradoxically, nor did they offer any cases involving depression.

Feldman (1976) has formulated a family-system model of depression, providing a framework for paradoxical intervention. Feldman's model integrates the intrapsychic concept of cognitive schema with interpersonal concepts. The intrapsychic concept of schema holds that the depressed individual attributes negative qualities to the self in response to specific life stresses. Beck (1974) has stated: "The depressive's negative ideation leads to sadness; he labels the sadness as a sign that his life is painful and hopeless. These negative interpretations of the affect further reinforce his negative attitudes. Hence, a vicious circle is produced" (p. 73). The intrapsychic process of self-depreciation is triggered and/or reinforced interpersonally. In a marital or familial context the process of reinforcement of the depression is postulated to be circular rather than linear. Feldman states that complementary cognitive schema are triggered in both spouses, which sets a repetitive pattern of mutual reinforcement into motion.

For example, the nondepressive spouse may be sad or do something to which the depression-prone spouse overreacts by becoming depressed. The depressed spouse may then trigger omnipotence and/or protectiveness from the mate, which perpetuates the depressed spouse's sense of helplessness. The cycle may begin at several points or in several different ways. The most important concept is that both spouses depreciate themselves in a circular model. The self-depreciation of the depressed spouse is more directly manifested. This depressed spouse may withdraw in a passive-aggressive manner, become overtly hostile, or make independent self-assertions. On the other hand, the self-depreciation of the nondepressed spouse is not experienced consciously. Thoughts of self-depreciation are defended against by playing rescuer. Thus, if a depressed spouse begins to improve, the non-depressed spouse will unconsciously attempt to produce a relapse in the service of his own defensive mechanism.

Watzlawick and Coyne (1980) presented a case in which depression was treated in a male following a stroke. They did not propose a general treatment strategy for depression but described the mostly paradoxical interventions which they used in treating one case.

The case involved the treatment of a 58-year-old professional who became depressed following a second stroke. The family, particularly the wife, had responded to his depression by encouraging the father to fight off his depression by trying harder to not be depressed. The pattern of behavior reinforcing his depression followed the model proposed by Feldman (1976). The client had been referred for family therapy. He agreed it would be useful for his family, but not for himself. He did not attend sessions.

The first strategy the therapists used was to restrain the family in their expectations. The family was to think about helping the father make one small change in his behavior that would assist him in returning to normal activities and then help him make that change. This strategy did not work but did give the therapist more information about the interaction between the client and his wife.

In the second session, the wife was instructed to change her usual way of helping her husband. She was told to make mistakes and appear disorganized. She was to further depreciate herself for inconveniencing her husband. This strategy was designed to shift her from a rescuing to a victim stance. She was to become more helpless than him in order to shift him to a rescuing position. This strategy was a partial success. In order to help his wife, the client began to do more for himself and his wife.

The third intervention (session three) involved giving the family a simply paradoxical directive which was congruent with their attitude that they must help their father. They were told, "You must encourage him by discouraging him." For example, whenever the client complained of pain, the wife was to be overly sympathetic and help him to bed. In short, the client's statements about himself regarding his limitations, attributes, etc. were to be exaggerated by his wife and family. This strategy is one of restraining and positioning. The wife discouraged his attempts to "do more" and accepted his negative attributions by exaggerating them. This strategy produced further recovery. The client began to do more for himself.

In the final session, the restraining directive was reinforced. A three-month follow-up showed that the client had improved steadily until another stroke. Interestingly, the client's psychological response to the third stroke was one not of depression but of self-determination.

In a later chapter on long-term treatment, a case demonstrating a wide range of paradoxical techniques useful in treating depression is presented. This case involved a man who had a long and severe depression. However, there are many instances of clients' talking about feelings of sadness or depression which are mild or temporary. We have found several successful strategies for these short-term cases, which we will briefly describe.

First, we relabel the depression. We say, "It is good that you are able to get in touch with your sad feelings. It makes you whole. It is appropriate for you to be depressed about x, y, or z and it is surprising you aren't more depressed. Furthermore, you can use your depression to learn about yourself and what you need to change."

Secondly, we talk about how most people don't know how to be depressed and how they tend to fight depression excessively. The depression is then scheduled. The client is instructed to set aside a certain time each day and just be depressed. We say, "Be as depressed as you can be and more; go ahead and think about the worst things possible. Exaggerate your depression and be sure to go the full length of time you have set aside, even if you have to force yourself. During the day, if you start to feel depressed, make a note of what you're feeling depressed about and save it for your next depression time." The client is told this assignment will be painful and will not make things any better for the first few days. It will work only if practiced on a regular basis.

The next step is to cut down the depression time by always prescribing more time than the client states is needed. When the depression is partially resolved or under control, a paradoxical prediction is made (a relapse is predicted) and the client is told that the scheduling may be necessary again if a relapse occurs.

Scheduling depression has been an extremely effective technique. In many cases no further work is necessary on the depression itself. In other cases work is done to modify the cognitive schema and help the individual learn how to use self-reward.

PARADOXICAL INTERVENTION WITH CHILDREN

While paradoxical treatment of children in family settings is not new (Selvini Palazzoli et al., 1974; Weeks and L'Abate, 1978), using paradoxes with children outside the family has only recently been demonstrated. L'Abate and his students have pioneered the investigation of paradoxes with children in inpatient treatment centers. Jessee and L'Abate (1980) have suggested that the use of paradox with children in inpatient settings can not only change a child's behavior but also modify the system around the child. They have noted that paradoxical interventions with children can be of great potential since these techniques require limited verbal ability and insight, have immediate effects, and are particularly suitable for oppositional individuals.

Jessee and L'Abate (1980) offer a few guidelines for the application of paradox. They state that it is inappropriate to use this method with disorganized or mentally retarded children. The child should be fairly normal and at least five years of age. The paradox should be given in a simple manner in the child's own language. Jessee and L'Abate have observed that a good prognostic sign was anger from the child when the paradoxical prescription was given.

One of their favorite strategies for dealing with problem behavior is called the "winner's bet." The child's inappropriate behavior is described and a bet is made with the child that the behavior will continue since s/he can't control it. If the child does not misbehave s/he wins the bet. However, if the behavior continues, the child must also agree to teach the therapist how s/he goes about misbehaving. If the child wins the bet, s/he has exhibited control over her uncontrollable behavior. If s/he loses the bet s/he must think about and enact the behavior consciously in order to teach the therapist.

Although the children discussed in Jessee and L'Abate's (1980) paper are not being treated in the context of their families, the techniques can still be linked to the family.

In one of their cases an 11-year-old boy had been hospitalized following several court appearances for stealing. The boy stole things both in and outside the home. Most of his thefts were of machines similar to the ones his father made at work. The boy's father was rarely home but his mother was home constantly and had been depressed for years.

The boy had allowed the female hospital staff to become close to him but was distant from the male staff. The therapist (Jessee) told the boy that he finally realized how the boy could let him know when he wanted to spend time with him. The boy was told that when he wanted to spend enjoyable time with a male staff member, he was to steal a magazine on machines that would be placed on a counter for him. The boy was further told that taking the magazine would help the male and female staff get together to discuss his behavior since they were always so busy. He was congratulated for helping them get together.

The boy reacted to the paradox with astonishment, which quickly converted to anger. He never did the task, nor did he steal anything else again. He returned to his family a short time later free from the behavior which had led to his problem. There were clear signs the parents had changed their behavior as well.

Jessee, Jurkovic, Wilkie, and Chiglinsky (1980) extended L'Abate's (1975, 1976) theoretical and clinical work in a paper on positive reframing with children. They argued that positive reframing has several advantages for children. First, the standard nosological system focuses on individual psychopathology and emphasizes only the negative or pathological. Positive reframing shifts the emphasis to the positive, thereby shifting the label bearer's perception of herself and the perceptions of others (e.g., the other children in the ward or center). Second, the child may view herself in strictly "bad" or "mad" terms. A positive reframe gives the child a greater sense of control and implies that her behavior has a good and useful function. An elevation in self-esteem follows. Third, positive reframing can change dyadic and triadic interactions in a more useful direction, especially when grownups and children are locked in power struggles.

Jessee et al. (1980) have observed that reframing at the group level is the most effective. That is, all the members of the child's group should receive the message for maximum effectiveness. For example, they point out that reframing "arguing as a way to improve one's speech" would have no effect. However, telling a group that they "argue only with people they care about or want to get closer to" does have an effect. This emphasis on involving the group or context is consistent with the systemic model of including all the persons involved with a problem.

Jessee et al. (1980) have speculated that a child younger than five probably will not respond to a paradoxical intervention. Their hypothesis is based on a cognitive/developmental perspective. They reason that the child should be capable of formal operational thought because reframing operates at the level of meta-reality. In short, the child should be able "a) to differentiate classes or conceptual wholes from their concrete members or parts and b) to change from one criterion for classifying objects (or behaviors) to another using the same class member" (p. 14).

However, they limit this hypothesis to the manipulation of the conceptual context. They believe positive reframing may be used to change the emotional context, and hence behavior, at much earlier ages. Reframing a child's tantrum in a humorous and supportive way may change the emotional context and eliminate the behavior. The question of age needs further clinical and careful empirical attention, especially with regard to the issue of what kinds of paradoxes work with children of different age groups or cognitive stages. It is clear from the cases presented by these researchers that a variety of techniques work well with children from nine years of age and up.

The use of paradox with children in treatment centers also illustrates another new application of paradox. Paradox has rarely been used in inpatient treatment centers and it has never been used in any systematic way. Bergman (1980) has presented a number of cases involving the use of paradox in community homes for the chronically disabled and retarded. A variety of techniques have been successfully used, including prescription, reframing, restraining, and prescribing a ritual. Bergman has reported an impressionistic success rate of 90%.

These clinicians have shown us that paradox is not limited to just individual, marital, or family therapy. We are just beginning to learn how and when it can be used in different settings and with different kinds of clients. These findings suggest active clinical experimentation with the ultimate goal of empirical validation.

9

Paradoxical letters

The use of written communication in psychotherapy is not new (Pearson, 1965). Albert Ellis (1965) serendipitously found that when, due to laryngitis, he wrote down his interpretations for clients rather than verbalizing them, his clients seemed to progress faster. He also noted that therapy in written form parcels out the person of the therapist, thus allowing the techniques of psychotherapy to be tested in a more controlled fashion.

Burton (1965) also considered the pros and cons of written therapeutic communication. He stated that some of the problems of written communication might be: a) dissociative, i.e., placing emphasis outside the therapist-client interaction; b) too much emphasis on the cognitive at the expense of the affective; c) used mechanically; d) used by the therapist to avoid direct confrontations; e) used by the client to avoid externalization by introspections. On the positive side, he believed written communication could be: a) a creative act and a catharsis if written by the client; b) used to provide data for content analysis; c) more integrative of contextual factors; d) reductive of the time required for treatment; and e) used in special emergencies.

Selvini Palazzoli et al. (1978a) have become the most significant advocates of using written paradoxical communication. The Milano team uses paradoxical letters in working with families. They have reported being tremendously successful using these letters although they have presented no empirical data to support their claims.

For the past several years, both straightforward (linear) and paradoxical letters have been investigated at the Family Study Center at Georgia State University under the direction of L'Abate. Paradoxical letters have been given to individuals (children and adults), couples, and families. While much of this research has been clinical or impressionistic, like Palazzoli's, an empirical study has also been conducted. Our empirical study is reviewed in the chapter on research.

Our interest in investigating written therapeutic communication emerged for a variety of reasons. First, anything worth remembering is worth putting in writing. Verbal messages can be forgotton, ignored, repressed, confused, distorted, or otherwise belittled and sidetracked. Second, written messages are a permanent record that can be read repeatedly. Therapists are well aware that clients need to hear the same statements many times before they have any impact. A client can be instructed to read a written message on a prescribed basis, perhaps increasing the efficiency and effectiveness of therapy. Finally, written communication is another way of intervening therapeutically. The verbal modality has become exalted. Verbal communication is just one mode of communication. Written communication is, in fact, the basis of our most serious adult enterprises. Therefore, it could be argued that it is more binding than verbal communication. The psychological impact of a written message may be greater than that of a verbal agreement.

Written messages may be particularly useful in certain situations. When verbal messages have failed to work, the next step could be to try written messages. We have used written messages frequently in attempting to break impasses and interfere with repetitive, destructive patterns. Written messages are indicated when there is externalization, denial, avoidance, and lack of awareness. Issues which are vague or ambiguous may be crystallized through written messages. Lastly, issues surrounded by hyper-emotionality may be depersonalized through the written word.

Our research has focused on both linear and paradoxical letters (Wagner, Weeks, and L'Abate, 1980). In order to better understand what we call a paradoxical letter, linear letters will be described first. A linear letter is written in a straightforward, easy-to-understand style. These letters provide direct feedback to the client, much like the verbal feedback given in the form of insights, interpretations, or confrontations. The following letter illustrates a linear message given to a couple.

A Linear Letter

Dear _____:

I have really enjoyed these sessions with you and I am quite fond of you both. You have a good sense of humor and care a lot about how the other acts and feels. You both seem to be working on communicating effectively with each other.

I have the impression, though, that sometimes you focus on money problems to avoid confronting issues more sensitive to you both. When you blame or put each other down and fail to deal with issues directly, communication and growth of the relationship remain at a standstill. Just because one of you behaves in a hurtful way does not justify the other one's behaving in a similar way.

Although you seem to have a lot of commitment to this relationship, you tend to use your friends to escape from marital responsibilities. By making your friends more important than your marriage, your involvement with them detracts from your relationship with your partner. I think you have to decide whether you want to be married or whether you want to remain single.

Sincerely,

Paradoxical letters are more difficult to describe than linear letters. At best, only general guidelines can be offered for the construction of paradoxical letters. Over the years we have used a variety of formats and our ideas about what works best have gradually emerged.

Writing a paradoxical letter requires the expenditure of additional time and effort. Even a short letter may require an hour to compose, edit, and revise. The letter forces the therapist to consider the intervention carefully. It helps the therapist distance from the intervention in a way that is different from making interventions in a session. Moreover, the intervention must be self-contained. It must target a specific behavior to be changed and then be precisely formulated to make that change.

The letter may be constructed and given to the client(s) immediately after the session. The disadvantage of this approach is that the client must wait while the therapist prepares the letter and the therapist is pressured to compose the letter quickly. Letters composed under these conditions may not be as precise as they could be. The advantage of this approach is that the therapist can give the client(s) the letter and observe their reactions. But this also has a disadvantage. The client(s) may try to undo the bind created by the letter. In order to prevent this counter-therapeutic event from occurring, the letter should be read to the client(s) or given to them—and then the session ended immediately.

We recommend that the letters be written after the session and then mailed to the client(s) the next day. Under these conditions, the therapist has plenty of time to think through the interventions to be used.

We usually find that letters require time to be effectively formulated. The day after the session finishing touches can be made on the letter. Sometimes the delay helps the therapist gain a different perspective on the problem, resulting in the formulation of an entirely new letter. One of the consequences of using paradoxical letters is that the therapist is usually limited by the number of letters that can be developed simultaneously. Letter-writing is so time-consuming and mentally demanding that only a few cases can be treated at any particular time.

The length of the letter sent to the client is vitally important. We suggest using short letters. Normally, the letter should not exceed one page and it should contain no more than two or three points. Letters which are longer or contain too many points seem to be shotgun approaches. They suggest a confused therapist and are likely to confuse the client. The letter should be concise and precise.

A problem that is common to all letters is their readability. The client(s) must be able to understand the words. It is easy to forget that clients may lack reading skills even when their vocabularies appear adequate. The therapist should attempt to match the reading comprehension level of the client(s) to the extent possible.

The paradoxical letter may involve only one method or it may involve the combination of several methods. Our guidelines on the "how" of paradoxical intervention can be followed in conjunction with the methods presented. We have used virtually every method with clinical success in letters. As we stated earlier, there has been one combination of methods which has been particularly flexible and clinically effective—the use of positive connotation, reframing or relabeling, prescription, and restraining in the same letter.

The therapist needs to be careful not to be prescriptive in the sense of being evaluative or judgmental. Shoulds or oughts are to be avoided. Prescriptions are made in the paradoxical sense. In short, the client is placed in the bind of being told not to change that which is desired to be changed. The elegance of a paradoxical strategy is that the client discovers a solution; it is not provided for the client ready-made.

Almost all letters are perceived as cryptic, obscure, confusing, perplexing, or noncommonsensical in nature. The letter is rarely seen as direct or clear. The ambiguity of the letter helps to secure the client's involvement, since the person or system receiving the letter must work on deciphering its meaning.

We have used paradoxical letters in a variety of situations. In some cases we have used letters beginning after the first session. These were cases we felt strongly would be resistive or where we detected a great deal of resistance or reactance during the first interview. In other cases the paradoxical letters followed an initial period of assessment during which straightforward interventions failed. The use of paradoxical letters is probably best reserved as a means of last resort. If straightforward interventions fail and then verbal paradoxical interventions fail or seem to lack the impact they need, then it is definitely appropriate to use the letters.

Once the use of letters begins, it does not need to be a routine practice, although our most common pattern has been to use letters on a continuous basis for a while until significant change has occurred. It is, however, possible to use them only when an impasse is reached or when the therapist wishes to punctuate the importance of certain changes. The letters may serve all the functions mentioned earlier, plus add a shock effect to the treatment. Clients do not expect to receive written communications from therapists, except bills.

We have given letters to many couples who were not in therapy; rather, they were functional and dysfunctional couples participating in marital enrichment programs developed by L'Abate and his group (1975; L'Abate, 1977a). These enrichment programs were designed for couples asking for help with their relationship. Enrichment programs are not intended to help resolve specific problems. They are broad-based, manual-directed, structured exercises that can be delivered by mental health professionals with a minimum of training and/ or experience. Usually a cross-sex team of enrichers works with a couple over a period of eight weeks. There is a structured intake or diagnostic session, six enrichment sessions lasting one hour each over six weeks, and a follow-up session.

The next three cases demonstrate the use of paradoxical letters in the context of marital enrichment. All the couples participated in the marital enrichment program offered through the Family Studies Center at Georgia State University. The couples knew they were a part of a research program on marital enrichment and they were told they would receive a letter after their fourth enrichment session.

These sessions were carefully documented with notes in order to track the process of change. Enrichment produces first-order or gradual change in most cases. Paradoxical letters usually produce a rapid and dramatic change. The process notes enabled us to determine whether the letters produced the intended change.

Case 1

Bill, 24, and Janet, 22, had been married three years when they came to the Family Study Center for the Marital Enrichment Program. Bill had owned a small business but sold it in order to return to college as a freshman. His wife had already completed her degree and was working in a technical occupation. Bill had not planned to enter college but did so after Janet's repeated suggestions. He felt Janet had pushed him into selling his business and going to school. Janet was supporting them by working approximately 60 hours a week and carefully budgeting their money.

Janet married Bill when she was 19. Her father was an alcoholic. She reported being distant from her family and never receiving any affection from her parents. She and her father frequently fought. Her marriage had enabled her to escape from an unbearable family environment. Since her marriage, her parents had divorced and her father had stopped drinking. Bill's family was close, even though his father was also an alcoholic. He reported being particularly close to his mother. They would talk over the telephone several times a week.

Bill and Janet chose the Conflict Resolution Enrichment program. This program is designed to help couples learn how to reduce their fights and fight constructively. The couple had stated that their main problem was arguing. They felt they needed to work on reducing their arguments, learn to appreciate one another, come to terms on differences of opinion, and give up the idea that she was always right and he was always wrong.

During the first three enrichment sessions several patterns of behavior became apparent. Janet would initiate an argument and Bill would retreat. She was the aggressor. She would start an argument with the idea that she was justified and right. She was aware that she used her arguments to manipulate him. She wanted to control his behavior and define him. She also wanted to elicit some kind of response from Bill. He reacted to her by intellectualizing and then leaving the situation. One of his strategies for getting out of an argument was to call his mother. Janet already felt a great deal of strain with Bill's mother because she said his mother was too involved in their lives. When Bill called his mother she felt hurt, unloved, and angry. The arguments and the triangulation of Bill's mother had produced a situation where the couple did not feel intimate or close.

She resented Bill for his relationship with his mother. She felt that the continuation of their relationship would make her turn out just like her father. She thought her father was an angry and hostile person. Bill wanted to avoid Janet. He could no longer deal with her attacks. He began distancing from her to protect himself and their relationship.

At the end of the fourth enrichment session, the couple was given the following letter:

Dear Bill and Janet:

The purpose of this letter is to deal with all the aspects of your relationship that we have observed above and beyond the enrichment process. We want to put these observations in writing because what we have seen is far too important for us to consider verbally. By putting our observations in writing, we will all have a better opportunity to reflect on them.

(This paragraph is standard for letters given to couples in the enrichment program.)

We are impressed by the way in which you use conflict to achieve intimacy and closeness and that you maintain your own individuality through your fighting. We're glad that you care enough to fight instead of being indifferent to each other.

(Fighting is given several positive connotations. Raises the question of why they use fighting to achieve intimacy, maintain individuality, and express caring.)

We have a suggestion to help you become more intimate through your fighting. The next time one of you feels unloved and wants attention, don't tell the other, but start a major fight. The next time the other one of you feels you are getting too intimate through your fighting, get out of the fight by retreating into your shell, or by being rational and logical, or by leaving the room.

(Transactional prescription — Their fighting sequence is prescribed.)

We wonder whether it is possible for both of you to be united at the same time. As long as you emphasize being right, you force the other person to be wrong and you cannot be united. Only by giving up being right or wrong can you be united together. Are you strong enough to unite?

(A straightforward message ending with a challenge. Being strong is relabeled as uniting.)

We enjoy working with you both and appreciate your efforts in entering into the sessions so actively.

(An apparently straightforward message with a hidden positive connotation. The couple would begin to argue in the sessions. These attempts to argue are redefined as being actively involved with each other, which is good.)

Sincerely,

It was standard procedure to avoid talking about the letter in the subsequent sessions unless the couple wanted to discuss it. The reason for this was to avoid undoing the bind the letter created. If a couple did want to discuss a letter, the enrichers were instructed to repeat what was in the letter and be evasive. The enrichers were to also say that the letter was to be discussed more fully in the follow-up session.

Bill and Janet did not comment on the letter in any of the following sessions. However, the enrichers noticed several changes in the session after the letter was given to them. The enrichers reported that the couple appeared more intimate, reserved, and playful with each other. They did not display the tension they had in the previous session. The most significant change was that the couple reported no fights in the weeks following the delivery of the letter. In previous weeks they had reported having at least one major fight a week.

By the sixth session Bill had decided to take a part-time job. The couple did argue about this fact in the session. However, Bill did not retreat. He asserted himself and used the fair fighting model they had been learning.

In the follow-up sessions the couple was asked about their reactions to the letter and the changes they thought they had made during the enrichment process. Janet said the letter was a "phoney." Bill wasn't sure what he thought about it. They both agreed that they were fighting less and felt closer to each other. Janet said she had stopped her attacks on Bill's family.

Case 2

Frank, 31, and Susan, 32, had been married 13 years when they participated in our Marital Enrichment Program. They had one daughter, seven years old. Frank was working in a professional field and Susan was a student.

Frank was the oldest of six children. His family was poor. His father was an alcoholic. Frank ran away from home at 14 but returned at the age of 17. He said his whole family consisted of failures. He was the only child to go beyond the ninth grade. His parents had eventually divorced and he felt obligated to help his brothers and sisters.

Susan's family was in many ways the opposite. Her parents were wealthy. Susan reported being extremely overprotected in her development. She was not allowed to engage in the normal developmental tasks because she was "daddy's girl." When she married it was against her father's wishes. She had not learned how to drive a car at the time of her marriage. Shortly after their marriage they both entered a Bible college. They separated for a short time during the time they were in college.

The couple said there were two major problems in their relationship. The first was Susan's dependence. Frank complained that she was totally dependent on him. He felt she clung to him and he said he felt he was being smothered. Susan agreed that she was too dependent and wanted to become more independent. The second problem concerned the expression of feelings. Susan complained that Frank never showed her any emotion. She was aware of not feeling any expression of love or warmth from him. Susan said she could not express anger. She expressed her feelings by either crying or showing Frank affection. She believed if she were to ever show any anger toward Frank he would leave her forever. Frank could not express anger either. Unfortunately, he had become angry with a couple of family members in the past and they died shortly thereafter; consequently, he associated anger with death. The fact that neither spouse could deal with anger had lead to the development of an ironclad rule that they must never fight. Even if it was clear to them that they were angry, they had to deny it or pretend that they weren't before they could go to bed.

This couple was most concerned with the imbalance in their relationship, which prompted them to select the Marital Equality Enrichment Program (L'Abate et al., 1975). Their mutual goal was for Susan to become more independent.

This couple represents the classic parent-child marriage. The wife had assumed an extreme one-down position, which placed heavy caretaking demands on the husband. While it appeared the wife was quite helpless, she used her position to manipulate or control certain aspects of the relationship. Ultimately, her powerlessness was an attempt to bind Frank to her in the same way a master is expected to take care of his slave. This relationship appeared to be very strained.

They had polarized to the point where a more extended form of intervention would have to be necessary to help this couple make the changes they wanted. Since we only had a short-term enrichment contract at the time the letter was delivered, we did not believe it would be appropriate to present a prescription which would destabilize the system too much. The following letter was given to this couple:

Dear Frank and Susan:

The purpose of this letter is to deal with all the aspects of your relationship that we have observed above and beyond the enrichment process. We want to put these observation in writing because what we have seen so far is too important for us to consider verbally. By putting our observations in writing, we will all have a better opportunity to reflect on them.

(Standard introductory paragraph.)

We want to congratulate you for being such an extraordinary couple by never misunderstanding each other. You both seem to have an in-depth understanding of each other's feelings. It is obvious that you have devoted much thought to this pursuit. Consequently, we feel your thoughtful understanding will enable you to continue your present degree of sharing feelings.

(Positive connotation of rule not to fight. The rule is defined as understanding and sharing their feelings perfectly. This couple carefully controlled their feelings. They understood the mutual need to protect each other and the relationship by not fighting.)

We are impressed by the amount of influence you both have in your marriage. We want you to continue to use the enormous power you have. But in order to protect the roles you have set up in the relationship, one of you should continue to use your power to control the relationship while denying this power, while the other pretends to be helpless. At all costs you should continue to cooperate with each other by keeping the roles we've described.

(The rules of the relationship are prescribed. It is suggested that they both have power in the relationship. Then the letter describes how they both use power to protect the relationship.)

We find you both to be warm, intelligent and caring individuals. We look forward to continuing our work together.

(A positive closing statement to the couple.)

Sincerely,

Susan and Frank never commented on this letter. At the end of the enrichment program several small changes had been noted and validated by the couple's self-reports. Susan said she had become more assertive with Frank. She reported being more direct and open with him. She was doing more for herself and felt more self-sufficient. Frank said he was showing her more affection and sharing more feelings with her. They agreed that Susan had made the most progress during the program and they also felt more satisfied with their relationship.

In this case, the reactions to the letter were not immediately apparent. There were no sudden or immediate changes following the letter. This fact makes it difficult, if not impossible, to parcel out the impact the letter actually had on their behavior.

Case 3

Joe and Sally were both 32 years old and had been married six months when they participated in the Marital Enrichment Program. Sally had been married once before at the age of 19 for a period of 11 years. She had custody of two pre-adolescent girls. Joe had also been married and divorced.

This couple wanted to improve communication in their relationship. They also said they wanted to keep the romance alive. The Marital Negotiation Program (L'Abate et al., 1975) was selected because of its emphasis on marital communications.

The enrichers noted how this couple appeared to be in an extended honeymoon stage. They would deny any problems or differences. Instead, they focused only on the good times they had together. Their relationship appeared to be a series of dates rather than an ongoing commitment. The most unusual feature of this marriage was how they defined their roles as partners. They verbalized being lovers rather than marital partners. They said their relationship was negotiated on a day-to-day basis. As long as it was fun and exciting, they intended to stay together. If it changed, they both vowed to separate. There were no long-term goals for this relationship and they denied having any expectations of each other. They stressed their need for individuality and individual growth. It just so happened that they were very much alike. They also believed they would lose part of themselves if they were to commit themselves to each other.

In this case we hypothesized that Joe and Sally were trying to protect themselves from the hurt and failure they had suffered in their previous marriages. They avoided talking about hurts and conflicts. They were extremely cautious about becoming intimate (e.g., being able to share hurt) and assuming marital and parental responsibilities.

The following letter was given to the couple:

Dear Joe and Sally:

The purpose of this letter is to deal with all the aspects of your relationship that we have observed above and beyond the enrichment process. We want to put these observations in writing because what we have seen so far is too important for us to consider verbally. By putting our observations in writing we will all have a better opportunity to reflect on them.

(Standard introductory paragraph.)

In working together over the past several weeks we have come to know you as caring, sensitive, and needing individuals who are working hard at your relationship. We appreciate your sincerity with us as well as your articulateness and candor.

(A linear statement about the positive aspects of their relationship.)

We are impressed by the way in which you are supporting each other's growth as committed lovers apart from your marriage and family.[a] Continue to be protective of each other's individuality and growth, and continue to move slowly towards forming a new integrated relationship and facing the task of being married and being parents.[b]

(a. Positive connotation of their support. Raises the question of

*how they are supportive of each other but unable to do so in
their marriage.
b. Restraining statement. Instructs them to "go slow" in being
married, etc.)*

We wonder if your commitment to each other's growth can be
best actualized by a commitment to your marriage and family?

*(A reframing question. Implies that actualization is part of mar-
riage.)*

We appreciate your hard work in the enrichment program
and have enjoyed our time with you.

(Closing statement.)

Sincerely,

In the session following the letter a number of new observations
were made. Joe and Sally appeared depressed and angry. Sally complained that she had too many responsibilities and she wanted Joe to
assume all the responsibilities for her children. She started questioning how much she wanted to share with Joe. She expressed being
scared of letting him nurture her. Joe was also questioning his commitment to the relationship. He discussed how he felt about the future
of the relationship and his responsibility for the children.

In this case, the immediate effect of the letter was to make explicit
the ambiguity of their relationship. All the issues they had avoided
dealing with in negotiating a marital relationship emerged in the following session. In the follow-up session the couple reported liking the
letter but not fully understanding it. They said they discussed it at
length. The issue of individuality vs. being marital partners was still
salient for them. They had decided it was more important to be individuals than marital partners. They re-affirmed their position that a
change in their relationship would probably lead to its dissolution.

This letter appears to have had a dramatic yet temporary effect on
the couple's relationship. It helped them to deal with some important
marital issues for a short period of time but in the end they decided to
re-affirm their original position of stressing the need for individuality.
This case points out the need for follow-up work when a change is
made. Had the couple not been participating in a structured program,

the issues they raised following the letter should have been dealt with specifically. Within the context of an enrichment program, it may prove more beneficial to present several letters.

There are certain patterns and problems which appear frequently in highly dysfunctional families. These patterns or problems can be managed in a variety of ways, including the use of written paradoxes. The next few letters represent some paradoxical approaches to dealing with these common patterns. In each case a written message was given to the family.

Reframing Positively

This method may be used in families when the children are acting out to protect the parents' relationship. The parents in these families feel defeated by their children and sometimes by each other. The parents may say they support each other while each secretly feels the other is not being a good parent. The defeating pattern can be reframed in order to tie it to success, enjoyment, caring, protectiveness, closeness, intimacy, etc. The following is a typical letter, much like the ritualized prescriptions used by Selvini Palazzoli et al. (1978b). The rules are:

1) Father will read this letter to other members of the family.
2) The letter will be read after dinner on Monday, Wednesday, and Friday evenings.
3) Mother will remind Father to read the letter.
4) Please do not discuss the content of this letter with anyone outside of counseling.

Dear _____ :

We [the parents] are appreciative of your protecting us because as long as you act up neither Mother nor I will need to look at ourselves and deal with our middle age. You will also help your brother to stay the way he is.

Consequently, we will understand that any time you blow up

it will be to protect us and your brother. We hope, therefore, that you will continue protecting us, because we need it.

Prescribing the Defeat

After reframing a behavior, the next step is to prescribe the behavior. Since the defeat is now a positive expression, it follows that the family should assist, continue, and even escalate, i.e., increase whatever they are doing to defeat each other. To make sure that the reframing and prescription are not going to be ignored or forgotten, it is helpful to put them in writing and to ritualize them, i.e., "Read this letter after supper on alternating days, either Mondays, Wednesdays, and Fridays, or Tuesdays, Thursdays, and Saturdays," as the Milano group recommends (Selvini Palazzoli et al., 1978b). This letter can be given to the child from the last example to read to his parents following these instructions:

1) To be read by son to other members of the family.
2) Please read on Mondays, Wednesdays, and Fridays after dinner.
3) Mother is to remind son to read and if she forgets, father and daughter are to remind.
4) Do not discuss contents outside of counseling.

Dear _____:

I [the therapist] am impressed with the way in which you show how much you care about this family and especially your mother. I feel you need to be congratulated for having violent temper tantrums, because these tantrums serve as a safety valve for what your father and mother cannot do. I admire you for the way in which you show your loyalty to your mother.

If this is the way you want to protect your parents from each other and continue keeping them apart, you should continue to blow up, but do this on Monday, Wednesday, and Friday of each week. Be sure to break some inexpensive item in your home and continue these outbursts, because if you stop, they might get back together.

The prescription of the behavior usually helps the child control the behavior that is problematic. This type of letter may help the parents see their part in the problem such that they begin to change spontaneously.

Congratulating the Family

In some families there is a game of divide and conquer. There are alliances and coalitions between and among family members which make order impossible. The family is split into several factions, with each bidding for power. The following message has been used to deal with this pattern:

> Dear _____:
>
> I am impressed with the ability you have developed to defeat each other. This keeps your family together and unchanged. To succeed by defeating is hard to master, but when instructions are unclear and not negotiated, then it is easier to not follow through.
>
> I admire you for wanting every family member to feel the power of defeat. You are assured of this power as long as instructions are given without everyone having an investment in them. One person can then use this against another, and in this way keep the family the same.
>
> I want to congratulate the family for knowing how to be happy by defeating and by being defeated. Since this seems successful, I would encourage you to continue doing what you are doing and by no means would I encourage Mother and Dad to share authority and responsibility with each other, because this change could break up the family.

This circular letter not only gives the family a more positive description of their relationship, but promotes an evaluation of the family system. In very resistant families this is a way to begin establishing and strengthening parental boundaries.

Admission of Defeat and Helplessness

This is a favorite ploy used by the Milano group (Selvini Palazzoli et al., 1978). Such an admission seems to mobilize family members into an attempt to do the opposite, that is, win. Even better, one should start therapy with the full realization (Andolfi, 1980) that underneath the pleas for help there is a hidden agenda that pulls for defeat in each and every family. This hidden agenda is present and needs to be present from the outset of each therapy. If and when the therapist becomes aware of defeat or the possibility of defeat, the following type of message may be useful:

> Dear _____:
>
> I am aware that, because of the power of this family, I am feeling a real sense of defeat and helplessness. I do know I have power that you cannot speak to, but yours is also special. You are a special family that I cannot fight with. I don't know where I could have found a better family than you to defeat me.

This verbal message provides the family with an incentive for continuing their therapy. Not only does this admission of defeat on the therapist's part assure the family's continued participation in therapy, in order to win, but the parents also learn something about the strength of their influence when they are united.

Reinforcing the Declaration of Impotence

The strategy of declaring impotence described by Selvini Palazzoli et al. (1978a), and others is generally considered a one-time brief intervention. When it becomes necessary to use this strategy, the therapists may need to reinforce it and make a paradoxical prediction. Even though the clients may say they feel confident in the therapist, the therapist may want to predict that they are sure they will ultimately let the clients down. In order to reinforce the declaration of impotence and help the clients examine their reasons for not being able to change, a second message may be given to the family. The message is a general statement that could be used with practically any family:

> Dear _____:
>
> Your standards for living are so high that few individuals, including me, can really live up to them. You should be congratulated for your search for perfection (and equating perfection to goodness and imperfection to badness). In spite of all the pres-

sures to lower your standards, we hope that you can keep them up because this world needs people like you who can uphold standards against all pressures both inside and outside the family. We doubt whether we can live up to your standards and wonder whether we will ever be able to meet them any time in the future. Keep up the good work! We will fail to meet your standards and wonder whether we really can help you.

CONCLUSION

Paradoxical letters can be a useful adjunct to the practice of linear and paradoxical therapy. They may be used in a variety of situations and may be the treatment of choice in a limited number of cases. In this chapter, we have described the process of letter-writing and the structure of the letters. Our examples have been for the short-term use of these letters. There are resistive cases where the therapist may choose to use paradoxical letters throughout. In the next chapter, we present a case demonstrating the long-term use of paradoxical letters.

10

Case studies in paradoxical psychotherapy

The literature on paradoxical therapy abounds with short-term or one-time paradoxical interventions. This fact reflects the immediate effectiveness of paradoxical interventions. Many times only one intervention is needed to remedy a client's problem. We could add more to this literature by presenting some of our more dramatic "miracle" cures. However, there are many cases where intervention needs to be extended over a period of time. The literature on protracted paradoxical intervention is very sparse. This lack of attention to extended case studies has given some therapists the impression that all paradoxical techniques should produce immediate and lasting results. We believe paradoxical interventions need to be tracked or followed up. Perhaps, the reason so many therapists have become disappointed with this approach is because they tried a paradoxical intervention once with a client and the client did not improve or had a relapse.

The purpose of this chapter is to present cases where a variety of therapeutic techniques, mostly paradoxical, are employed over a number of sessions. Each case demonstrates how paradoxical techniques have been used to deal with cases with multiple problems, to reinforce previous interventions, or to prevent the client(s) from having a relapse.

CASE 1: PARADOXICAL INTERVENTION IN AN INDIVIDUAL AND A FAMILY

Our first case demonstrates the paradoxical treatment of both an individual and a family. The family was seen for just a few sessions and then the mother was seen for several months. This case also exemplifies the use of paradoxical letters. For the first few months of treatment a paradoxical letter was mailed to the client(s) the day after the sessions. The client(s) was seen by the senior author and a male clinical psychologist* who was interested in learning paradoxical psychotherapy.

The client was an overweight 37-year-old white woman with three children, Sara, 15, Ann, 14, and Dave, 11. Norma, the mother, had been married for a brief period of time to an Indian and had one child from this marriage. The husband had deserted her. Her other two children had different fathers, but she told all three that they had the same father. The children were very different physically. Norma had had six psychiatric hospitalizations by the time we saw her. She had a total of 18 weeks as an inpatient and literally years of experience in day treatment centers; she had been in therapy with numerous staff members in our hospital system. Most of her diagnoses were of some schizophrenic type with one diagnosis as manic-depressive.

Norma had been seen by several therapists in the clinic. In fact, she had become a legend. She was known as a chronic patient with whom it was impossible to work. This information suggested that she might be a candidate for paradoxical treatment.

Norma was referred to our clinic by the day treatment program she was attending. She had been complaining about her 14-year-old daughter having temper tantrums and wanted some help. She also wanted someone to explain her "mental state" to her other two children.

---

*Thomas Ryan, Ph.D. was the co-therapist on this case.

Although we knew a great deal about this family before they came for the first session, we decided to conduct a typical first session and obtain a clinical-social history and set goals for treatment. The family arrived for their first session with the mother leading the way down the clinic corridor and the children scattered along the way behind her. The children entered the treatment room one-by-one and scattered to different corners of the room. The oldest daughter pulled one chair to a corner and turned it toward the wall so that she could place her head in the corner. Ann sat in the opposite corner and Dave sprawled out in the middle of the floor. Norma asked them to straighten up once and then gave up. The oldest daughter interrupted the session at that moment to announce that she was in this session against her will and would not come back. The mother looked at us and said she would try to make her come back but said she had had little success in controlling her children.

We attempted to structure the family and obtain the information previously mentioned. It shortly became clear that Norma wanted to bring her children in for treatment without being there herself or, if she was, without taking an active part. She told us she wanted the family to understand each other, the children to stop fighting, and the therapists to explain to her children why she had been hospitalized the last time. Norma was clearly uncomfortable with us and with trying to control her children. The children must have sensed her discomfort because they began to distract shortly after the session started and continued to escalate their behavior. The session was in chaos after just 20 minutes. Sara would sporadically pound her head on the wall while mumbling things. Dave was singing, blowing bubbles with his chewing gum, and picking on Ann. Ann overreacted to Dave's annoying gestures and moved over to Sara, whereupon Sara and she started arguing. The mother sat helplessly and said this was the way things were at home all the time. Our attempts to structure the family up to this point had failed just as miserably as the mother's attempts.

We shifted to a paradoxical strategy to deal with the family's behavior. Initially we sat quietly for a minute just watching the family. Then we began to chat with each other about how dull and uninteresting the family appeared. After our short dialogue we relabeled the chaos in the family. We told them they must really care about each other to try so hard to keep each other busy and entertained. But, we also said, we had seen what they were doing hundreds of times and it was very boring for us to watch and probably boring for them to do it. We then started telling them how they could do what they were already doing better. A challenge to be more creative was issued. The children's initial reaction was to ignore us. We continued to prescribe what they were doing and they began to test us by being even more distracting.

Finally, they began to calm down and waited to see what we were going to say or do next. Sara had turned toward us and finally proclaimed that the therapists were "bananas." The strategy we employed had disrupted or exploded the chaotic pattern of the family and had also shown the children that we were, in fact, "crazier" than mother. We had previously learned that the children thought their mother was crazy. They expected her to be hospitalized any day by the clinic. The fact that we acted crazier than the mother may have made us appear less threatening to the children and perhaps to Norma.

The first session ended without any goals being set with the family. We had accepted the responsibility for setting the first goal. This goal was to eliminate the chaos in the family and reduce the bickering among the children.

The mother's mood during this session was depressed. Her inability to control her children was one source of her depression. The children distracted and acted playful but they were far from happy. They too looked sad. Our hypothesis was that the family chaos was a protective mechanism to avoid depression.

A letter was written after this session and mailed the next day. Norma had been told to expect a letter with some homework from us. The statements in the letter are numbered and then analyzed.

Letter One

Dear Norma, Sara, Ann, and Dave:

(To be read at supper table by Norma)
I was very impressed with the sadness and hurt in your family in our last session. I am glad that two of you were able to express your sadness.[1] It is important when you are sad and hurt to be

able to share it with other family members. A family that shares its hurt really loves one another.[2]

However, I have grave misgivings about how much you should share at this time. I think it is much too soon for you to communicate these feelings to each other.[3] Instead, each of you should continue to protect the family from its sadness by distracting or keeping each other busy.[4] You might even elect one family member to really focus all your attention on, or maybe someone in the family has already decided to take this role. This person could be responsible for starting fights and misbehaving.[5] It should be a very responsible and loyal member of the family, which will make the choice easy since one of you is already acting in an overly responsible manner (but enjoying it).[6]

This family is also in a silent crisis.[7] Someone has changed recently, which has the family confused and uncertain about the future. The confusion and chaos in the family are actually part of the preparation for the family's forthcoming growth and change.[8]

Warning: The family should be prepared for a big fight on Wednesday night.[9]

Analysis

1) Cryptic statement—Raises the question of who expressed sadness. Designed to unite family in guessing who.

2) Relabeling—Sharing hurt equated to love.

3) Restraining—Previous statement tells them it is good to share hurt but now they are warned that it may be risky.

4) Positive connotation—Distraction is said to protect family, which puts them all on the same level.

5) Prescription—The fighting is prescribed.

6) Relabeling—The most distracting member of the family is relabeled as the one who is responsible and loyal.

7) Cryptic statement—What is a "silent crisis"?

8) Relabeling—Remember this is a chaotic family. There is no predictability or certainty. Their confusion is relabeled as preparation for growth.

9) Paradoxical question—Our next session was scheduled for Thursday. The oldest daughter said she would not return. Hence, we expected a fight about her attendance on Wednesday night, if not earlier.

The next session began very differently from the first. The family walked in together. Sara, Ann, and Dave sat on the floor in front of their mother in a line. They were quiet as they looked directly at the therapists.

Norma initiated the session by saying she wanted to talk about the letter. She said she was angry about it and then started to question us about various parts. She had read the letter to the family at the dinner table as we had instructed. The family accurately guessed why we predicted a fight on Wednesday night. Norma said they guessed who had expressed sadness in the first session and had agreed among themselves. The family could not agree about other parts of the letter. The important point is that they spent time together trying to decipher a message about the family. The letter had united the family in a serious way around an issue.

Norma reported a change in the family (although she did not attribute those changes to the letter). The family did not have a single fight during the last week. Norma told us the family was too busy talking to each other and having fun. The children had their own news to report. Each child took his or her turn telling us about the spaghetti-throwing fight they had after receiving the letter. We used the spaghetti fight to elicit a positive mood in the session in which the children talked to each other and Norma. The chaos we observed in the first session was completely absent in the second session.

The main issue we felt we needed to deal with in the second session was Norma's anger. Our history of Norma told us she would not directly confront others, including therapists. She would deny being angry and then explode later. Her other strategy was to play one therapist against another. She probably knew more mental health professionals than anyone in the clinic, which made it quite easy for her to defeat a therapist in this way. Norma was asked to elaborate on what made her angry about the letter but she refused to discuss it. She claimed, however, to have taken the letter to a social worker for her reactions. A note was written on the back of our letter which stated that our letter was nonsense. The tone of the note was hostile. We knew from the handwriting that Norma had not written the note, but we could not be sure who wrote it.

The presence of this note warned us that Norma would try to undo treatment by playing us against other therapists. We told her she should continue to get help from others and we appreciated all the feedback we could get. We then contacted the other therapists who worked with her in our system and told them to expect Norma to complain about us. They were instructed to tell Norma that we had been in touch with them. They were to make a detailed list of her complaints and send them directly to us. Norma never attempted to triangle any other therapists in the future. These two moves show how we were able to bind off any difficult situation in the future. The client who plays this kind of game must not be given any options to undo treatment. We had defused any power she might have had by prescribing this behavior and contacting other therapists.

The second letter reinforces the changes which resulted from the first letter, in addition to dealing with Norma's denial of anger.

Letter Two

Dear Norma, Sara, Ann and Dave:

We enjoyed working with the family Thursday. We felt the family was having fun and it was exciting to watch. We also saw a lot of care and love in the family. However, we are concerned about the family not having any fights in the last week. While this kind of progress is good, we feel that the family has gone too fast.[1] We still think it's a good idea for the family to have at least one fight a day. You could make each member of the family responsible for starting a fight on different days.[2]

Norma, we felt that you were angry with us and holding it inside. We admire your ability to control your anger, but we feel that you should let us know when you're angry by showing us.[3] We had expected you to be much angrier on Thursday and expect that you will be angry with us many times in the future.[4]

What continues to concern us most about the family is its sadness. While the family was not as sad this Thursday as last Thursday, we are afraid that one of two things will happen. The family will either slide back to being sad and keeping each other busy, or, as the family improves, one member will get worse.[5] If the family keeps improving, you should pay close attention to each other to see who gets worse. The minute the family sees one person getting worse, all the members of the family will have to go back to the old way of behaving in order to protect that person.[6]

We hope the family studies each letter as well as they studied the first one. Feel free to show it to all the mental health experts you like. However, the family is the real expert on understanding these letters since they are written in a way that only the family can *begin* to understand.[7]

Analysis

1) Restraining—The family is told they have made a desirable change too rapidly.

2) Prescription—The symptom of fighting is prescribed in a certain way.

3) Relabeling—Norma's control of her anger is relabeled as a special ability. The idea that she cannot or could not control her anger is changed.

4) Paradoxical prediction—Norma is told she should have been angrier and that she will be angry with us in the future. This statement gives her permission to be angry with us and to show us that she is angry.

5) Paradoxical prediction—We predict the family may have one of two types of relapses.

6) Prescription and positive connotation—The symptom is prescribed under specified conditions for the protection of the family members.

7) Prescription and cryptic statement—Norma is told to show the letters to others. The family is told the letters cannot be fully understood. This statement challenges the family to try to understand the letters.

The family's response to this letter was to not have any fights in the following days. Norma acted angry with us in the next session over the statement that someone should be elected each day to start a fight. Her anger seemed to be a sham. We hypothesized that she was testing us to see how we would respond to her anger. The mood in the family continued to improve. Norma exercised more control over her children during the session. She reported having more control over them and had established order in the house.

Norma confided to us she had been a "nut" but she was determined not to have to go back to the hospital. Her description of herself indicated that she still felt she might be a "nut" requiring future hospitalization. Now that the family was organized enough to be workable, we asked Norma to clarify some goals or changes the family would like to make. Norma described several problems in the family. However, she felt pessimistic about the potential for changing those problems. She felt helpless and hopeless. When we attempted to focus on the positive aspects of the family, Norma would not take any credit for them and diminished her value. She was locking herself into a position of "It's hopeless but you help us."

The next letter was formulated to deal with Norma's sense of hopelessness. The usual therapeutic strategy would have been to encourage Norma by providing support, understanding, and clarity. In short, the therapists would take a one-up position in which they would imply they have some solutions. Norma had defeated enough therapists for us to know this strategy would be ineffective. We decided to be more pessimistic than she appeared to be.

Letter Three

Dear Norma, Sara, Ann and Dave:

We want you to know that we were serious about what we said about who would be the next nut or problem in the family. Families do develop habits which are hard to break. Therefore, someone in the family might start doing poorly in school, setting fires, getting in trouble, getting depressed, or developing other problems.[1]

We are struck by how willing members of the family are to make other people responsible for their behavior. While we admire your willingness to take responsibility for other people, who is responsible for you? When you make others responsible for you, then when you do well it is someone else's joy and when you fail it is someone else's fault. Are you strong enough to take credit for both your successes and your failures?[2]

We feel rather helpless and hopeless about how we will be of help to the family. We feel certain that at some point we will let the family down. We don't know when or why this will happen but we know it will happen. We suspect the family is already feeling let down by us.[3]

Analysis

1) Paradoxical prediction—Future problems are predicted. Part of this paragraph was designed to help Norma focus on specific problem areas. Problems in the family are also normalized to some extent by reframing them as their habits, a shift from the medical model to the normal.

2) Linear statement—Responsibility is discussed in a straightforward manner. The final sentence is a challenge emphasizing success. Norma believed she was a failure. She refused to accept successes.

3) Hard restraining—We declare our impotence, past, present, and future.

The next session was a special session just for Norma. With the encouragement of another counselor Norma had become interested in acquiring some vocational skills. She had never worked full-time for any extended period. Her two most stable jobs had been driving a school bus and babysitting. She said she was interested in being a clerk or secretary. A meeting was held in which a vocational rehabilitation specialist came in to discuss what Norma needed to do to participate in a training program. Norma was hesitant to ask questions. She was not sure she was ready to go to school. A few weeks later she did begin a training program. She was an excellent student.

The whole family returned for their next regular appointment. Norma took the lead in this session by telling us things weren't as bad in the family as we had suggested in our letter. In fact, she said the family was getting along fine. She then started talking about herself. For the first time, Norma actually began to talk openly about her own problems. At this point, the children were dismissed from the therapy room for several reasons. Norma had indicated that she wanted to talk about herself rather than her problems with the family. Talking with her alone provided us with the opportunity to explore issues without concern for what her children might believe. The children were also likely to interpret any statement of personal problems as further evidence that mother was crazy. Finally, there had been a blurring of generational boundaries in the family. By sending the children out, we were beginning to set limits for adult (parent) vs. child (family) issues.

Norma talked about feeling sad or depressed. She felt disorganized and powerless. Most of all she was concerned about Christmas, which was only 25 days away. Her financial situation was grim. No money was available for presents. The session consisted of three parts. First, we obtained an inventory of her individual problems. Secondly, strategies for finding a temporary job were discussed. Finally, her depression over Christmas was normalized and a paradoxical assignment was given. The assignment was to spend one hour a day worrying and feeling depressed.

This session also ended with a decision being made by Norma to discontinue family therapy. Norma realized that her family was reacting to her condition. She believed she needed help for herself in order to be able to help her children. We agreed to see Norma individually with the understanding that we would help her with family issues as they arose.

Letter Four

Dear Norma, Sara, Ann and Dave:

We are glad that you feel good enough about the family to stop the family sessions at this time. We agree that the family has made good progress, although we don't understand how since we had just gotten started with the family sessions. We want to congratulate the family for having the ability to change itself.[1]

We are glad that you, Norma, were strong enough to ask for help for yourself. We know the Christmas season will be a difficult one for you because you cannot provide for your family the way you would like. Feeling sad about this fact is perfectly normal. Also, with all the worries that you have right now it was no wonder that your "head" was not working right today like you told us.[2]

As we suggested in the session, we believe it is important for you to set aside one full hour each day in which to worry and experience your sadness. By taking conscious control of these things, you will learn how to control them rather than letting them control you.[3]

Analysis

1) Linear statement—This paragraph praises the family for making changes. We take no credit for the changes. Furthermore, we accept her request for individual help without questioning the needs of the family.

2) Linear statement—This paragraph was designed to normalize Norma's depression and confusion.

3) Prescription—The prescription given in the session is restated in the letter, i.e., be depressed.

The next session was held just a few days before Christmas. The primary purpose of the letter had been to warn Norma about how difficult the Christmas season might be for her. We expected her to relapse at this point. The fact that she did not experience a relapse showed that the treatment was working. The last letter had helped to normalize an experience she might have otherwise labeled "crazy."

Norma had searched successfully for some temporary jobs after the last session. She reported being busy preparing for Christmas. Her financial situation was improving such that she believed she would be able to provide presents for her children. Norma had also been helping other people out in their Christmas preparations. An elderly woman had asked her to help her buy presents and take her to shop. Norma helped her without accepting any money. She was pleased to be able to help someone else. Norma was demonstrating that she could be helpful and effective with others. She began to make a number of positive statements about herself. The only problem she reported was feeling upset by a dream in which a baby died. The dream was analyzed using a Gestalt approach. Her dream turned out to be an anniversary reaction to the death of a close friend's baby.

The next letter was sent to Norma just a few days before Christmas. Norma was coping effectively and we wanted to praise her. We did not want to raise any new issues at this time so we issued a warning to her.

Letter Five

Dear Norma:

I am glad that things are going so well for you. You seem to be standing up to the pressure of Christmas well.[1] Just remember that when things slow down you will probably experience a low period.[2]

I like the way you are doing for others. It is commendable that you have taken care of yourself well enough that you can help take care of others.[3]

Analysis

1) Linear statement—Praise.

2) Paradoxical prediction—Christmas had given Norma a goal. She wanted to make it a happy experience for her children. We speculated that she would experience a low period following Christmas. If she did feel low our prediction would help to normalize the experience as well as show that we knew what would happen.

3) Relabeling—Taking care of others is reframed as taking care of self. Norma had believed she could take care of others but

not herself. This statement changes the meaning attributed to taking care of others.

Four days after Christmas we had another session. Christmas had been a pleasant experience for the whole family. She told us Christmas stories with more affect and humor than we had seen up to this time. Her affect was reinforced by our listening and sharing a couple of stories of our own. Her temporary jobs had served their purpose. Norma was now interested in finding a steady part-time job while she completed her training. We discussed how she might look for a job, pointing out that the job market was very tight.

In this session a new issue emerged which stemmed from her anger over her repeated hospitalizations. Perhaps this issue arose because Norma felt she could now talk openly about what made her feel angry and depressed. She felt her hospitalizations had been necessary but she objected to the way she was treated during her confinements. She was also unhappy and bitter about the treatment she had received in her day hospital program and from her individual therapist. She had learned that she could read her hospital chart, including our progress notes. She believed there were statements in her chart which were not true. She wanted to insert her own notes in her chart to "set the record straight." We agreed to help her with this task. She was praised for wanting to help the hospital get its charts in order.

Letter Six

Dear Norma:

We were glad to hear that Christmas was a good time for you. Your sense of humor in our session today was delightful. You seem to be doing great without us.[1]

We realize how difficult and stressful it is to look for a job. We expect that you will feel like giving up many times before you find something. You may begin to feel low after looking for a job for a while, which is perfectly natural. After looking for a job, many people give up and then feel depressed.[2]

You have asked to review your chart and set the record straight in our next session. We hope you think about the things you want to say thoroughly so you can set things straight with the center and be finished with it. We encourage you to be honest and not hold back in your comments.[3]

We're glad that everything is going so well for you. What concerns us is that sometimes just when things start to go right they get undone and fall apart. Can you think of ways things might fall apart? What can you do to stop it?[4]

Analysis

1) Linear statement—Praise and reinforcement. We accept no credit for helping her.

2) Paradoxical prediction—This statement suggests that looking for a job will be depressing and she may give up. By making these predictions, we hope to normalize them if they do occur and place them under our control.

3) Relabeling and prescription—Norma's request to read her chart could be interpreted as paranoia. We told her it was good for the hospital and for her. The goal of therapy was to help Norma reach the point where she would no longer need therapy or any service provided by the hospital. By prescribing this task to her we imply that she will begin finishing her relationship with the hospital by becoming more involved with it.

4) Paradoxical prediction—We continue to be more pessimistic than Norma by predicting a relapse.

The next session was primarily devoted to Norma's reading her chart and making notes. One therapist (Weeks) sat with her while she reviewed the chart. Norma did have one complaint before this session got underway. She wanted to know why we were always so pessimistic. She said we could find the dark lining in any cloud. Her response was triggered by the last letter. She claimed she was getting sick of "letters like that." I said we would consider her request and even make up good things if we had too. We did not send a letter to her following this session because she used it to review her chart.

The next week Norma returned with a handful of notes she wanted added to her chart. She wanted us to read them first and comment on them. We complied with her request and started reading. We had decided before the session to select statements with which we could agree and exaggerate on them. We planned to focus on incidents which would produce anger. It was not difficult to find incidents (real or not) which would produce anger in her. We exaggerated her complaints. The therapists expressed their anger and indignation, suggesting that Norma begin to make complaints to all sorts of official persons and organizations. She responded by saying she didn't have time to help the hospital with its problems. She had enough to do to take care of herself. What struck us more than anything else was the fact that Norma's notes were clear, intelligent, and well-thought-out. Most of her complaints seemed reasonable, although trivial. She objected to relatively unimportant statements we made about her in our progress notes.

Norma did not allow us to read all of her notes. She stopped us about midway through the session to discuss her feelings about her inability to remember things that had happened to her. She could not remember things she knew she had done. She had asked her family and others to fill her in on different events and was distressed by her memory gap. Talking about her past made her feel sad. She was realizing that she had lost a part of her life that she could not recover. She had been thinking about her past since the last session. These thoughts had made her feel depressed. She found herself worrying at bedtime, which produced insomnia. This appeared to be the first time Norma had stopped to consider her past. She was becoming more introspective. A need to understand her past was beginning to emerge.

Letter Seven

Dear Norma:

We are really impressed with the way you have reacted to your chart. Your comments on the chart were well-written, clear, logical, and truthful. Very few people could have been as objective as you were in writing down your reactions.[1]

Your concern about your past (the gaps) is a big step for you. You're really putting your life together so you can begin to really think about the future.[2] There is one danger in what you are doing. People who have "lost" part of this past and are strong enough to realize it like you always feel somewhat sad or depressed about it. You should expect to feel low as long as you are dealing with the issue about your past. It is a perfectly normal reaction which lasts for some time and is the stage before making a lot of future plans and feeling happy.[3]

We want you to spend one hour this week at bedtime worrying and giving in to your depression. You should think all of your worst thoughts and feel as low as you possibly can. This task will be difficult at first but later will help you get in charge of your depression rather than it taking charge of you.[4]

Analysis

1) Linear statement—Norma was praised on her notes to her chart. We used the notes to refer to her ability to write clearly. This maneuver also encouraged her efforts in becoming a secretary or clerk.

2) Relabeling—Norma's concern about her past is preparation for the future.

3) Positioning and relabeling—The fact that she can't remember part of her past is accepted. She is given permission to feel depressed about it and then her experience is relabeled as preparation for the future.

4) Prescription—Her worrying and depression are scheduled at bedtime.

Norma arrived for the next session upset. She had had an argument with a friend earlier the same day. She had also had an argument with another friend earlier during the week. In both cases she felt she had been used and was angry. She did not know how to assert herself so she allowed others to take advantage of her. By the time she reached our office she was ready to explode. She claimed everyone hated her. Initially, we accepted her position (positioning) that everyone hated her. After we pursued the "evidence" with her for a while, she said she was being irrational. She just didn't know how to stand up to people. If she did stand up for herself, she thought she would lose her friends. A short discussion on assertiveness followed. Norma decided it wasn't worth it to have friends if she couldn't assert her rights. She was warned that she might lose some of her friends if she did stand up for herself.

Norma had talked about her friends from time to time. We had learned that all of her friends either were or had been patients at the hospital. In fact, her best friend was a very disturbed woman with whom she had taken turns, or so it seems, being hospitalized so their children would have care. We realized that eventually Norma would need to make other friends. She was encouraged to make friends in her training program and eventually she did form a couple of relationships.

Letter Eight

Dear Norma:

We must admit that we were hesitant to believe you when you told us everyone hated you. However, the evidence you gave us was overwhelming. It is amazing that you can function at all with people doing all those terrible things to you.[1] All we can do is suggest that you avoid people as much as possible and protect yourself from the inevitable hurt, tension, and conflicts that go with getting involved with people.[2]

Analysis

1) Positioning statement—We fully accept the statement that everyone hates her.

2) Prescription and Restraining—Her tendency to avoid others is prescribed and she is told to restrain herself from getting involved with others in order to protect herself.

Norma decided after reading our last letter that she would have to stand up for herself or have no friends at all. She talked about how she had started to set some limits with her friends. One of her friends had been calling several times each day and into the late night hours. Norma told her she could not accept any calls after 10:00 p.m. because she needed to sleep. Her friend tried calling late a couple of times. Norma reminded her of her needs and hung up. They continued to be friends but the late calls stopped.

We believed Norma had reached a transition point in her life. She was doing well in her secretarial/clerical training program. She felt she was getting her life and family in some order. The future was beginning to look hopeful for her. For the past several years her life had in some way revolved around the hospital. Now she was moving toward something completely different. We wanted to prepare Norma for the future as early as we could. Our goal was to help her survive independently. We raised questions in a challenging way in our sessions about the difficulties of being a student, finding a full-time job, and so on. Norma defied our challenges by responding positively. She said she would be able to handle things as they happened. She realized she would have failures and setbacks but maintained that these things were part of living.

A new strategy was developed to help Norma begin to make her transition. First, we believed it was imperative for Norma to see herself as competent. She needed to know she could survive in the outside world as a self-sufficient and independent woman.

Norma would say from time to time that she was a survivor. She used the term survivor to denote the fact that she had lived through her hospitalizations. We suspected she also used the term to refer to her ability to manipulate the system, although she believed she had been victimized by the system. Norma knew from the beginning of therapy that I (Weeks) was a psychology intern with the hospital. In order to strengthen Norma's identification with me, I began to talk about how I too had been victimized by the hospital, e.g., low pay, long hours, poor working conditions, etc. I pointed out how I felt I was treated even worse than the patients she had described to me. I told Norma I still had several months to go to complete my "stay" and I didn't know how I could survive it. I asked her to tell me what she had done to survive her ordeal with the hospital. In addition, I started discussing the difficulties of getting a job. Of course, I was overly pessimistic about my future.

Norma responded just as we expected. She talked about having hope and gave me encouragement. She even offered to write me a letter of recommendation. When we switched back to pointing out difficulties she might encounter, she was even more "resistant." The strategy had reinforced her sense of competence and hope. This strategy was used several times over the remainder of treatment. It would just so happen that I would have a similar problem a week or two after one of Norma's complaints. She never failed to be encouraging.

The following letter was sent to Norma by me (Weeks). The co-therapist did not sign this letter.

Letter Nine

Dear Norma:

I am glad that things are going so well for you and your family. You seem to be pulling everything together and you look hopeful about the future.[1]

You should prepare yourself for some setbacks, problems, anxieties, and depression. You know by now that just when things start to go right these things are likely to happen.[2]

I would also like to ask a favor of you. You have learned a lot about what it takes to survive in the hospital system. What can you tell me to help me get through the next few months? Could you write down your ideas and send them to me in a letter?[3]

Analysis

1) Linear statement—Encouragement and recognition of her strengths.

2) Paradoxical prediction—Another prediction of doom to inoculate her against problems and challenge her to continue her struggles.

3) Reversal—This strategy is similar to declaring impotence. I take a one-down position which forces her out of the victim role she had habitually assumed.

Norma reacted strongly to our letter but not to the part we expected. She ignored the request for help. The letter we received from her repeated her objection to our pessimistic predictions. Her letter was openly angry about our prediction.

We expected Norma to still be angry at the beginning of our next session. We wanted to continue our strategy of being pessimistic about the future while praising Norma for her progress. We also wanted to recognize her anger and deal with it in an appropriate way. This fact placed us in a bind. If we continued to be pessimistic, then we would be ignoring Norma's anger. If we stopped our strategy, then she might experience a relapse. Our solution to this problem was for the therapists to disagree. I (Weeks) would continue to be overly pessimistic, while the co-therapist would be optimistic. The co-therapy model also allowed us to play out any ambivalences in Norma we detected.

Norma was, in fact, angry when she arrived for her session. She wanted to discuss her letter. The therapists responded briefly to her and then began to argue between themselves about Norma's situation. Norma felt she had won the battle since one of us agreed with her. The remainder of that session was spent in helping Norma do some problem-solving. The Department of Social Services was making revisions in some policies. Norma had been informed that her assistance and food stamps might be reduced. Instructions were given about whom she should contact.

Letter Ten

Dear Norma:

We are pleased that things are going so well for you. Perhaps we were wrong in worrying that you would have a 90% good/ 10% problemsome week. You have had so much experience expertly navigating bureaucratic systems that you may do better than we would in the same circumstances. However, we are still a little concerned about the amount of new stresses you are assuming with school and still caution you to be prepared for a 7% bad week.[1]

Analysis

1) Paradoxical prediction—We continue to predict problems but reduce our estimate.

The next session was relatively uneventful. Norma had started her second term of training. She was doing fine in school, making new friends, and finding her home life enjoyable. At the end of this session, I (Weeks) predicted another relapse while my co-therapist disagreed.

The letter sent this week suggested that two letters had been sent. In fact, only one letter was actually sent. The purpose of this letter was to praise Norma but imply that one of us (Weeks) disagreed. The letter makes a paradoxical prediction by implication.

Letter Eleven

> Dear Norma:
>
> As Gerald might have written, he and I can't agree about what feedback to include in this week's letter.
>
> I feel you are making wonderful progress and I'm very pleased. You handled your first class very well even when first classes are usually very stressful. The fighting among your children seems to have calmed down dramatically, which can only be attributed to your good interventions.
>
> I feel you justified in being quite proud of your accomplishments.

The relapse we had been predicting for the past several months finally occurred—or so it appeared. The timing of her relapse was interesting since it occurred just after our most positive letter to her. Norma complained that she was having difficulty falling asleep because her thoughts were racing. She brought notes to the session which described her problems and strange feelings she claimed to experience. Her complaints were all of a nonspecific nature. It was not clear to us whether these were real complaints or some kind of test. The only complaint we were not suspicious of was her insomnia. We knew Norma was a coffee drinker and she had a reputation for medicating herself. She had, in fact, told us she had a closet full of drugs but did not take them. Norma admitted to the fact that she had been drinking more coffee at night. She estimated that she would drink up to 20 cups an evening! We explained the need for her to cut down on her coffee drinking and not to drink coffee in the evening. She agreed it would be a good idea to drink less coffee. It would also save her some money.

The other nebulous problems she had written down posed more of a therapeutic problem. Was she testing us or were they really problems that upset her? We decided to maintain our paradoxical position while closely monitoring the problems she presented. Congratulations were offered on the good job she had done of recording her problems. We explained how our sessions would be more useful and productive if she had a number of specific problems. In fact, we mentioned feeling that our last few sessions had not been approved of by our supervisor because there were no *real* problems. In short, we implied that we were in trouble for continuing to see her because she didn't have enough problems. Thus, she could help us if she were to bring in all her problems. A prescription was given at the end of the session for her to try to race her thoughts even faster when she went to bed. The letter following this session was signed only by Weeks.

Letter Twelve

Dear Norma:

I was able to sucker Tom into betting me a dollar that you could race your thoughts for 15 minutes. He felt that you have the exceptional mental power and control to do it, plus he said you could take some Elavil, which would help your thoughts race anyway. I agree that you have good mental control but think this task is impossible for anyone.[1]

I appreciate the notes you let me read. I told my supervisor about some of the things you wrote, which got him off my back.[2] I hope you continue to write these clear and insightful notes and include all of your problems, weird feelings, and unusual thoughts. The more the better.[3]

Analysis

1) Reframing—The first sentence of this paragraph states that we have made a bet on one of her symptoms. The purpose of the bet was to increase her resistance to us because betting on

someone's symptoms would not be perceived to be in her best interest. We wanted her to resist our instructions to race her thoughts. This bet was also designed to communicate our lack of concern over the severity of the symptom. The second part of the paragraph puts the client in a bind. If she races her thoughts, then she has "exceptional mental power and control." If she doesn't have any racing thoughts, then the symptom has disappeared.

2) Reframing—Note-writing is frequently considered pathological. We have reframed the situation so that her notes mean she is helping us as well as the therapeutic process.

3) Symptom prescription—Her note-writing behavior is prescribed, which indirectly prescribes her problem: weird feelings and unusual thoughts.

Norma surprised us in the next session. We thought we had placed her in a bind such that one of us could pretend to win the bet. When we asked her about racing her thoughts, she started laughing at us and said we were both suckers. She had decided not to tell us whether she had done it or not. Her attitude toward us and her complaints indicated that she no longer experienced the problems she had claimed to have earlier. She had also managed to escape from one of our binds without realizing it. She knew, however, that at some level she had turned the tables on us and she was delighted about it. When asked about the other problems and the notes we had requested, she said things had straightened out. She then changed the subject. We probed some around the problems she had presented earlier until we were convinced they were probably pseudo complaints. She never mentioned any of these problems again, nor was there any evidence that any of the problems were occurring.

A few weeks earlier Norma had expressed concern over not being able to remember parts of her past. She had also mentioned not being able to remember certain parts of her childhood. We had suggested she begin checking things out with her family. She had not seen her parents in 15 years, nor did she want to see them in the future. Yet, she did want to understand her family more fully. A commitment was made to work on a genogram, a psychological family tree, when she obtained more information. This past week Norma had talked with an aunt who was very familiar with her family. The aunt had given Norma some information about the family which reaffirmed her feelings of not wanting to see them. She had learned that she was an unwanted child and that her sisters had all been sexually molested by her father. She also obtained information about her brothers and sisters regarding their adjustment. Norma was encouraged to obtain more information so that we could work on the genogram in the next session. She was appropriately upset and saddened over the information she had obtained.

Letter Thirteen

> Dear Norma:
>
> We want to congratulate you on pulling one over on us. I guess we'll never know who won the bet. That's probably a first for you.[1]
>
> We were amazed at how well you handled the information you got about your family. Any regular person would have fallen apart probably. We like the way you want to put all the pieces together so you can understand things better.[2]
>
> We feel badly that we may have been selling you short. Unfortunately, it took us a long time to discover your inner or hidden strength which has allowed you to *survive* against all odds . . . even us.[3]

Analysis

1) Cryptic statement—What are we really telling Norma? We are telling her in an indirect way that she actually defeated us by escaping from our bind.

2) Linear statement—Norma is praised for her interest in her family and searching for her past. The second sentence of this paragraph implies that she is stronger than most people.

3) Linear statement—This is the first time we both directly acknowledge Norma's overall strength. We believe Norma may

have reached the point where paradoxical predictions of
doom and gloom are no longer necessary. We also declare our
incompetence as therapists, which helps to empower her.

Norma did not report any problems at the beginning of the next
session so we proceeded to work on her genogram.

The genogram session was a draining experience for all of us. Norma was one of 13 children and had a large extended family. While we
had hoped to help Norma develop some ties with her family members,
we could not find a single individual who was functional enough to be
of help to her. It seemed that Norma was the healthiest member of her
family. We decided it would be more helpful to encourage her to develop a social network outside her family.

Letter Fourteen

Dear Norma:

We were fascinated by your family tree. It annoys (typo—
should have been amazes) us that you managed to escape from
such a sick family with so few problems.[1] It is an even greater
achievement that you can be a helpful mother to your children
when you never had a mother of your own.[2]

We realize that talking about your family will dredge up old
memories that may best be put aside. We expect you will feel low
as we continue to put the pieces of your family together.[3]

Analysis

1) Linear statement—The second sentence was intended to
   reinforce Norma's health. However, a typographical error
   slipped by us (annoys for amazes). Norma thought we were
   telling her she was really sick or we wanted her to be sick
   (nuts). The statement thus became a paradoxical prediction.

2) Linear statement—This statement reinforces Norma's concept as a mother. It also points out the fact that her mother
   was never emotionally available for her. This statement was
   designed to help her grieve over the support she did not receive from her mother.

3) Paradoxical prediction—Sadness is predicted to be a consequence of her genogram work.

In the next session we continued with the genogram work in order to detect any other patterns Norma had replicated in her life or might replicate in the future. Few new patterns were found because of Norma's lack of information about her family members.

Norma had learned that her food stamps and aid from the Department of Social Services were being reduced. She had been to the Department of Social Services several times during the last week to work out a better arrangement. She had been shuffled from one person to the next. She felt frustrated, angry, and powerless. Just when she thought her life was beginning to have some direction, the support she needed to achieve her goals had been reduced. Norma still thought she could just slide by if there were no extra expenses. We were already amazed at how well she lived on her present income. Norma had not shown signs of relapsing following the last positive letter sent to her. Thus, another letter was sent.

Letter Fifteen

Dear Norma:

I was sorry to see you looking so tired and hassled yesterday. It's obviously very draining to be a single parent in today's world, but I think you are to be commended for doing such a good job of holding the family together; maintaining an atmosphere of love in the household; going to school to improve the family's income; etc.[1] In fact, considering the degree you are hassled by the Department of Social Services, I'm just a little surprised you're not feeling even more drained than you appeared.[2]

Analysis

1) Linear statement—This statement emphasizes the positive things Norma was doing.

2) Relabeling—Norma's drained appearance was labeled in such a way that we are impressed by it rather than concerned.

An individual who begins to make major changes in her life usually goes through a period of confusion. Many clients report feeling disorganized, directionless, purposelessness, disoriented. Life may seem unreal. The individual may try to relive old experiences or recapture old relationships, knowing in advance that it is not possible, yet trying anyway. The confusion individuals experience is simply a part of the process of change.

Norma had entered just such a phase in her next session. Her life had been changing but she didn't know what to expect. Her relationships with her old friends were strained because she was in school and had some sense of direction. She was having to make decisions about the future, such as where she wanted to live and work, and kind of work she wanted to do. She was experiencing the same kind of confusion a student feels when she has just graduated from high school or college. However, Norma reacted to her confusion more severely than someone in a developmental crisis. She believed her confusion might be a sign of another breakdown coming. Her confusion was not acceptable to her. She defined confusion in a pathological manner.

Our letter was formulated in such a way that we did not attempt to change Norma's pathological view of her confusion. Instead, we minimized or normalized the problem. In addition, we used the session to let Norma know this problem was one we had expected. We reframed her confusion as part of getting better—not worse.

Letter Sixteen

Dear Norma:

After talking things over we have decided that you are suffering from a "transient change disorder." The symptoms of this disorder are rapid change, confusion, and sadness. It is a temporary disorder that takes time to work through.[1] We do want you to begin keeping a record of when you are feeling confused, how long these periods last, and how severe they are (rate them on a scale from 1—mildly confused, to 10—very confused).[2]

People suffering from transient change disorders are in the process of making major changes in their lives and moving on to a higher plane.[3] On the other hand, it means giving up a lot of things that were once good.[4]

P.S.—from Barbara the secretary.
>   Hope this letter is a little better. I reminded Gerald that his handwriting is illegible and causes difficulty in trying to type a decent letter. I guess it was a lost cause—his handwriting is still unbearable.[5]

Analysis

1) Reframing—This is an example of pathological reframing. The pathological frame of reference Norma attributed to her confusion was not changed. She wanted her disorder diagnosed. We complied by giving her a disorder which "explained" her symptom plus giving her the expectation that these symptoms would disappear.

2) Linear statement—A behavioral technique was prescribed which is generally used to obtain baseline data. We used this technique to help her "distance" or objectify her confusion.

3) Reframing—Meaning attributed to confusion changed from pathological to health framework.

4) Restraining—Making positive changes results in both good and bad consequences. Change means sacrificing things that were once good.

5) Metaphor—Shortly after Norma began her clerical/secretarial training she caught a typographical error in one of our letters. She was proud she had the ability to find something having to do with the hospital that was objectively wrong.

We had our typist misspell one word in each letter sent to her beginning after she started talking about being a secretary. There were several reasons for this strategy. First, we wanted Norma to feel she didn't have to be perfect in her academic work. Second, it was a way to make us look more human. We always apologized for our errors while giving her credit for being sharp. Third, the errors were a metaphor representing the fact that we were not perfect or always right.

She expected hospital staff to always say they were right even when it was apparent to everyone that they weren't. The postscript to this letter served to disqualify the previous letters. It suggests that she hasn't received a "decent" letter and that I (Weeks) was unbearable.

Norma responded to our postscript by exclaiming that we should have her working for the hospital. She teased us about keeping all the psychiatrists and psychologists in line if she were to work in the hospital. When we told her she would have to work 24 hours a day to keep the psychiatrists straight, she replied by saying she wanted to work in an office where there were no hassles. This playful dialogue among us was a metaphor representing Norma's separation from the hospital. She had reached the point where she could joke about the staff rather than feel angry and upset.

Reframing and prescribing Norma's confusion had been helpful to her. She realized she was not confused as frequently or as much as she thought she was. The complaint was still present but its meaning had changed. She now said her confusion was OK. She decided to take one day at a time. The fact that she had made this kind of perceptual change meant she would be able to cope with other changes more effectively.

Most of the next session concerned Norma's friends. As Norma's situation improved, she had more and more difficulties with her friends who were still in the day hospital program. Her friends demanded that she visit them during the day at the hospital and be available to them by phone in the evening. Norma was beginning to structure her life in such a way that she no longer had the time or patience to listen to their unending complaints. She was willing to help them but felt she was being abused. We agreed that her friends had used her. We also continued to encourage her to develop other friendships.

Letter Seventeen

Dear Norma:

I am still not sure you realize how difficult it will be to deal with your present friends once you start your career. I am afraid they will not understand you, and you will feel rejected by them and have trouble setting some limits with them. It's never too early to plan for the future.[1]

Analysis

1) Paradoxical prediction—By predicting difficulties with her friends, we hoped to inoculate her against those problems or make them less severe for her.

Norma had shown considerable improvement since the beginning of her therapy. She had become amenable to therapy. Her attempts to resist and manipulate us had stopped. She was thinking clearly, responding appropriately, showing appropriate affect, and had some order and direction in her life. Her self-concept of being chronically sick (nuts) had changed to one of a person with good attributes and potential. The sessions with her were not as difficult as our early ones. The game-playing she had used early on had turned into genuineness. Relating to her had become easy because she was able to relate to herself congruently. The need for paradoxical strategies had diminished to the point where we were sending her mostly linear letters.

On the basis of these improvements, a decision was made to stop sending letters and shift to seeing her bimonthly, rather than weekly. These plans were discussed with Norma in our next session. She felt comfortable in making the transition. In fact, she said the weekly sessions had recently become too frequent for her.

We saw Norma for six more sessions on a bimonthly basis. Most of the work in these sessions centered around her developing social and parental skills. The problems she presented were specific. They were mostly related to making further adjustments in her new life-style.

After the six sessions Norma was still doing well. I (Weeks) was terminating my internship and relationship with Norma. The co-therapist continued to see Norma on a monthly basis.

A year later Norma had completed her training. She had experienced no psychological problems. Her children were all doing exceptional work in school. In fact, two of them had won awards for outstanding achievements. Unfortunately, Norma had experienced several medical problems which had prevented her from working. In addition, two of her closest old friends had committed suicide. She had felt sad over their deaths but did not let these events stop her from moving forward. Eventually, Norma accepted a part-time job in a store close to her home. She was happy and optimistic about her future.

CASE 2: PARADOXICAL TREATMENT OF DEPRESSION*

Mark was a 67-year-old white male who came to the clinic seeking help for depression. He was neatly dressed and appeared to be in excellent physical health. Mark had recently retired from a job as a specialty salesman. He and his wife Sally, 60, had moved from a large city to a housing development in the country. His wife had worked part-time, which meant they could afford to retire without much concern about money. They had two adult sons who were both single. Both sons were artists. One son lived in a commune.

Mark had a long history of depression. His mother had become depressed just before his father died. She was hospitalized for several weeks. One year after his mother's depressive episode Mark became severely depressed. He was hospitalized for three weeks and then treated as an outpatient for two years. Mark was 23 at the time of his first hospitalization. His depression worsened to the point where he could not function adequately in his original occupation as an entertainer. His depression forced him to leave show business in search of another occupation. He found a position in a specialty shop where he became a highly successful salesman. However, he continued to struggle with depression. He was unable to go to work some days because he felt too depressed. Luckily, Mark was considered invaluable by the owner of the store who tolerated his absences.

Mark had been in and out of treatment for his depression with psychiatrists for at least 30 years. He had been hospitalized several times and received no less than 10 electroconvulsive treatments. Two years before we saw him he had been hospitalized one month, treated with ECT, and given more antidepressants. His psychiatric treatment for the past several years had been chiefly chemotherapy.

When Mark presented himself at our clinic he exhibited many of

---

*This case was treated by the senior author and Evelyn Salch.

had one full hour each morning in which there were no interruptions. The session was ended promptly after we gave these instructions. As the couple made their way from our office, Mark looked back over his shoulder to say he might prove us wrong about having a "low" week. His response cued us that we had been on target with out interventions.

Mark and Sally returned to our office the next week with Mark looking much better. He was talkative and animated. He said he was afraid to try the assignment (he called it his meditation time), but did it because we were the doctors. The first couple of days had been difficult. He had no trouble being depressed during his meditation time. By the end of the week he reported he could not force himself to be depressed for a whole hour. The most significant change was that he had no "low" during the whole week. He said the past week had been better for him than any week in the past 30 years. His improvement during the past week had even surpassed our expectations. Sally was also impressed with his change in mood.

The content of Mark's meditation was explored in this session. Those thoughts which were unreasonable were subjected to a rational-emotive therapy analysis. The reasonable thoughts that depressed him, such as mother's senility and poor health, were normalized. They were labeled as normally depressing thoughts. He was given the same assignment, except he was to reduce the time to 30 minutes a day.

Mark stated in the next session that his lows were completely gone. He was grateful that we had given him a plan. No one had ever given him a plan before. He was clearly optimistic about being able to control his depression—in fact, overly optimistic.

We used this session to work on how Mark dealt with anger and hurt. Depressed individuals often do not know when they are having these feelings or how to express them. Mark fit our expectations. He rarely got angry, although he did say he could express feeling hurt when he was depressed. Sally was in better touch with her hurt and anger so we had her model these feelings for Mark and then had them share their feelings with each other. This strategy helped Mark assert himself and began the process of clarifying underlying marital issues. For example, Mark had been angry with Sally for years over sending their oldest son money.

The 30-minute meditation was reassigned. We also predicted that Mark would have a "low" during the coming week. Our rationale was that things were going too well. When he had the low he was to pay close attention to the moment he started to come out of it and then extend it 30 more minutes. Mark was upset by our prediction and assignment. He thought he was in better control than our prediction indicated.

Mark proudly announced in the following session that he had experienced no low as we predicted. We acted perplexed over his report and then tried to fabricate a low out of the past week's events. Mark and Sally were unwilling to buy any of our "interpretations" that he really did have a low. They did report having an argument during the last week. They had fought over sending money to their oldest son. Sally said she could not remember when Mark had been so assertive with her. She verbalized being pleased with her "new husband."

As is often the case, when one partner begins to improve, the relationship deteriorates. Our next move was intended to deal with this issue. In this session we began to point out some of the risks of Mark's becoming too assertive with Sally. We suggested getting depressed rather than angry as one way to protect the relationship. They both acted insulted when we made this suggestion. We asked them to think about it and then prescribed that he cut his meditation time to 20 minutes a day.

Mark's next visit marked several weeks without a low. He had improved at a surprising rate. There were signs of both individual and marital changes. We asked Mark whether he was really ready to give up a "habit" he had had for 30 years. Of course, we knew he would say he was. We cautioned him about his answer. What, he asked, would the negative consequences of giving up his depression be? They thought about this question and said he would receive less attention, sympathy, and affection from Sally. We agreed but said those things were just the tip of the iceberg.

In Chapter 7 (pp. 126–131), we presented the concept of "negative consequences," using this session as an example. After we completed our use of this technique, we still acted unconvinced about his giving up the depression completely. We prescribed a relapse. Mark was instructed to select any eight-hour period during the next week in which to act as depressed as possible. He could not tell Sally that he was faking but was to assure her it was real. He was further instructed to pay attention to how he triggered this depression, how he maintained it, how he stopped it, and how Sally reacted to him. Sally was, of course, present while we gave Mark these instructions. She was told she should try to guess when he was going to "pull" his depression. She was to respond to Mark just as she would during any real depression. Neither one liked this assignment. They saw this assignment as an inconvenience because they had a busy week ahead.

Mark carried out the faked depression just as we had assigned it. He reported that it was difficult to pretend to be depressed. He said he much preferred to be doing other things. Mark said he learned two things from this assignment. He realized how he could use depression to control Sally and express his anger indirectly. The fake depression allowed him to avoid doing some things he did not want to do, as well as to obtain attention and affection from Sally. He also used the depression as a cover to express his anger over sending their son money. Sally had tried to guess when Mark was going to be depressed but was unsuccessful. She said she was not sure whether his depression was real or faked so she went along with it as usual. For her, this meant pampering Mark and later getting impatient with him. We used Mark's insights to question the couple again about the value of giving up the depression. Once again they said the depression must go. The prescription to be depressed 20 minutes a day remained intact.

Mark had been talking about finding a part-time job since one of our early meetings. He said he wanted to get out and he liked to meet people. The Christmas holidays were approaching, making more jobs available. During the next week Mark began a job as a part-time salesman in a large store selling the same kind of merchandise he had sold all of his life. The first day of his job had been both physically and psychologically straining. Mark experienced a "low" the first evening of his work and the next day. Two factors seemed to trigger his low. The first was the fact that he faced a new experience. He did not adjust to changes easily. He also experienced a loss of self-esteem and pride. He had moved from a respected position in a fine store to being a part-time salesman being paid minimum wage. His loss and readjustment were handled in a straightforward way. Framing his new job as a loss rather than a gain helped him realize that feeling low was normal. In short, we normalized the experience for him.

The other part of his job which triggered his depression was anxiety over making mistakes. Mark's first day was for training. He had to learn new procedures and how to operate a new and more complex cash register. He described feeling that he would make a mistake, causing others to think less of him. His overconcern or anxiety over making mistakes was treated paradoxically. We instructed him to make one small mistake during the next week, which would make him look foolish; then, he was to psychologically step back and watch people's reactions.

Mark thought about the kinds of mistakes he might make at work but he did not do the task. He said there would be nothing to gain from it since the problem had cleared up anyway. We told him if he did start to feel concerned with making mistakes again he would have to do this exercise.

Mark had been in treatment for some time with only one relapse. After our initial sessions our basic strategy had been to predict relapses. We were running out of plausible reasons why he should have a relapse. With the Christmas holidays approaching we told him that people prone to depression usually become depressed during the holidays. We gave him a number of reasons why people become depressed during this time. We talked about lack of money, missing family and friends, old memories coming to the surface, and the idea that one should be only happy during Christmas holidays. We told him he would be in a "danger" period from December 15 to January 15. His depression period was also reduced to 15 minutes per day. Every Monday during this period he was to spend an hour considering the following questions as pessimistically as possible: 1) What could I lose this week (psychologically or physically)? 2) What could happen to make me feel bad about myself? 3) What could happen to make me feel helpless or hopeless? Mark defied our prediction by making it through the period we designated without a single low.

Death had been an ongoing issue for Mark because of his mother's condition. We began discussing their attitudes toward death. There was a myth in Mark's family that people do not mourn over death. Members were to mourn in isolation and silence. Aside from talking about the effects this myth would have, we also had Mark read Kübler-Ross's book, *On Death and Dying.*

We then learned that Mark had never visited his father's grave. He was afraid such a visit might trigger a deep depression. He was advised to make a visit to his father's grave with his wife and one of his sons during the Christmas holidays. He and the family did make the trip. Mark reacted with tears and sadness. His reactions were all appropriate and he knew they were appropriate. He felt relieved and thankful to be able to grieve normally.

At the end of the Christmas shopping season Mark lost his job. The store had told him they could probably keep him as a permanent part-time employee, but their business was unusually slow, causing Mark to be terminated suddenly. Mark felt disappointed and sad but was not devastated by an event which he said a few months earlier would have thrown him in a deep depression. He took a couple of weeks to vacation before beginning another job search. He later found another permanent part-time job. The way Mark handled losing his job gave us the opportunity to label his depression a normal reaction (i.e., "normal depression"). We congratulated him on being ready to experience normal depression in the future.

Our initial strategy of scheduling Mark's depression was next reduced to five minutes a day. Some days he reported it was hard to go the five minutes. We continued over the next several weeks to work on two other issues while we began to taper the number of weekly sessions. One of the issues we focused on was how Mark and Sally expressed anger and hurt. They were beginning to argue more openly. We predicted a number of fights while framing them as one of the "bad" side effects of Mark recovering from his depression. They countered that their arguments were good for them. We responded to this statement with puzzlement and said we hoped they could continue to prove us wrong.

The other issue we focused on was Mark's activities. The retirement village where they had relocated offered a wide range of activities, including a small theatrical group. When treatment began Mark was playing golf from time to time but otherwise stayed home. We encouraged him to get involved in different things, especially social activities. Mark had the idea that if he got involved Sally would be lonely. We maneuvered Sally into giving him permission to do things even if it caused her to get depressed. This, in fact, was his real fear.

Mark started swimming, playing pool, cards, and golf with other men, and became active in the theater group. He started writing jokes, limericks, and songs. On several occasions he brought his artistic productions to our sessions to try them out on us first. He even wrote several poems related to his previous depression and his therapy with us.

We saw Mark and Sally until mid-summer, with our last sessions spread one month apart. The last few sessions were brief. They were enjoying their retirement with both its pleasures and stresses. Mark felt he wanted to continue his five minutes a day of meditation. He had defined it as a way to prevent problems from occurring or to problem solve in advance.

CASE 3: PARADOXICAL INTERVENTIONS
WITH A SINGLE-PARENT FAMILY

Until recent years, the single-parent family has usually been conceptualized as an aberrant family form in comparison to the intact family. Today, the notion of the single-parent family as an alternative and viable family form is cutting across all socioeconomic classes and gaining acceptance among the lay public and professionals. Any clinical practitioner, especially a family clinician, can expect a large part of his or her practice to consist of troubled single-parent families. This is especially true in light of the statistical reports that five million single parents are raising ten million children, and that the single-parent family is growing almost ten times as fast as two-parent families (Ogg, 1977).

Despite the increase in single-parent families, there still exists a paucity of theory and models for how to intervene in changing a dysfunctional single-parent family into a functional single-parent family. Notable among those handful of therapists who have published their work with single-parent families are Hallett (1974) and Peck (1974), who utilize a transactional analysis model of intervention; Goldman and Coane (1977), who devised their own four-step model for intervening with divorced single-parent families; and Kaplan

(1977), who has written about the use of structural family therapy.

The following clinical case report* demonstrates the use of paradoxical therapy with a single-parent family (SPF). To our knowledge,
there are few publications on the use of paradoxical therapy with
SPF's. Exceptions are to be found in Haley's (1973) report on the case
of Milton Erickson in which Erickson treated a divorced mother and
her eight-year-old son around a power struggle issue; and in Haley's
(1976) report of the single-parent case involving an eight-year-old
girl's fire-setting problem and her older brother who was identified as
a "parental child." The concept of "parental child" advanced by
Haley (1976) is analogous to Boszormenyi-Nagy and Spark's (1973)
concept of the "parentified child." Accordingly, the "parental child"
functions as an adult caretaker of other children in the SPF household
without the power that is needed for this responsibility. The presence
of a "parental child" is commonly found in dysfunctional SPFs. However, a child in a SPF would also be considered to be "parentified" if
the child functioned as a pseudo-spouse and caretaker to the parent,
who is unwittingly using the child as a substitute for the missing
spouse. In other words, the child who is identified as parentified is expected to function more like an adult than as a child, which can lead
to power struggles and a blurring of generational boundaries within
the family.

In the following case report, one of the major problems in the SPF
was that the 11-year-old daughter was parentified and presented herself as an adult equal in power to her mother. For example, on many
occasions the daughter was consulted and co-decided with her mother
on issues around household responsibilities, her mother's career decisions, and matters related to her mother's boyfriend. The parentified
child allegedly had the same power as the parent, except on those occasions when the parent tried to reassert authority over the child.
Then, the parentified child became confused and resisted letting go
of the illusory power that accompanied the parentification process. In
protest, the parental child resisted the parent by escalating maladaptive behaviors. The parentification process had become even more
complex in this case of a divorced SPF, where the absent parent was

---

*This case was treated and reported by Jackie Johnson and the senior author.

involved. The daughter overidealized her father and threatened to run away from her mother whenever her mother tried to reassert her parental authority and set age-appropriate limits with her daughter.

The family of treatment consisted of the mother and daughter who had been living alone in the same household for the last three years. The daughter was an illegitimate child whom the mother admitted to having put up for legal adoption shortly after birth in order to manipulate the father into marrying her. The mother could not tolerate being without her child and quickly took the necessary steps to regain custody. One of the issues that surfaced during the course of therapy was the mother's feelings of guilt over allegedly rejecting her daughter and believing that someday her daughter would reject her. Partly because of the mother's guilt, she often vacillated between the extremes of setting unreasonable limits with her daughter, e.g., no sweets are to be eaten, to setting virtually no limits.

The daughter saw her father as all-understanding and accepting of her regardless of what she did. The daughter was blind to any faults in him and overidentified with him. His contact was infrequent with his daughter, about once a month, and often the contact was initiated by the daughter whenever some conflict occurred with her mother.

The mother appeared to be depressed and ambivalent about accepting her parental responsibilities. One of the major issues that became troublesome to work with in the course of therapy was the mother's refusal to decrease her outside commitments; the mother worked full-time in the evenings as a nurse and was a full-time college student during part of the day, taking an overload of courses every quarter. As a result, the mother delegated many responsibilities to the daughter and became overly critical of the daughter when she did not live up to expectations.

The daughter experienced low self-esteem, was overburdened with the mother's adult expectations of her, and sorely needed age-appropriate parental limits.

The presenting problem that led the mother to seek therapy was her daughter's threatening to run away from home to be with her father and her acting-out behaviors, e.g., calling a false fire alarm, wearing dirty clothes on occasions, being remiss in her personal hygiene, and so on.

Early in the course of therapy, the major therapeutic goals were to deparentify the daughter through realigning generational boundaries and reinstating the mother's parental authority; help the mother and daughter engage in age-appropriate behaviors, such as establishing their respective social support systems; encourage the mother to confront herself over her guilt and depression; and bring the absent father into therapy.

The course of therapy consisted of 33 sessions that occurred over a 14-month period. After the initial interview sessions, the daughter and mother were seen for eight individual sessions by each of the authors in order to separate them from their overinvolvement with each other. They were told at the beginning of therapy that they would be seen together after a few individual sessions. During this period, the diagnostic picture of the dynamics of this SPF was completed and rapport and trust were established.

During the first few joint sessions, it became clear that our therapeutic efforts to move this family were failing. The mother and daughter continued to behave like two spouses in marital conflict, and the mother resisted any confrontations around her overcommitments. Further, both the mother and daughter were firmly entrenched in their power struggle, as the daughter behaved as an equal to her mother and her mother continually failed to set appropriate parental limits, while simultaneously criticizing her daughter. It was at this point that we reevaluated our strategy and decided to use a forced holding technique.

Our first therapeutic task was to help the mother establish some kind of control over her daughter. To achieve this goal we used a therapeutic technique which involved having the mother hold or sit on the child and ask the child, "Who is the boss in the family?" The details of this technique have been reported in another paper (Johnson, Weeks, and L'Abate, 1979) and in a similar recent paper (Friedman et al., 1978). This technique did help put the mother in control, but it also led to a great deal of resentment and anger from the daughter directed toward the mother and therapists. During the week following this session, the daughter responded to the mother's requests but was sullen much of the time. In several subsequent sessions with mother and daughter, we worked mostly with the mother. These sessions were devoted to how the mother was parented and how she reacted to her daughter when she was younger.

The daughter would sit in silence during these sessions; when her mother said things with which she disagreed, she would engage in distracting behaviors, such as humming or singing or plugging her ears with her fingers. We were unsuccessful during this period in reestablishing rapport with the daughter. We then decided that linear therapy and forced holding had been ineffective and shifted to a paradoxical approach.

Since the daughter resisted our efforts to engage her in therapy, we decided to have mother and daughter sit back to back in the sessions and requested that the daughter not speak. In the following session, the daughter opened up both verbally and emotionally. As she cried, she talked profusely about all her problems with her mother. Both the mother and daughter reported feeling very hopeless about their relationship.

Rather than offer encouragement, which had been our strategy in the past, we took the paradoxical stance of expressing our helplessness about being able to help them and expressed hopelessness about the future of their relationship. Specifically, we talked about the possibility of the daughter going to live with her father and how in just a few short years she could leave home altogether. Since the daughter had already talked about going to another country, we talked about where she might go and suggested that South America would be far enough that she would not have to have any contact whatsoever with her mother. Both mother and daughter looked depressed at the end of this session and the mother cried at one point. She had never cried in a session up to the present one.

In the next two to three weeks the situation between them improved. They were now cooperative with each other around the house and did a few things together on the weekends. During these sessions we used a restraining strategy of offering no support or encouragement and predicting more problems. Several sessions were devoted to how the daughter had idealized the father. We had the daughter write poems about her relationship with her mother and father (she had told us previously that she liked to write poetry). The poems helped the daughter gain more insight into the idealization of her father, whom she began viewing more realistically. However, there were still a number of issues that the mother felt needed to be resolved. The issues all centered around controlling her daughter's behavior.

Our next strategy was to try a paradoxical "behavioral" approach in changing their relationship. Interestingly, the mother had implemented a behavior program of her own about a year prior to entering therapy. The program had initially worked but collapsed after two to three weeks because the mother had turned the program over to her daughter, including having the daughter reinforce herself.

The therapists pointed out to the mother that behavioral programs were difficult to formulate and implement and that we would have to proceed very, very slowly. Our strategy was to proceed so slowly that the mother would become motivated to make the desired changes on her own. One session was spent just "thinking" about using a behavioral program. This session was followed by two sessions whereby mother and daughter set up goals and consequences for every aspect of the daughter's behavior. During these two sessions mother and daughter argued over what goals and consequences should be used, which resulted in the mother becoming angry and impatient.

After several sessions of mother and daughter disagreeing on a behavioral program and the therapists playing incompetent, the "restraining" strategy had produced frustrations in the mother but not enough so that she would take charge of the relationship. The therapists decided to unilaterally take charge of the "behavioral program." First, we asked the mother what would be the smallest acceptable change in her daughter. She responded that something had to be done about her daughter's excessive use of the telephone (an issue that had been raised in several prior sessions). At this point the therapists offered "the behavioral program" to solve this problem. The program offered was very complex and completely unmanageable. It involved giving the daughter a certain amount of money at the beginning of each week for not using the phone. Whenever the daughter used the phone, she would have to pay certain amounts of money, depending on when and how long and how frequently she talked. There were also fines and bonuses built into the system. The mother readily agreed to this program, but the daughter felt angry and de-humanized by the program. In fact, she said, "the program made her feel like a robot."

In the next session the mother reported that this system worked for two days and then collapsed. However, when the system failed, the mother had decided that "it was time to put her foot down." The mother monitored her daughter's phone calls during the week and, when she talked too long, the mother had told her in strong and certain terms to get off the phone. The daughter, sensing that her mother was in charge, complied. Interestingly, the daughter looked somewhat relieved in the session following the mother's taking charge. Not only had the mother taken charge of her daughter in terms of the phone, but she took charge in several other ways. The therapists congratulated the mother on her new behavior but acted perplexed. They said they would drop the behavioral program until problems with the phone started again (a paradoxical prediction). Both mother and daughter seemed relieved that we were willing to drop the "pay telephone idea."

During the next few sessions we worked on consolidating the mother's gains of being in charge of her daughter by predicting relapses (i.e., mother would not be able to take charge of various areas and would complain about it to her daughter). For example, one of the problems had been the daughter's leaving her clothes out. We decided to prescribe the symptom in this case. We asked the daughter to intentionally leave some of her clothes out and for the mother to try to catch her as soon as she did it. The daughter did not follow through on this task. In fact, she spontaneously started washing her own clothes, to her mother's delight.

During the next month mother and daughter started to interact more positively with each other and their peers. They would hug in the sessions and looked forward to doing things together. At this point we asked the mother to pretend that she would like to go back to the way the situation was when it was at its worst and describe what she could do to accomplish that goal. The mother was able to articulate a list of ways she could set things up so that she and her daughter would be at odds. This question was designed to bind off the old relationship the mother had with the daughter.

After many of the problems with the daughter had been dealt with, we shifted the therapeutic focus to the mother's problems. If we were to use traditional diagnostic labels, the mother in this case could have been classified as an obsessive-compulsive and depressive personality. Whenever she was feeling depressed or out of control, she would over-organize, including over-organizing her daughter's life. This pattern had been seen often in the previous sessions, with little progress having been made when the mother was feeling depressed or out of control. We confronted the mother on her behavior and discussed how it was probably an attempt to avoid feeling depressed. She agreed that there were many depressing aspects about the way she had been living and she was willing to make changes. The mother's tendency to over-organize was worked on paradoxically in the context of the relationship with her daughter.

First, we gave the daughter's previous undesirable behaviors a positive connotation. We told the mother that her daughter's behavior had protected her from her depression and her sense of inner turmoil by keeping her busy. The daughter's face signaled recognition when we made this statement and the mother agreed. We instructed the mother to become super-organized the next time she felt confused or depressed. We further told the daughter to be acutely aware of her mother's moods so that whenever she saw her looking confused or sad she was to engage in some of her previous behavior to keep her mother busy. In the next few sessions the mother became cheerful and reported that for the first time in years her house and yard were not perfect, that she was enjoying making friends where she went to school, and that she was quitting one of her jobs. The daughter became equally cheerful. The daughter was having parties with her friends at the house, doing well in school, and she and her mother were laughing and enjoying each other in and out of sessions.

In our final session we discussed how they could each go back to being their old miserable selves and then prescribed that they might want to do this from time to time as a reminder of how things had been. They were also told that having a planned relapse could be a valuable learning experience. This strategy was used to further bind off a relapse and prepare them for future relapses.

In summary, the mother had successfully reasserted her parental authority over her daughter while also allowing the daughter to explore her own identity in age-appropriate ways. Further, the mother had given up her workaholic role and need to distract herself from her feelings by being an over-organizer and complainer. Also, she had begun to explore outlets with people her own age, thereby creating her own support system separate from that of the daughter. Although we were never able to bring in the absent father, as he refused to come, his daughter had demythologized her feelings for him. The absent father was no longer overidealized and triangulated into the mother-daughter relationship as a way to deal with the conflicts of the single-parent family.

A one-year follow-up contact with the mother and daughter revealed that this family was still functional. They were coping quite well with the normal ups-and-downs related to life-cycle changes associated with a growing adolescent daughter and a mother who has to let go.

11

Research

There has been a dearth of research on paradoxical psycho-therapy. Despite the fact that hundreds of case studies have been reported demonstrating the unusual effectiveness of this approach, there has been very little empirical work of any kind. There are several possible explanations for this lack of empirical research. The most obvious reason is the paucity of paradoxically trained therapists. Even those with a background in paradoxical therapy have used a limited number of methods. This approach to therapy has been evolving. It is difficult to research an approach to therapy until the theoretical principles and techniques have been delineated. The first such effort was made just a few years ago by Watzlawick et al. (1974). Another possible reason for lack of empirical investigations is that the leading paradoxical therapists have been clinicians in non-academic settings. Consequently, they have been more interested in reporting on what works than in producing rigorous empirical investigations which the academic would find essential for promotion and tenure.

All the reasons we have listed for the failure to research paradoxical therapy are changing. Many more clinicians are receiving training in this approach, including those on university faculties. More importantly, researchers have become interested in explicating the theoretical principles and methods of paradoxical therapy. These changes should stimulate much more empirical research in the near future.

Most of the research to date has been done by a very small number of researchers on paradoxical intention (Frankl, 1959). Paradoxical intention is a specific method. The theory underlying the application of this technique has been well defined and its application has been illustrated many times over (see Weeks and L'Abate, 1978).

The technique of paradoxical intention is the same as paradoxical prescription. In both cases, the symptom is prescribed, as we have described already. In our review of empirical work, we are careful to discuss just how paradoxical intention was used. This attention is given in order to show that the researchers are, in fact, investigating a method of paradoxical psychotherapy.

RESEARCH ON PARADOXICAL INTENTION

One of the earliest studies on the effectiveness of paradoxical intention was reported by Gerz in 1966. He treated 51 cases over a period of six years. He does not report his screening procedure, if any, nor was any other basic information given for the clients. Gerz decided on the basis of his clinical judgment whether the clients had made considerable improvement. He reported success rates of 75.8% for phobics, 66.7% for obsessive-compulsives, and 68.8% for pseudo-neurotic schizophrenics. Most of these clients had been in treatment previously.

Gerz's (1966) research focused specifically on the treatment of phobics and obsessive-compulsives. Of his 29 phobics, 22 recovered completely, five improved significantly, and two showed no improvement. Of the six obsessive-compulsives, four recovered completely while two were improved enough to work. The only other information given about the clients and the course of treatment was what one could infer from reading two case studies. The length of treatment was not given for any of the groups of cases. He did point out that paradoxical intention produced rapid results for acute cases but chronic cases needed up to two years.

It was apparent from Gerz's article that his application of paradoxical intention was the same as that of symptom prescription. The phobics were told to do or think of that of which they were most afraid and, in fact, to exaggerate it to the point of absurdity. The obsessive-compulsives were given the same kind of formulation. A perfectionist was given some instructions to say to himself, "I don't give a damn anymore. Hell, who wants to be a perfectionist. I hope I get sued very soon, the sooner the better." Gerz went on to tell him to get sued several times so he could get his money out of his insurance. In addition to prescribing the obsessive thought, Gerz told him to become a great mistake maker in the office. In both of the cases presented and in the general description of his technique, symptom prescription was clearly being used. However, it should be noted that humor was an integral part of the prescription, in accord with Frankl's (1967) guidelines for this technique. Many of the prescriptions made by paradoxical therapists, as well as later logotherapists and researchers of paradoxical intention, do not intentionally add the element of humor that Gerz used.

Gerz's (1966) study stimulated a more rigorous study of paradoxical treatment in the treatment of obsessive thoughts. Solyom, Garza-Perez, Ledwidge, and Solyom (1972) used four men and six women clients in their study. The average age was 31 years. All the clients were chronically ill, an average of 9.2 years. They all had previous psychotherapy and drug therapy. The period of treatment lasted six weeks, each client being seen for one hour a week. The clients were given a simple explanation of the technique. Then they were instructed to obsess more.

Each subject served as his/her own control. The clients were told to pick two obsessive thoughts of equal strength. One thought became the control thought while the other was treated. The initial assessment for each subject consisted of several objective scales plus a 0-4 rating for several dimensions of the obsessive thoughts. Even though data were collected objectively, the results of the study were not statistically presented. Instead, Solyom et al. reported that for the ten target symptoms, five were eliminated completely, three were unchanged, and two clients failed to apply the technique as instructed. The improvement rate for the target symptom was 50%. A 40% specific effect was obtained due to the fact that both control and target thoughts improved for one client.

Ascher (1979) conducted a study on the use of paradoxical intention in the treatment of psychogenic urinary retention. Three males and two females ranging in age from 19 to 47 years participated. Three of the clients had experienced the problem for over 20 years, five years being the shortest duration. The symptom was assessed by the use of a 100-point rating scale. Each time the client attempted to urinate, s/he was to rate the degree of discomfort. Baseline data were collected during the first two weeks of assessment. In the following eight weeks all the subjects received in vivo systematic desensitization. After the eight-week period those clients who were dissatisfied with their progress were told they could continue in a paradoxical intention treatment. All the clients continued for at least a few sessions. After clients were given the rationale underlying paradoxical intention, they were instructed to enter the bathroom and go through all the activities associated with urinating but not to urinate.

The results of this study were presented in means for each week of treatment. All subjects showed improvement in the behavioral program. When the paradoxical condition was instituted, about half the clients experienced immediate relief and terminated therapy. By the end of the sixth week following the behavioral program, every subject experienced little or no anxiety urinating. A six-month telephone follow-up revealed that the improvement had been maintained. One client reported difficulties from time to time but would treat himself using the paradoxical instructions.

A number of studies have been conducted on the treatment of insomnia by paradoxical intention. A time-series analysis was performed by Relinger, Bornstein, and Mungas (1978). They solicited a client with insomnia via a public service radio announcement. A 31-year-old housewife responded who had suffered from insomnia chronically for 20 years. She had treated herself by using over-the-counter drugs.

The researchers' dependent measures were eight different dimensions of sleep which the client would chart. The treatment program consisted of a three-week baseline, one-week of treatment at half-hour per day, and one-, three-, and twelve-month follow-ups on the dependent measures.

During the period of treatment the client was instructed to stay awake as long as possible in order to experience the exact thoughts and feelings that were keeping her awake. In order to control for the demand characteristics of treatment, the client was told that no improvement could be expected until the end of the treatment period. Least square analysis t-tests showed significant improvement on five of the eight dimensions of sleep. No change was present for the number of times awakened during the night during treatment but one month later that measure had improved. The follow-up showed that the effects of treatment not only persisted but had improved at the twelve-month mark.

Another study on the paradoxical intention of insomnia was conducted by Ascher and Efran (1978) in the context of a behavioral program. Five clients were treated who had suffered from insomnia from three to 12 years. The dependent measure was latency to sleep onset. Their treatment consisted of a two-week baseline period, followed by a ten-week behavioral program (deep muscle relaxation, systematic desensitization, and covert conditioning). After the ten weeks of behavioral treatment, two weeks of paradoxical treatment followed, with three clients receiving one rationale for staying awake longer, while the other two were given a different rationale. After two weeks of paradoxical treatment, four of the clients received no treatment and one returned to the behavioral program.

The means of sleep latency onset showed some improvement during the behavioral treatment but a rapid reduction in onset latency when paradoxical instructions were used. A one-year telephone follow-up showed that all the clients were satisfied with their sleep behavior. The use of different rationales made no apparent difference in the effectiveness of the paradoxical instructions.

A controlled group study on paradoxical intention and insomnia was carried out by Turner and Ascher (1979). This was the first controlled group study of paradoxical intention. Fifty subjects were randomly assigned to five treatments: progressive relaxation, stimulus control, paradoxical intention, placebo control, and a wait-list control.

The outcome measures were obtained from the daily scores on a sleep questionnaire. Following a ten-day baseline period, each client received 30–45 minutes of therapy once a week for four weeks. The data showed that all three treatment groups improved significantly. However, there were no differences among the treatment groups. The researchers hypothesized that the lack of differences among treatment groups could be accounted for in two ways. The random assignment of clients to groups could have meant a mismatch of specific sleep difficulties with treatment. Their second hypothesis was that the group might be responsive to some feature of treatment common to all the groups.

A partial controlled group replication of the previous study was made by Ascher and Turner (1979). Twenty-five clients who had suffered from insomnia for an average of eight years participated in this study. The clients were randomly assigned to three treatment groups: paradoxical intention, placebo, and no-treatment control. Clients in the experimental group received four weekly sessions of treatment. They used the same sleep questionnaire in this study as in the former study (Turner and Ascher, 1979) to collect baseline and post-therapy data. Unfortunately, no follow-up was performed. The effectiveness of paradoxical therapy for insomnia had been replicated in controlled experiments.

The further development of paradoxical techniques led to an interesting study comparing two methods for the delivery of paradoxical intention (Ascher and Turner, 1980). Forty insomniacs who had a nine-year mean duration of the problem were selected for this study. The dependent scores were taken from a sleep questionnaire. There was a ten-day baseline period followed by 30–45-minute sessions once a week for four weeks.

The clients were randomly assigned to four groups. Two groups received paradoxical instructions. Both these groups were told to remain awake as long as possible under the conditions natural for sleep. The rationale given to these two groups immediately prior to the paradoxical directive differed. The first group was told about the relationship between performance anxiety and sleeplessness. In short, worrying about falling asleep produces sleeplessness, which in turn exacerbates the inability to fall asleep. The second group was told that it was necessary to become aware of any anxiety-provoking thoughts before going to sleep so that these thoughts could be treated in a systematic desensitization program. Members of the control group were required to construct an 18-item hierarchy of bedtime activities which were paired with six neutral images twice a day but not within two hours of bedtime. The last group was placed on a waiting list with the assurance they would receive treatment.

The only group to show significant improvement was the first paradoxical intention condition group—those subjects who were told about the relationship between performance anxiety and sleep. The second group did no better than either control groups.

The researchers speculated that the second type of paradoxical procedure did not work because the subjects were actually trying to comply with the instructions in order to receive treatment. Moreover, the subjects in the first paradoxical group were given a reasonable explanation in addition to being told the instructions were the treatment.

RESEARCH ON PARADOXICAL PSYCHOTHERAPY

There have only been two empirical investigations on the effectiveness of paradoxical therapy. The first study could be considered empirical in the sense that specific questions were asked and data were presented.

Weakland et al. (1974) reported some data on the effectiveness of their paradoxical work at the Brief Therapy Center. Their data were collected over a six-year period in which 97 cases comprising 236 individuals were treated. Their cases were obtained through a variety of sources with no screening for acceptance in treatment. The clients were from every socioeconomic class, ranging in age from five to over 60, and included both acute and chronic problems.

The clients were treated for a maximum of ten sessions, usually weekly. Because their approach was goal-oriented, they decided to evaluate the outcome of treatment on the basis of whether the specific goals of treatment were achieved. The researchers had the clients interviewed after treatment by a therapist who did not participate in the treatment. The interviewer asked five questions: a) Had the goal of treatment, which was specified, been fulfilled? b) What was the status of the main complaint? c) Had the client sought treatment elsewhere since termination? d) Had improvement occurred in other areas not specifically dealt with in therapy? e) Had any new problems appeared?

On the basis of these questions, the researchers divided the cases into three groups: a) complete problem resolution (success); b) clear and considerable problem resolution (significant improvement); and c) little or no change (failure). They reported a success rate of 40%, a 32% rate for significant improvement, and a failure rate of 28%. In short, 72% of the cases improved over an average of seven sessions. We do not know from their report how long a period elapsed until the follow-up. They did state it was a short-term follow-up since resources were not available for a long-term follow-up.

Wagner, Weeks, and L'Abate (1980) conducted a study to determine the effectiveness of written linear and paradoxical messages with couples. The couples who participated in this study were all part of a marital enrichment program. Fifty-six were equally divided into four groups: a control group; enrichment; enrichment plus a direct, straightforward linear letter; and enrichment plus a paradoxical letter. The enrichment program required six weekly sessions. At the end of the fourth session the couples in the letter groups received either a linear or paradoxical letter.

The results of this study showed that all three experimental groups made significant improvement in marital functioning. However, the paradoxical group did not differ significantly from the other two experimental groups.

There are several reasons why the enrichment plus paradox group did not change as much as expected. The paradoxical letters were generally directed toward specific aspects of the relationship while the pre-post assessment devices were global. Secondly, only one letter was given to the couples in the letter groups. The use of any technique once may not be enough of a test of its validity. Finally, all the couples in this research were nonclinical. They did not present with specific problems nor were they resistive. The use of paradoxical techniques with such couples may be unnecessary and inappropriate to produce change.

The primary value of the study is not found in its results. A research methodology is being proposed for the study of paradox and other techniques which renders more information about the *process* of therapy. The enrichment programs are all manual-directed. The use of written messages gives us a written record of the technique used. In combination, the use of these two research procedures allows us to understand what actually happened to produce change by parcelling out the influence of the therapist and the distortions rendered in case reports.

This review of research shows that paradoxical intervention/symptom prescription has been demonstrated to be effective in the treatment of certain specific disorders. Other research either failed to demonstrate effectiveness or was so methodologically weak that the results must be interpreted very cautiously.

The most important value of the research done up to now may be that of developing a methodology of how to research paradoxical therapy. Many of the studies conducted were single-subject design. This type of design is relatively new in psychotherapy research and has been used primarily in the investigation of behavior therapy. The foregoing studies revealed its usefulness in studying paradoxical intention. The two major advantages of a single-subject design are that just one subject is needed and it is ideally suited to begin to discover whether a technique changes behavior. The single-subject design is most appropriate for procedures which are designed to change specific behaviors independently from other behaviors (Leitenberg, 1973). It is therefore well suited for paradoxical therapy because some of the techniques are designed to change a very specific behavior.

One of the possible problems of single-subject design is that some of the designs appear appropriate for the investigation of only linear therapies. In the ABA_1B_1 design, the behavior being treated is subjected to baseline, treatment, no treatment, and treatment again. The behavior is expected to improve in a linear fashion so that when no treatment occurs the problem behavior shows no improvement or increases in frequency. Paradoxical interventions tend to produce immediate results which are purported to be lasting. If this assertion is true, then the last two phases of the ABA_1B_1 design will fail to detect any changes. There are other variations of the single-subject design which may prove useful for studying paradox. For example, a multiple baseline design could be used to study the serial treatment of several different symptoms. A researcher could identify several symptoms amenable to paradoxical prescription and treat each one in turn. Those symptoms treated would remain unchanged while those being treated would change, thus, demonstrating a treatment effect. Once a technique has been shown to be effective using this design, the research can then proceed to controlled group studies.

Controlled group studies on paradoxical therapy must be designed to assess symptom resolution very specifically. Global assessment procedures are inappropriate because paradoxical therapy is goal-oriented. One of the problems of all psychotherapy research is that the treatment described may not actually be what transpired in the sessions. Our model represents an effort to overcome this difficulty. The enrichment process can be described precisely because it is manual-directed. The paradoxical intervention is given in written form, which parcels out problems associated with therapists' making the intervention. Unlike our first study, the therapist may give several letters to reinforce the first. The clients could also be instructed to read the letter on a prescribed basis to reinforce its effect.

The future success of paradoxical therapy lies in its clinical utility and demonstrated effectiveness. Paradoxical therapy has reached a stage of development where empirical research is a necessity. History now teaches us that those therapies which are empirically supported have been most accepted, respected, and clinically refined (Corsini, 1979).

PHENOMENOLOGICAL RESEARCH ON PARADOXICAL INTERVENTIONS

Practically nothing has been written about the clients' reactions to paradoxical interventions or their experience in therapy. Yet, we are often asked to describe the kinds of reactions we receive from our clients. The purpose of this section is to describe the kinds of reactions that have been noted and give some reactions from clients. We have just started to ask clients to describe their experience of therapy so we can make few generalizations at this time.

Reactions to paradoxical interventions, both written and verbal,

vary widely. We have observed emotional reactions ranging from in-
difference to humor, puzzlement, surprise, shock, confusion, anger,
denial, and hurt. Yet, we cannot remember a single case where a paradoxical intervention produced an emotional reaction which led to the
client's dropping out. Instead, a well-timed, precisely targeted intervention seems to have the effect of "hooking" the client. It seems to capture
the interest of the client in a special way. We believe the intervention
communicates our understanding of their paradoxical situation without commenting on it directly. The client may prefer this situation to
an explicit confrontation, especially if one is working with a couple or
family where not commenting on behavior has an adaptive purpose.
Making this kind of contact with a client is a unique experience. The
therapist is communicating with the client on two levels and sometimes the client appears to recognize this fact. The session is transformed into a situation that feels like both a game and a deadly serious
struggle. The fact that the therapist communicates on two levels may
also be reassuring. The client knows at some level that she is in her
predicament because of confused communication and now she has
found someone who recognizes that fact and controls confusing
messages in a helpful way, rather than being controlled by them, as is
the client.

The most common emotional reactions we have observed to paradoxical interventions are humor and confusion. Both these reactions
seem to indicate that the intervention is on target. Most clients are upset by their symptoms. If they can laugh at the symptom, see it as absurd, or gain some distance from it, then the symptom has acquired a
different emotional meaning. Humor itself is paradoxical. The punch
line of a joke contradicts or meta-communicates on the previous lines.
It could be argued that a humorous response indicates a reframing of
the problem from something to feel sad about to something to feel
glad about. The other response, confusion, suggests to us a perceptual reorganization. Even in straightforward therapy clients go through
a period of confusion which could be called experimentation, trying
on a new self, searching for identity, or becoming a new person. Furst
(1978) has also found that the therapeutic process can be conceptualized as reinforcement, confusion, change, and reinforcement.
Minuchin (1974) refers to the same phenomenon when he talks

about creating an imbalance in a family system. In paradoxical therapy the change is rapid and sometimes instantaneous. The client will
slip into a trancelike state during which an old experience is reorgan-
ized in terms of a new framework. The period of confusion preceding
reorganization may be brief or it may last some time.

Emotional reactions to the letters may also change over time. Initial
reactions of anger, hurt, and disbelief have often been followed by acceptance, objectivity, and confusion. In one case a woman read a letter with disbelief and hurt. She later said she felt the therapist had
"written her off" as hopeless. After her initial reaction, she examined
each statement in the letter carefully, realizing that she had not really
been interested in changing. The letter had given her the motivation
to change by helping her resolve her basic ambivalence between doing more of the same or trying to be different.

It is important to note that, whatever the client's emotional reaction, the therapist should not change positions unless there are very
good reasons to do so. The best way for a client to attempt to undo a
paradox is to have a strong emotional reaction which proves the therapist wrong. The paradoxical therapist must be able to accept, even
want, clients leaving the office confused, bewildered, hurt, angry,
and so on. It is tempting to help a confused client become uncon-
fused. In those cases, the therapist is in effect asking the client to see
reality his/her way. Clients have the ability to process their own feelings if they are given the time. Their feelings reflect the binding situation in which they find themselves. Their feelings motivate them to
find the solution that not only is the most workable for them, but also
feels right.

Aside from the emotional reactions clients may display, there are
two other dimensions to be considered, verbal as opposed to behavioral compliance and change. The client may verbally disagree with
the intervention but show a behavioral change. This reaction appears
to be common for many of the techniques, particularly restraining
techniques. Or, the client may verbally agree as well as make a behavioral change. This reaction is common for certain types of symptom
prescriptions. Finally, the client may verbally comply and make no
behavioral change. These reactions indicate that the intervention was
not properly designed. The only statement that we can now make

with some confidence about these patterns is that an intervention greeted with strong verbal disagreement or affect is likely to produce a behavioral change.

Phenomenological research on this type of therapy should prove most interesting. We have just recently started asking our clients about the "way we work." One case we treated involved a professional couple who were living together. Many of the interventions used with them were prescriptions and paradoxical predictions. They were asked to write a description of what it was like when we gave them those "crazy, unusual, bizarre or weird" homework assignments. This couple had become interested in our approach to therapy since they were familiar with more traditional techniques from previous therapy. In fact, the husband had read several of our articles, in addition to *Change* (Watzlawick et al., 1974). The couple said they discussed our method of therapy together and the male partner wrote their reactions. While they said they agreed on its content, there is an interesting disclaimer at the close of their statement. The couple was also asked to comment on any ethical problems they saw with this approach. Their comments are presented in unedited form.

Paradox Therapy

Experience:

Approaching problems in a paradoxical mode invariably results in a tension-resolution process. The first feeling that I usually have is fear. I tend to try to avoid doing the paradox exercise, and have to keep myself firmly in line to do it at all. Once I've submitted myself to the exercise, however, I find it intriguing, and often comical.

In the tension building stage, my "I" becomes acutely apparent. Moods that could be thematized as "What will happen to me" tend to manifest. I get a little self-conscious and sometimes feel silly.

During the resolution phase, the "I" becomes far less important. I feel playful and good humored. I would say that the process works very effectively on areas in my consciousness that have gotten stuck, and torture me repeatedly with no resolution. In these cases, efforts of will tend to give energy to the block—

rather than whittle it down. This is perhaps because blocks tend to present themselves ambiguously—there is always something to be gained by keeping them. Thus, the will will often cross itself up, pushing both directions (for and against the block) at the same time.

Using paradoxical methods, I find myself emphasizing the counterpart of the will—surrender.

As with any creative process that I'm familiar with, I consciously will myself to a point where I can surrender to the events at hand. I consciously create the dream that has been bothering me, and then consciously play it out. "*I*" become actor, rather than acted upon. In doing so, the block loses its special enchantment and recedes to the "alternative concept/behavior" level.

Since alternatives don't need to be argued with, after successful paradox resolutions, I don't spend much time thinking about problems that previously took up an inordinate amount of my energy.

P.S. Alice thinks it's all a crock of shit. She also says that paradox therapy gives the client an underlying positive message that is intrinsically therapeutic, i.e. What you are experiencing/ thinking is OK, though it may need modification for the sake of harmony.

Alice later wrote the following poem about the therapy.

PARADOX THERAPY

You cannot kill crabgrass
a neighbor once told me
It'll even crack cement to grow.
Like so, the paradox probes.
It'll push through a block of concrete
as wide as life and
as long as dread.

Taking this principle to heart,
mind, and psyche as well,
the paradox therapist has thrived.
One family whose sickness

stank like a gangrenous curse
got a license in therapy
to grow even worse.

At home on a venomous night
they threw a spaghetti fight.
The wife cleaned it up,
all the noodles and sauce,
except for a spot on the moon,
that frankly, no sane man would touch.

Next day when they stomped to the doctor's,
refusing to see him again,
they spat out these words on the spot:
"You'll have to get well on your own."

Another, quite nuclear family,
put through their paradox paces,
fell madly in love with their illness
and refused to relinquish their spaces.
To continue they threatened to sue,
so what could their therapist do?

He brought on a paradox naturally,
that ate them all up in the raw
and thus he got rid of their flaw.
In this age of determine disaster,
it helps to keep often in mind
that for living there's nothing like dying.

The husband did write a short statement on the ethics of paradoxical treatment.

I don't really see much of an ethical problem associated with therapy in general. People come in voluntarily, and are supposed to be responsible for their own psyches. Providing no powerful mood modifying drugs are used, the participant always has free choice to participate in the exercises or not.

However, I would expect the therapist to show some discrimination concerning the abilities of the client to productively assimilate the therapist's guidance. The more powerful the method, the more responsibility the therapist has. It's clear that paradox therapy is a powerful treatment, operating on levels that a less sophisticated client may not be aware of—the creative use of fear and tension.

Considering the worst—a client disintegrating under the care of a paradox therapist—my own feeling is that the client is ultimately at fault for giving his power away with so little discrimination. Though not exactly responsible, the therapist would in most cases be in error and should be censored.

The reader should note how these clients said the prescriptions produced a fear response. There are times when clients are afraid to carry out prescriptions. The two situations which seem to consistently produce this reaction are prescribing depression and fighting. The depressed person is afraid of staying depressed and the couple told to fight are afraid the prescribed fight will have the same consequences as a real fight. One way to deal with fear of doing a task is for the therapist to proclaim his fear that the client will not be able to do the task (e.g., I'm afraid you won't be able to get depressed enough) and then agree with the client that it is a difficult but necessary request. When a relationship is involved the therapist may want to exaggerate the negative consequences. For example, if the husband says his wife really will stop talking to him when he provokes a fight, the therapist can have his wife talk about all the worst actions she could take. These must be exaggerated such that a humorous mood is created. When the couple can laugh about the worst consequences in the office together, they have already united to do the task at home.

The reactions of the next client confirmed more of our observations. The most surprising reaction of this client was his spontaneous amnesia for some of the tasks. He could remember doing something, but not what. He further knew they were "weird" tasks. This same client also reported being able to remember the linear tasks which were given at about the same time the other tasks were given.

When I agreed to write my reactions to some of the exercises my psychologist had recommended, I thought my problem would be deciding which one of the many crazy exercises did I want to describe. Much to my amazement, however, I found that I could not remember the exercises. This fact may not strike the reader with any force but I can assure you that the appropriate word to describe my reaction is amazement. For months my feelings about the exercises were "I need help and I am paying this jerk good money and he gives me dumb exercises."

I am going to provide my reactions to three different exercises. The first reaction will be to a general set of exercises that were aimed at working out problems in a relationship. The second reaction will be to an exercise that aimed at dealing with my depression. The final reaction will be to an exercise that was to deal with feelings of incompetence at work.

Reaction #1

I was living with a woman that I cared for very much. We had been living together for a little more than a year and planning to be married. The relationship appeared to be perfect. We were in the same general kind of work and therefore talked about our work a great deal. We enjoyed many of the same kinds of things, e.g., sports and travel, and we did these things together. Sex was super. We probably had sex on an average of twice a day. Our friends thought our relationship was perfect and commented to this point often.

Within this "perfect" relationship, however, I was miserable and felt like the relationship was exhausting me. My partner was certainly no better off so we decided to seek professional help. Her basic complaint was that I did not talk to her about my feelings and therefore, she felt excluded. I felt so close I could not breathe. It seemed the more I tried to give her what she wanted, then the more she wanted and the greater my failing. Her reaction was just the opposite, she felt the closer she tried to get the more I pulled away.

After a couple of meetings with the psychologist, he had us doing a number of exercises or homework assignments. Most of these assignments I cannot remember. I do remember, in a general fashion, one of the assignments. The assignment was that we could plan and do things together only on odd number days. I thought the assignment was crazy. I did not see any way that such a silly assignment could help us. I felt my partner and I had a problem in communicating with each other and further the basic problem was my inability to share feelings and be as close as my partner wanted.

I did, however, go along with the assignment without protest. My feelings at the time and my reasons for doing the assignment seemed to me less than honorable. I thought "This assignment is not going to do a damn thing for us. This psychologist is a fool. I know my partner will do anything he says—to the letter. Thus, the assignment may not solve any problems but if I go along with it, then on even numbered days I can relax, do some things I want to do, and most important I will not be in that miserable failure position during these days and evenings."

By joint agreement, my partner and I continued the assignment for two weeks. At the end of the two weeks she was ready to stop but I wanted to continue. Simply put, I was enjoying myself very much on even numbered days and was enjoying the relationship very much on odd number days. My partner agreed. She was enjoying herself and the relationship much more.

I can only say upon reflection that what I saw as a dumb exercise stimulated some of the most important learning of my adult life. I began to think seriously about myself as a person with rights. It sounds and looks foolish to think and write the following statements. I discovered that you don't have to give up yourself for a relationship and that, for me, any relationship that demanded that I give up self for the relationship is not worth it.

Reaction #2

A relationship that was very important to me had ended. My oldest son wanted to come and live with me. My ex-wife would not even talk about the problems she was having with my son. Things were going very badly at work. Among other things I had failed to get a promotion that I believed I deserved. These major items and some minor ones had me so depressed that I could barely function.

I went to see a psychologist and was given, what I believed, a crazy assignment. I was told that it was a very normal reaction for anyone in my situation to be depressed. Then I was told you can't stop being depressed at this moment but you can manage the depression. I was told to pick an hour during the day that I could be free from interruptions. During this hour I was to think about all the things that were depressing me. Further, I was to tell myself that the situation was even worse than I thought. For example, I had not got the job at work because I was competent, thus I would probably be fired and never get another job. After I spent this hour then I couldn't think about those things again until the next day. When things came up during the day I was simply to remind myself to think about that during the hour on the following day. If something seems really important, then I was to write it down so that I could be sure to think about it the next day.

My general reaction to this assignment was that it was crazy. I thought the psychologist didn't believe I was depressed. If you could manage depression, then you could just stop being depressed. If you made the situation sound worse than it was, you might come to believe it and then be even more depressed. Thus, I thought I had an assignment that could not possibly help me and could possibly make me even more depressed.

I am not sure why I even started to do the assignment. I think the reasons for attempting the assignment were: 1) I did have confidence in and respect for the psychologist; 2) I surely did not know what to do and even a crazy idea is better than no idea; 3) I thought maybe I was so confused that I didn't know a good idea from a bad one; 4) I thought maybe this assignment was so damn weird it might work; and 5) I think I was desperate enough to try anything.

For that set of reasons and perhaps others I decided to try the assignment. The results were amazing, the damn thing worked. Within three weeks I was functioning for most of my day at a reasonable level of efficiency and effectiveness.

Reaction #3

I was having and had been having feelings of professional inadequacy. I had a good deal of professional success but I thought that was probably due to luck and political manipulations. I had the thought that it was simply a matter of time before everyone knew that I was incompetent. I had spent a good part of my career getting jobs that I thought I couldn't handle. My thoughts were if I can get this impossible job and do it, then I will know that I am competent. I would get the job, be successful at it for three or four years, and then decide I had better change jobs before my colleagues found out I was incompetent. So, then I would get a job that was even more difficult than the one I was leaving.

I told this story to a psychologist. He suggested that I go in to work the next day and behave incompetent. My reaction was— No! I was not going to let everyone know that I was incompetent. The psychologist then suggested that I pick a relatively safe work situation and behave incompetently. I reluctantly agreed to try the assignment.

During the next months I attempted the assignment at least a dozen times. I was never able to behave incompetently throughout an entire situation. I would begin the assignment and people would start to look at me strangely and I would stop. I decided that I was behaving too incompetent, thus I tried in several situations to behave just a little bit incompetent. This strategy did not work because I was getting the same reactions from people.

All of the above situations were relatively safe because I was selecting situations that involved a small number of people and the issues were relatively unimportant. I decided in these situations even a fool was expected to behave competently. So, I picked a situation that involved a large number of people and the issue was crucial for the organization. I selected an alternative to address the issue and marshalled my argument for the absurd alternative. I started to present the alternative. I was no more than half way through the alternative and as I looked around the room most of the people were nodding their heads in agreement or giving other signs of support. I thought "Good Grief!"—if they accept this alternative it will take us six months to get out of this mess. I then moved away from the absurd alternative to an alternative that would deal with the issue.

I don't feel that I ever implemented the assignment. I have not or don't remember talking with the psychologist about it. But now for the strangest comments—somewhere during this three to six month process I stopped feeling incompetent. I don't know when it occurred or how it occurred. During this time I had a lot of other things happening in my life but I have a strong hunch that the weird assignment helped.

12

Professional and ethical issues

The introduction of paradoxical methods, like other methods, will probably be met with resistance from some clinicians. Therapists who have been trained and are practicing one way will find it difficult to change their working habits. Their typical ways of intervening have become easy and comfortable for them. They have a system which already works and they feel confident about their skills. A new way of working would threaten their security. Learning a new approach would require more work, and the loss of confidence associated with doing the tried and true. Paradoxical therapy would be more threatening to clinicians than other methods because it does not make sense within traditional views of therapy.

The clinician who is unfamiliar with the theoretical basis of paradoxical therapy might argue that there is no way the specific methods could work. We have seen a number of traditionally trained therapists who believed an intervention would make the problem worse because the symptom was prescribed. Their lack of understanding of the paradoxical method and commitment to other techniques make it difficult for them to see the reason for an intervention, even after a lengthy explanation.

The unfamiliar clinician confronted with having to deal with paradoxical methods has one excellent argument at his disposal. The practitioner can point out with much justification that it has not been demonstrated to be effective. Most of the evidence supporting its use has been in case reports. Empirically oriented therapists who think about problems in a linear fashion could easily reject paradoxical therapy as having nothing more than a placebo effect.

The issue of professional acceptance has thus far been discussed in very broad and general terms. The question of acceptance may become concrete if a therapist attempts to work paradoxically. It must be recognized that every therapist works in a social context. Even the therapist in private practice deals with other clinicians through meetings, workshops, and clients moving from one therapist to another. Many therapists work in group practices and clinics where their work is indirectly or directly viewed by others. The therapist's approach may be seen in staff meetings, supervision, case conferences, case disposition, and training. Suppose a group of therapists decided they wanted to form a study/peer supervision paradox group. Suppose the clinic hired a therapist who already had this type of training. How would the staff react to a form of therapy that is not only new, but contrary to the principles of common sense and traditional psychotherapy?

The therapist can expect the same range of emotional reactions from staff that can be expected from clients. Some therapists will accept the new form of treatment with puzzlement; others will be angry that a treatment of "no value" is being "experimented with" in their clinic. For a variety of reasons the way the staff reacts can be helpful or hurtful to both the therapist's survival at that clinic and the quality of therapeutic work in the total clinic. The staff may reject, belittle, criticize, or ignore the paradoxical therapist. In fact, in some clinics there may be individuals who are so entrenched in one therapeutic modality that they reject all else.

Two problems are likely to arise for the therapist working in a group or clinic. The first problem is what to do with a therapist who can treat difficult cases quickly and successfully. In particular, what is done with those cases that others have treated or are treating unsuccessfully? Certain types of disorders have a long history of being labeled as having a poor prognosis. In addition, some therapists have their own notions about what is an impossible case. When a paradoxical therapist is introduced into this context, a situation exists where case disposition, supervision, and staff meetings are full of conflicts. The conflicts stem from the fact that a paradoxical therapist might view the case as one that is hopeful when another therapist would see it as hopeless. The therapist who sees the case as hopeless would then be forced to tactfully admit that he does not know how to treat this case. If the paradoxical therapist were then successful with a case the other therapist thought hopeless, then that therapist might feel incompetent. For these reasons the paradoxical therapist may initially need to go slow in introducing this method. One way to go slow is for the paradoxical therapist to join with the other therapist in declaring the situation to be hopeless, and consequently, worth one last try with something completely different. Declaring oneself to be the savior of a client only creates defensiveness in other staff members.

The other problem a paradoxical therapist is likely to have is more ethical in nature. Suppose a client has been in treatment for some time without showing improvement. The nonparadoxical therapist of that client may talk about resistance, lack of motivation, inability to change, secondary gains, and so on. The idea is that it is the client's responsibility to change and not the therapist's responsibility to facilitate the change until "the client is ready." A therapist with this attitude will decide it is ethical to treat a client for an extended period of time without making changes in the approach to treatment. This kind of situation can produce a great deal of impatience in a paradoxical therapist. He is trained to expect change quickly. When a change does not occur, the paradoxical therapist does not blame the client but examines the strategy being used. The responsibility of change resides with the therapist. The therapist must be able to change the method to fit the client. In the short run we believe it is best to approach lightly therapists who hold the attitude that it is the client's responsiblity to change. Ethically all one does is suggest that it is time to try something different. In the long run, paradoxical psychotherapy must prove its effectiveness clinically and empirically before one can claim it is the treatment of choice for a difficult case.

Once a paradoxical therapist has acquired a reputation of being effective, difficult cases will be awarded to him/her. The staff may evolve a new frame of reference for the paradoxical therapist. The therapist may be said to be no more effective than others, but simply a specialist in treating difficult cases, just as other staff specialize in this or that.

Relations with the staff can have an important effect on the success of treatment. Clinics usually have a group of "chronic" clients. These clients may have been treated by several of the staff. A paradoxical therapist then enters the picture. The patient is placed in a therapeutic double-bind. As we stated earlier, the client may try to escape from binds by trapping the therapist. But if this fails the client's next move could be to consult a previous therapist. This strategy is the same old game of playing one therapist against the other. In the case of paradoxical teams, the client may later contact a team member in order to evade the bind. Consequently, it is helpful if others either take a hands-off attitude with paradoxical cases or be informed about how to respond. For ethical reasons, it may be too difficult to inform other staff. However, the paradoxical therapist may find it useful to explain to the staff the necessity of referring the client to him/her only. Because the client could call at an odd hour in crisis, a clinic having a crisis team could also be given special instructions on how to respond to the client, provided certain ethical considerations are met.

The paradoxical therapist inhabits a different epistemological and methodological world than do most other therapists. Selvini Palazzoli et al. (1978a) have elegantly stated: "We are imprisoned by the absolute incompatibility between two primary systems in which human beings live: The living system, dynamic and circular, and the symbolic system (language), descriptive, static, and linear" (p. 52). We have observed that paradoxical therapists utilize both systems while most other therapists, especially individually oriented therapists, utilize only the latter. Theoretical and clinical conflicts are bound to occur between therapists who see reality in such a different way.

ETHICS

There are several different ethical issues surrounding the use of paradoxical methods. These issues related to: 1) how to use paradoxes; 2) when to use paradoxes; and 3) whether paradoxical therapy is unnecessarily manipulative.

All therapeutic techniques should be used responsibly. The therapist's responsibility to the client is to have the skill to know how to make an intervention correctly. The therapist who uses paradox as a gimmick because s/he read about a similar case is not acting responsibly. The paradoxical therapist needs sufficient training and/or supervision before attempting these methods. Not only is an intervention made in a theoretical vacuum likely to fail, but if it does work the therapist will not know what to do next. The symptom may then reappear, causing the client to lose faith in the therapist and terminate treatment. The paradoxical therapist must also take responsibility for keeping detailed records of the interventions made and following up on each intervention with careful accuracy. Paradoxical tasks create an enormous amount of information in the form of feedback about the therapist's working hypothesis and interventions. This feedback becomes part of the basis for future interventions. Disrespecting the significance of follow-up would be analogous to a physician who simply asks a patient how he or she feels after treatment without doing specific follow-up examinations.

Stanton (1981b) has mentioned several oversights and errors in strategic therapy which have the potential to become ethical problems. The therapist must be careful not to become "pat" in giving directives. Each intervention must be tailored to the client. A second problem is that of not remaining cognizant of the effect interventions may have on members of the client's system who are not in treatment. Third, the therapist might make a prescription without linking it to the rest of the family system. Such a mistake would at the very least perpetuate the idea that the family plays no role in that client's problem. Finally, the therapist must have sufficient skill and confidence in actually delivering the intervention. Otherwise the bind will not "stick."

When to intervene paradoxically was discussed in Chapter 4. The contraindications for paradoxical intervention include crisis situations, homicide, suicide, and situations where the client has been a victim of circumstance. Paradoxical intervention in these situations would most likely be unhelpful, and hence, irresponsible. The therapist should selectively choose the cases where this type of intervention would be helpful as a result of careful theoretical analysis and clinically proven applicability.

Paradoxical methods should not be used for their shock value. Although these methods sometimes produce a shock reaction, this is not their function. Nor should the therapist use this method because s/he has failed at everything else and thinks something "crazy" might work. The therapist who makes a paradoxical intervention on the basis of intuition rather than both intuition and analytical justification is behaving impulsively.

Paradoxical methods can be overused. A therapist who uses paradoxical techniques with every client is using the approach irrelevantly. Paradox is a method to be used in selected cases and usually in combination with a variety of other techniques.

Finally, there is the issue of whether paradoxical therapy is unnecessarily manipulative. This has emerged because paradox is an "insightless" form of therapy with an overtly Machiavellian quality. There appear to be three specific areas of ethical concern involved in the issue of manipulation: 1) definition of problem and goals; 2) selection of a method which is noncontrolling in the client's view; and 3) informed consent.

The first issue is *problem definition and goal selection*. Some consider it manipulative and unethical for a therapist to define the problem and select the goals of treatment. In fact, the working method of paradoxical therapy described earlier shows that a careful analysis of the problem is made *mutually*. In short, the therapist and client agree on what is to be changed. Furthermore, the method dictates that specific behavioral goals be established whenever possible. The assessment phase of paradoxical treatment is much like that of behavior therapy. Clinicians do not impose their own definition of the problem, nor is there an open-ended or ambiguous contract such as one sometimes finds in "humanistic" psychotherapy.

The second issue is that of *selecting an intervention method which is not restrictive, controlling, or intrusive* (Stoltz et al., 1978). Maley and Hayes (1975) have argued that methods which were viewed as restrictive, controlling, and intrusive are those interventions with the most *obvious* control. These methods often involve punishment, threat of punishment, or withdrawal of positive reinforcement. This whole issue can be circumvented, in part, if our guidelines are followed for the application of paradox. For primarily practical reasons we have stated that paradoxical interventions should be reserved for more resistive cases. Unless there are good reasons to use paradoxes from the beginning of therapy, straightforward types of interventions may be used. Only when those fail is the use of paradox indicated. Our reasoning follows the same principles applied in medicine. The treatment with the lowest risk is implemented first. Ultimately, the selection of treatment is guided by cost/benefit analysis. In cases where nothing else has worked, nothing is to be lost by making a paradoxical intervention. Moreover, it should be noted that no evidence has been presented to indicate any risk associated with paradoxical intervention. We have never seen a paradox produce deterioration in a client unless that was our method of helping the client reach his/her goal (i.e., to destabilize the system). At worst, what we have observed is simply no change. Clinicians unfamiliar with this approach seem to be concerned that the prescription will actually result in a continuation of the symptom. These clinicians do not understand the purpose of the intervention.

There may also be concern over the obvious control the therapist is exercising in the sense of the bind restricting the client. The question is actually one of how much conscious manipulation a therapist should use. Haley (1976) has said that clinicians are now recognizing manipulation as a part of therapy. He pointed out how therapy is a paid relationship in which one person provides a service for another. It is not a relationship based on friendship which presupposes such qualities as openness, honesty, and non-manipulation. If it is true that all therapies involve manipulation, why has paradoxical therapy been criticized for being too manipulative? In our experience those clinicians who make this claim want to deny that they are manipulative. They tend to define the therapeutic relationship as one like a friendship. Thus, the question of ethics becomes confused because there is no agreement on what type of relationship exists between therapist and client. The paradox of this situation is that the "non-manipulative" therapist must in fact be a good manipulator to be effective. Consequently, the "non-manipulative" therapist is unconsciously manipulative. At best, this situation appears unproductive for the practice of psychotherapy. If psychotherapy is a science, the therapist must be able to explain the purpose of interventions. A scientific approach to therapy demands a conscious and deliberate understanding of the treatment program.

Finally, it could be said that a paradoxical intervention is restrictive because it gives the person no choice. This view is true of a pathogenic double-bind. In our earlier description we showed how a pathogenic bind leads to a no-win situation. One fear is that an unethical therapist might use a paradox in a self-serving way. Erickson and Rossi (1975) reported on a significant limitation of double-binds relating to the motivations of the therapist. They suggested that binds would be accepted only if there was a positive meta-level to the therapy. In relationships where the meta-level is competitive or negative, the directive would be rejected. The client will accept the parameters of the bind only if s/he sees some benefit. It is possible that a client may accept the bind out of trust, but even in those cases there is a meta-structuring of the relationship.

The purpose of the therapeutic double-bind is diametrically opposed to that of the pathogenic bind. The former bind produces a win consequence even though the bind appears restrictive. A therapeutic bind exposes the illusion of alternatives described by Watzlawick et al. (1974). The bind is not an end in itself; it is a mechanism which allows the client to initiate his/her own change. The mechanism provides an experience which releases the client from a paradoxical situation. The counterparadox provided by the therapist moves the client to a different frame of reference. The new frame of reference is created by the client; it is never prescribed by the therapist. What is prescribed is, in fact, the existing frame of reference which has previously been defined in need of change. The meta-level structuring of paradoxical therapy is not one of restriction. On the contrary, the intervention allows the client the fullest expression of freedom in developing a new frame of reference. From the outset of therapy, the meta-framework has been one of initiating changes. The fact that clients respond to paradoxes by attributing change to themselves serves as evidence of this view.

The final issue concerning paradoxical therapy is that of *informed consent*. In the case of paradoxical therapy, the issue is whether the client understands and agrees to the methods used to change his/her behavior. It could be argued from the outset that most therapists, perhaps excluding behavior therapists, do not explain their treatment methods, so why should a paradoxical therapist? A counter-argument might be that most clients intuitively understand the methods because they make sense. The heart of the issue is not whether the client is told about what method is to be used. We have found that paradoxical methods work, even when they are explained to the client or when the client is a paradoxical therapist, if the task is acted upon. The real issue is that the client is being changed without insight or conscious recognition. Haley (1976) has dealt with this problem extensively. He maintained that no therapy is fully explicit. Otherwise, the therapist would have to constantly comment on the process of therapy. He further maintained that the lack of insight is a form of courtesy. Shameful events need not be discussed or remembered. Insightless therapy offers another courtesy. An insight provided by a therapist is always colored by the therapist's theoretical orientation. There is no pure insight. An insightless therapy avoids all the problems of a therapist imposing his/her values.

Some nonparadoxical therapists have also objected to the conscious manipulation used by paradoxical therapists as lying. They have rightly argued that it is unethical or deceitful to lie to the client. Haley (1976) has pointed out that "deceit" may be used either consciously or unknowlingly. In both cases, the outcome may be the same. The question of deceit or lying can be resolved only by placing it within the epistemological framework of paradoxical therapy. The paradoxical therapist who tells a client to have a symptom is not making a statement with the intent to deceive the client from his/her theoretical perspective. From a linear theoretical perspective, such a statement could be seen as a lie. The client may view such a statement to be both a lie and not a lie. The frame of reference in which s/he places the problem would make the statement a lie, but the purpose of therapy is to change the client's frame of reference, which makes it not a lie. The client may then see the statement to be a benevolent lie — one used out of kindness.

Clients have not shown any concern over the issue of lying in paradoxical therapy. It has been linear therapists who have questioned our method. From our perspective, linear therapists may sometimes commit the kind of lying of which they accuse us. A linear therapist might offer hope, encouragement, etc. to someone without believing it to be genuinely useful for producing a beneficial therapeutic effect.

This kind of "pat" encouragement may exacerbate the problem in some cases; hence, it is a malevolent lie. We do not wish to imply that it is never appropriate to be encouraging. In many cases, this technique is quite beneficial. However, there are clearly cases where a paradoxical approach is indicated. The symptom should be encouraged. If we define truth as that which works (a pragmatic theory of truth), then the injunction given to the client is true.

Paradoxical therapists arrange situations where the client appears to change spontaneously. Even if the client consciously understood the paradox, the change could still occur. What difference does it make whether the client is conscious of the bind? The fact that the client changes spontaneously and without the knowledge that the therapist had contrived the situation empowers the client. The client feels more in control of self. This sense of power may help the client approach future problems with a more positive attitude. The demoralization experienced over not being able to cope with the problems is also counteracted.

The issue of informed consent is no more of a problem for paradoxical therapy than it is for any other approach to therapy. The problem is that paradoxical therapy departs from the tradition of providing the client with insight—a tradition which holds that insight is necessary for lasting change to occur. What we face may be less of an ethical issue than an empirical issue. It is clearly unethical to use a therapy which doesn't work.

TRAINING IN PARADOXICAL PSYCHOTHERAPY

Who should be trained

The complexity of paradoxical psychotherapy has been emphasized throughout this book. The paradoxical therapist must have a solid foundation in system/communication theory and the principles of paradoxical therapy, and accept being highly directive in making interventions. A beginning therapist who lacks this foundation would not be ready to work paradoxically. The theory would be absolutely necessary in guiding the therapist in the when, how, and why of making paradoxical interventions. The beginning therapist also lacks the basic clinical skills to intervene paradoxically. Paradoxical interventions must be carefully formulated, appropriately timed, convincingly delivered, and followed up. In order to make paradoxical interventions, the therapist must first have the skills necessary to make active and directive interventions. The therapist would need to possess what Tomm and Wright (1979) have called executive skills. Executive skills refer to the therapist's ability to use his/her emotions in formulating an intervention and then competently making an overt intervention. Beginning therapists may be too anxious or overwhelmed by their own emotions to be emotionally-sensitive to the client. They may also feel uncomfortable about giving specific directives.

We have observed that family therapists can learn to work paradoxically more easily than individual therapists. As a group, family therapists are trained to be more directive than most individual therapists. They also have an understanding of systems theory. Consequently, it is easier to train most family therapists, provided they have met the minimal criteria mentioned earlier.

It is obvious that a client-centered, gestalt, or psychoanalytic therapist would have difficulty changing approaches or integrating paradoxes in his/her approach.

Training

There appear to be three ways one can learn to do paradoxical therapy. The first route is through academic or professional graduate schools. There are a few marital and family therapy programs in this country which provide training at the doctoral level in the use of paradox. The reader interested in this approach should write to all those programs for a description of the training. A comprehensive list of programs has been published in the July 1979 issue of the *Journal of Marital and Family Therapy*.

Clinicians who have completed their training can learn through workshops and externship programs at different institutes. A few of the better known training institutes are:

The Brief Therapy Center of the Mental Research Institute, Palo Alto, California

The Brief Therapy Project of the Ackerman Institute,
   New York
The Philadelphia Child Guidance Center,
   Philadelphia, Pennsylvania
The Family Institute of Washington,
   Washington, D.C.
The Institute for Family Studies,
   Atlanta, Georgia
The Wisconsin Institute for Family Studies,
   Milwaukee, Wisconsin

A comprehensive list of training sites and paradoxical therapy supervisors is scheduled for publication in a newly formed newsletter (May, 1980) called the *Underground Railroad*. This newsletter is published at the Wisconsin Institute on Family Studies, 6416 West Capitol Drive, Milwaukee, Wisconsin, 53216.

If a clinician is not able to participate in an externship program, s/he might be able to find a competent paradoxical supervisor in his/her area. In either case, the training should be contracted for a one- to two-year period. The trainee should treat just a few cases paradoxically at one time and should keep detailed process notes, if not audio- or videotaped recordings of the sessions for supervision. The reasons for these guidelines are explained in the third way to achieve training —the study-peer supervision group.

In some parts of the country it is simply impossible to find a supervisor to provide ongoing training. In such a case a group of experienced therapists may be able to train themselves by attending brief workshops and forming a study/peer supervision group. Training for the group would begin by attending workshops and then forming a study group to share information and discuss the different issues raised in this book. When they feel they have sufficient information, the therapists would become a peer supervision group.

The group should first be aware that learning to work paradoxically means giving up old ideas. Change, even for therapists, is not easy. The therapist's image of self may undergo a change during the early phase of training. Therapists who like to think of themselves as loving, caring, sensitive, feeling individuals may initially think practicing this approach to therapy is incongruent with their self-image. In short, the therapist's resistance to change may be a crucial issue in learning this approach. Being a paradoxical therapist violates the norms of what most therapists perceive to be their role. The group should be aware that such resistances will emerge. A therapist may not want to make a certain intervention when it is clear to the group that it is needed. The therapist might fail to follow through on an intervention or allow the client to escape from the bind. This kind of therapist resistance stems from lack of confidence in the intervention. In this situation, the therapist has not received enough support from the group to overcome old therapeutic habits. A therapist who understands how an intervention will work, what changes are likely to occur, and how a client may try to undo a therapeutic double-bind will be invested in making the intervention and following through.

The group serves as a sounding board for new interventions. A therapist learning this approach may feel that an intervention is appropriate but questions whether it is crazy, absurd, or "gimmicky." Again, the group helps to clarify the design of the intervention. Until the therapist feels confident that his/her interventions are properly formulated, s/he is not ready to practice this type of therapy independently. Confidence is gained by acquiring a theoretical/clinical background and having a history of success with the techniques.

A peer supervision group could begin with one or two training cases. One system for peer group supervision is to assign two members of the group as primary therapists while the other members observe from behind a one-way mirror. The observers could then have the primary therapists leave the room on a rotating basis during the session to discuss paradoxical strategy. Clients will find the first few minutes of this procedure somewhat distracting, but if it is done in a business-as-usual fashion the procedure will be readily accepted. Following the session the group may review videotaped segments as a way to gain further information about their working method. They can also discuss goals, predict the outcome of their interventions, and plan for the next session.

This type of training approach requires more concentration on cases. While it can be exciting, challenging, and highly creative, it can also be draining if too many cases are treated paradoxically. The quality of the experience far exceeds the quantity of cases treated. The group must restrain itself in order to protect the quality of the training. There may be a tendency to take on too many cases when some difficult or "impossible" cases show improvement. The successes of paradoxical treatment can be so reinforcing that the therapist falls into a dogmatic trap, namely, that there is only one method for every case.

References

Ackerman, N. Prejudicial scapegoating and neutralizing forces in the family group, with special reference to the role of "Family Healer." In J. Howells (Ed.), *Theory and practice of family psychiatry.* New York: Brunner/Mazel, 1968.

Adams, H. Toward a dialectical approach to counseling. *Journal of Humanistic Psychology,* 1977, *17,* 57-67.

Adler, A. Verdrangung und mannlicher protest; ihre rolle und bedeuting fur die neurotische dynamik, 1911. In *Heilen und bilden,* 1914.

Adler, A. *The individual psychology of Alfred Adler.* (H. L. Ansbacher and R. R. Ansbacher, Ed. and Trans.). New York: Harper and Row, 1956.

Andolfi, M. Paradox in psychotherapy. *American Journal of Psychoanalysis,* 1974, *34,* 221-228.

Andolfi, M. Redefinition in family therapy. *American Journal of Family Therapy,* 1979, *7,* 5-15.

Andolfi, M. *Family therapy: An interactional approach.* New York: Plenum Press, 1980.

Ansbacher, H. Adler's "Striving for Power," in relation to Nietzsche. *Journal of Individual Psychology,* 1972, *28,* 12-24.

Ascher, L. Paradoxical intention in the treatment of urinary retention. *Behavior Research and Therapy,* 1979, *17,* 267-270.

Ascher, L., & Efran, J. Use of paradoxical intention in a behavioral program for sleep onset insomnia. *Journal of Consulting and Clinical Psychology,* 1978, *46,* 547-550.

Ascher, L., & Turner, R. Paradoxical intention and insomnia: An experimental investigation. *Rehaviour Research and Therapy,* 1979, *17,* 408-411.

Ascher, L., & Turner, R. A comparison of two methods for the administration of paradoxical intention. *Behaviour Research and Therapy,* 1980, *18,* 121-126.

Ayllon, T. Intensive treatment of psychotic behavior by stimulus satiation and food reinforcement. *Behaviour Research and Therapy.* 1963, *1,* 53-62.

Azrin, N., Naster, D., & Jones, R. Reciprocity counseling: A rapid learning based procedure for marital counseling. *Behaviour Research and Therapy.* 1973, *11* 365-382.

Bahm, A. *Polarity, dialectic, and organicity.* Springfield: Charles C Thomas, 1970.

Bandler, R., & Grinder, J. *The structure of magic, Vol. I.* Palo Alto: Science and Behavior, 1975.

Basseches, M. Dialectical schemata: A framework for the empirical study of the development of dialectical thinking. *Human Development,* 1980, *23,* 400-421.

Bateson, G. *Steps to an ecology of mind.* New York: Ballantine, 1972.

Bateson, G., Jackson, D., Haley, J., & Weakland, J. Toward a theory of schizophrenia. *Behavioral Science,* 1956, *2,* 4.

Beahrs, J. Integrating Erickson's approach. *American Journal of Clinical Hypnosis,* 1977, *20,* 55-68.

Beck, A. Depressive neurosis. In S. Arieti (Ed.) *American handbook of psychiatry, Vol. 3*, Basic Books, 1974.

Beck, D. Research findings on the outcomes of marital counseling. *Social Casework*, 1975, *56*, 153-181.

Beisser, A. The paradoxical theory of change. In J. Fagan and I. Shepherd (Eds.), *Gestalt therapy now*. New York: Harper and Row, 1970.

Bergman, J. The use of paradox in a community home for the chronically disturbed and retarded. *Family Process*, 1980, *19*, 65-72.

Berne, E. *What do you say after you say hello?* New York: Grove Press, 1972.

Bertalanffy, Ludwig von. The meaning of general systems theory. In *General systems theory*, New York: George Braziller, 1968.

Binswanger, L. The existential analysis school of thought. In R. May, E. Angel, and H. Ellensberger (Eds.) *Existence*. New York: Basic Books, 1958.

Binswanger, L. *Being-in-the-world* (translated and with critical introduction by J. Needleman) New York: Basic Books, 1963.

Boss, M. *Psychoanalysis and daseinanalysis*. New York: Basic Books, 1963.

Boszormenyi-Nagy, I., & Spark, G. *Invisible loyalties: Reciprocity in inter-generational family therapy*. Hagerstown, Md: Harper and Row, 1973.

Brehm, J. W. *A theory of psychological reactance*. New York: Academic Press, 1966.

Brehm, J. W. *Responses of loss of freedom: A theory of psychological reactance*. Morristown, N.J.: General Learning Press, 1972.

Brehm, S. *The application of social psychology in clinical practice*. Washington, D.C., Hemisphere, 1976.

Burton, A. The use of written productions in psychotherapy. In L. Pearson (Ed.), *The use of written communication in psychotherapy*. Springfield, Il: Charles C Thomas, 1965.

Buss, A. Development of dialectics and development of humanistic psychology. *Human Development*, 1976, *19*, 248-260.

Calhoun, J. Abnormal psychology: Current perspectives. (2nd ed.) New York: CRM/Random House, 1977.

Clark, R. *Mental illness in perspective: History and schools of thought*. Pacific Grove, Calif.: Boxwood Press, 1973.

Corsini, R. *Current psychotherapies* (2nd ed.), Itasca, IL: Peacock, 1979.

DeShazer, S. Brief therapy: Two's company. *Family Process*, 1975, *14*, 79-93.

DeShazer, S. The confusion technique. *Family Therapy*, 1975, *2*, 23-29.

DeShazer, S. Brief therapy with couples. *American Journal of Family Therapy*, 1978, *6*, 17-30. (a)

DeShazer, S. The confusion technique. *Family Process*, 1978, *5*, 23-39. (b)

DeShazer, S. Investigation of indirect symbolic suggestions. *American Journal of Clinical Hypnosis*, 1980, *23*, 10-15.

Dewey, J., & Bentley, A. *Knowing and the known*. Boston: Beacon Press, 1949.

Dunlap, K. A revision of the fundamental law of habit formation. *Science*, 1928, *57*, 360-362.

Dunlap, K. Repetition in the breaking of habits. *Science monthly*, 1930. *30*, 66-70.

Dunlap, K. *Personal adjustment*. New York: McGraw-Hill, 1946.

Edwards, P. (Ed.) *The encyclopedia of philosophy*. New York: Macmillan and The Free Press, 1967.

Ehrenwald, G. *Psychotherapy, myth, and model*. New York: Grune and Stratton, 1966.

Ellis, A. The use of printed, written, and recorded words in psychotherapy. In L. Pearson (Ed.), *The use of written communication in psychotherapy*. Springfield, IL: Charles C Thomas, 1965.

Enright, J. An introduction to Gestalt techniques. In J. Fagan and I. Shepherd (Eds.), *Gestalt therapy now*. New York: Harper and Row, 1970.

Erickson, M. Psychotherapy achieved by reversal of the neurotic processes in a case of ejaculation precox. *American Journal of Clinical Hypnosis*, 1973, *15*, 217-222.

Erickson, M. Hypnotic approaches to therapy. *American Journal of Clinical Hypnosis*, 1977, *20*, 20-35.

Erickson, M., & Rossi, E. Varieties of double bind. American Journal of Clinical Hypnosis, 1975, *17*, 143-157.

Fabry, J., Bulka, R., and Sahakian, W. (Eds.) *Logotherapy in action*. New York: Jason Aronson, 1979.

Farrelly, F., & Brandsma, J. *Provocative therapy*. Fort Collins, Colorado: Shields Publishing, 1974.

Feldman, L. Depression and marital interaction. *Family Process,* 1976, *15,* 389-396.

Feldman, L. Strategies and techniques of family therapy. *American Journal of Psychotherapy,* 1976, *30,* 14-28.

Fisher, L., Anderson, A., & Jones, J. Types of paradoxical intervention and indication/contraindication for use in clinical practice. *Family Process,* 1981, *20,* 25-35.

Foa, U., & Foa, E. *Societal structures of the mind*. Springfield, IL: Charles C Thomas, 1974.

Foley, V. *An introduction to family therapy*. New York: Grune and Stratton, 1974.

Frankl, V. Sur medikamentosen unterstutzung der psychotherapie bei neurosen. *Schweizer Arshio fur Neurologie und Psychiatrie,* 1939, *43,* 26-31.

Frankl, V. *Man's search for meaning: An introduction to logotherapy*. Boston: Beacon Press, 1959.

Frankl, V. *The doctor and the soul: From psychotherapy to logotherapy*. New York: Knopf, 1965.

Frankl, V. *Psychotherapy and existentialism: Selected papers on logotherapy*. New York: Simon and Schuster, 1967.

Frankl, V. Paradoxical intention and dereflection. *Psychotherapy: Theory, Research, Practice,* 1975, *12,* 226-237.

Freud, S. Inhibitions, symptoms, and anxiety. In J. Strachey (Ed.) *The Standard Edition of the Complete Psychological Works of Sigmund Freud (Vol. 20)*. London: The Hogarth Press, 1959.

Friedman, R., Dreizen, K., Harris, L., Schoen., & Shulman, P. Parent power: A holding technique in the treatment of omnipotent children. *International Journal of Family Counseling,* 1978, *6,* 66-73.

Furst, H. *Modes of construction and their change through validation and invalidation*. Stockholm: Ramsays Tryckerier, 1978.

Gerz, H. The treatment of the phobic and obsessive-compulsive patient using paradoxical intention. *Journal Neuropsychiatry,* 1962, *3,* 375-387.

Gerz, H. Experience with the logotherapeutic technique of paradoxical intention in the treatment of phobic and obsessive-compulsive patients. *American Journal Psychiatry,* 1966, *123,* 548-553.

Goldman, J., & Coane, J. Family therapy after the divorce: Developing a strategy. *Family Process,* 1977, *16,* 357-362.

Grinder, J., & Bandler, R. *The structure of magic, Vol. II.* Palo Alto: Science and Behavior, 1976.

Grunebaum, H., & Chasin, R. Relabeling and reframing reconsidered: The beneficial effects of a pathological label. *Family Process,* 1978, *17,* 449-456.

Guerin, P. *Family therapy*. New York: Gardner Press, 1976.

Gurman, A. The effects and effectiveness of marital therapy: A review of outcome research. *Family Process,* 1973, *12,* 145-170.

Gurman, A., & Kniskern, D. Deterioration in marital and family therapy: Empirical, clinical, and conceptual issues. *Family Process,* 1978, *17,* 3-20.

Gurman, A., & Kniskern, D. *Handbook of family therapy*. New York: Brunner/Mazel, 1981.

Haley, J. The family of the schizophrenic: A model system. *Journal of Nervous and Mental Disease,* 1959, *129,* 357-374.

Haley, J. Whither family therapy. *Family Process,* 1962, *1,* 68-100.

Haley, J. *Strategies of psychotherapy.* New York: Grune and Stratton, 1963.

Haley, J. (Ed.) *Advanced techniques of hypnosis and therapy.* New York: Grune and Stratton, 1967.

Haley, J. An interactional explanation of hypnosis. In D. Jackson (Ed.), *Therapy, communication, and changes. Vol. II.* Palo Alto: Science and Behavior Books, Inc., 1968.

Haley, J. *Uncommon therapy: The psychiatric techniques of Milton H. Erickson.* New York: Ballantine, 1973.

Haley, J. *Problem-solving therapy.* San Francisco: Jossey-Bass, 1976.

Hall, C., & Lindzey, G. *Theories of personality (2nd Ed.)* New York: John Wiley and Sons, Inc., 1970.

Hallett, K. *A guide for single parents.* Mallbrae, Calif: Celestial Arts, 1974.

Hare-Mustin, R. Treatment of temper tantrums by paradoxical intervention. *Family Process,* 1975, *14,* 481-486.

Havens, L. *Approaches to the mind: Movement of the psychiatric schools from sects toward science.* Boston: Little, Brown, and Co., 1973.

Hughes, S., Berger, and Wright, L. The family life cycle and clinical interventions. *Journal of Marriage and Family Counseling,* 1978, *4,* 33-40.

Hughes, P., & Brecht, G. *Vicious circles and infinity: A panoply of paradoxes.* New York: Doubleday and Co., 1975.

Hull, C. *Principles of behavior.* New York: Appleton, 1943.

Jackson, D. The question of family homeostasis. *Psychiatric Quarterly Supplement,* 1957, *31,* 79-90.

Jackson, D. The study of the family. *Family Process,* 1965, *4,* 1-20.

Jackson, D. Family interaction, family homeostasis and some implications for conjoint family psychotherapy. In D. Jackson (Ed.), *Therapy, communication, and change.* Palo Alto, Science and Behavior Books, 1968.

James, W. *Pragmatism.* New York: World Publishing, 1907.

Jessee, E., Jurkovic, G., Wilkie, J. & Chiglinsky, M. *Positive reframing with children: Conceptual and clinical considerations.* Manuscript submitted for publication, 1980.

Jessee, E., and L'Abate, L. The use of paradox with children in an inpatient setting. *Family Process,* 1980, *19,* 59-64.

Johnson, J., Weeks, G., & L'Abate, L. Forced holding: A technique for treating parentified children. *Family Therapy,* 1979, *6,* 123-133.

Kantor, D. & Lehr, W. *Inside the family.* San Francisco: Jossey-Bass, 1975.

Kaplan, S. Structural family therapy for children of divorce: Case reports. *Family Process,* 1977, *16,* 75-83.

Karpman, S. Script drama analysis. *Transactional Analysis Bulletin,* 1968, *26,* 39-43.

Kelly, G. *The psychology of personal constructs, Vol. I and II.* New York: Norton, 1955.

Koen, R. An intra-verbal explication of the nature of metaphor. *Journal of Verbal Learning,* 1965, *4,* 129-133.

Kübler-Ross, E. *On Death and Dying.* New York: Macmillan, 1969.

L'Abate, L. Family enrichment programs. *Journal of Family Counseling,* 1974, *2,* 32-38.

L'Abate, L. A positive approach to marital and familial intervention. In L. F. Wolberg and M. L. Aronson (Eds.), *Group therapy 1975—An overview,* New York: Stratton Intercontinental Medical Books Corp., 1975.

L'Abate, L. *Understanding and helping the individual in the family.* New York: Grune and Stratton, 1976.

L'Abate, L. *Enrichment: Structured intervention with couples, families, and groups.* Washington, D.C.: University Press of America, 1977. (a)

L'Abate, L. Intimacy is sharing hurt feelings: A reply to David Mace. *Journal of Marriage and Family Counseling,* 1977, *3,* 13-16. (b)

L'Abate, L., & Collaborators. *Manual: enrichment programs for the family life cycle.* Atlanta, Ga.: Social Research Laboratories, 1975.

L'Abate, L., & L'Abate, B. The paradoxes of intimacy. *Family Therapy,* 1979, *6,* 175-184.

Lamb, C. The use of paradoxical intention: Self management through laughter. *Personnel and Guidance Journal,* 1980, *59,* 217-219.

Landfield, A. The compliant: A confrontation of personal urgency and professional construction. In D. Bannister (Ed.), *Issues and approaches in psychological therapies.* New York: Wiley, 1975.

Lederer, W., & Jackson, D. *The mirages of marriage.* New York: W. W. Norton, 1968.

Leitenberg, H. The use of single-case methodology in psychotherapy research. *Journal of Abnormal Psychology,* 1973, *82,* 87-101.

Lenrow, P. The uses of metaphor in facilitating constructive behavior change. *Psychotherapy,* 1966, *3,* 145-148.

Levitsky, A., & Perls, F. The rules and games of Gestalt therapy. In J. Fagan and I. Shepherd (Eds.), *Gestalt therapy now.* New York: Harper and Row, 1970.

Madanes, C. Protection, paradox, and pretending. *Family Process,* 1980, *19,* 73-86.

Madanes, C. *Strategic Family Therapy.* San Francisco: Jossey-Bass, 1981.

Maher, B. *Principles of psychopathology,* New York: McGraw-Hill, 1966.

Maley, R., & Hayes, S. Coercion and control: Ethical and legal issues. paper presented at the *Conference on Behavior Analysis and Ethics,* Morgantown, W. Va., June, 1975.

Marcuse, H. *Reason and revolution: Hegel and the rise of social theory.* London: Routledge and Kegan, 1954.

Maslow, A. Some educational implications of the humanistic psychologies. *Harvard Educational Review,* 1968, *38,* 685-696.

Masters. W., and Johnson, V. *Human sexual inadequacy.* Boston: Little, Brown, 1970.

Miller, S., Nunnally, E., & Wockman, D. Minnesota couples communication program: Premarital and marital groups. In D. H. Olson (Ed.), *Treating relationships.* Lake Mills, IA: Graphic Publishing Co., 1976.

Millon, T. *Modern psychopathology.* Philadelphia: Saunders, 1969.

Minuchin, S. *Families and family therapy.* Cambridge, Mass., Harvard University Press, 1974.

Minuchin, S., Rosman, B., & Baker, L. *Psychosomatic families: Anorexia nervosa in context.* Cambridge, Mass. Harvard University Press, 1978.

Mozdzierz, G., Macchitelli, F., & Lisiecki, J. The paradox in psychotherapy: An Adlerian perspective. *Journal of Individual Psychology,* 1976, *32,* 169-184.

Newton, J. Considerations for the psychotherapeutic technique of symptom scheduling. *Psychotherapy: Research, Theory, and Practice,* 1968, *5,* 95-103.

Newton, J. Therapeutic paradoxes, paradoxical intentions and negative practice. *American Journal Psychotherapy,* 1968, *22,* 68-81.

Ogg, E. *One-parent families.* Public Affairs Committee, 1977.

Olson, D. *Treating relationships.* Lake Mills, IA: Graphic Publishing Co., 1976.

Papp, P. (Ed.) *Family therapy: Full length case studies.* New York: Gardner Press, 1977.

Papp, P. The Greek chorus and other techniques of family therapy. *Family Process,* 1980, *19,* 45-58.

Pearson, L. (Ed.) *The use of written communication in psychotherapy.* Springfield, IL: Charles C Thomas, 1965.

Peck, B. Psychotherapy with fragmented father-absent families. *Family Therapy,* 1974, *2,* 27-42.

Rabkin, R. *Strategic psychotherapy: Brief and symptomatic treatment.* New York: Basic Books, 1977.

Raskin, D., & Klein, Z. Losing a symptom through keeping it: A review of paradoxical treatment techniques and rationale. *Archives of General Psychiatry,* 1976, *33,* 548-555.

Relinger, H., Bornstein, P., & Mungas, D. Treatment of insomnia by paradoxical intention. *Behavior Therapy,* 1978, *9,* 955-959.

Riegel, K. Dialectical operations: The final period of cognitive development. *Human Development,* 1973, *6,* 346-370.

Riegel, K. Subject-object alienation in psychological experimentation and testing. *Human Development,* 1975, *18,* 181-193.

Riegel, K. The dialectics of human development. *American Psychologist*, 1976, *31*, 689-700.

Rimm, D., & Masters, J. *Behavior therapy: Techniques and empirical findings*. New York: Academic Press, 1974.

Rogers, C. *Client-centered therapy*. Boston: Houghton Mifflin, 1951.

Rohrbaugh, M., Tennen, H., Press, S., White, L., Raskin, P., and Pickering, M. *Paradoxical strategies in psychotherapy*. Paper presented at the American Psychological Association, San Francisco, August, 1977.

Rohrbaugh, M., Tennen, H., Press, S., & White, L. Compliance, defiance, and therapeutic paradox. *American Journal of Orthopsychiatry*, 1981, *51*, 454-467.

Rosen, J. A method of resolving acute catatonic excitement. *The Psychiatric Quarterly*, 1946, *20*, 183-198.

Rosen, J. *Direct psychoanalysis*. New York: Grune and Stratton, 1953.

Rosenthal, R. *Experimenter effects in behavioral research*. New York: Appleton-Century-Crofts, 1966.

Rosenthal, R. The Pygmalion effect lives. *Psychology Today*, 1973, *7*, 56-62.

Rossi, E. Psychological shocks and creative movements in psychotherapy. *American Journal of Clinical Hypnosis*, 1973, *16*, 9-22.

Rychlak, J. *A philosophy of science for personality theory*. New York: Houghton and Mifflin, 1968.

Rychlak, J. *Introduction to personality and psychotherapy*. New York: Houghton and Mifflin, 1973.

Rychlak, J. The multiple meaning of dialectic. In J. Rychlak (Ed.), *Dialectic: Humanistic rationale for behavior and development*. Basel: Karger, 1976.

Sander, F. Fried's "A case of successful treatment by hypnotism (1792-1893)"—An uncommon therapy? *Family Process*, 1974, *13*, 461-462.

Saposnek, D. Aikido: A model for brief strategic therapy. *Family Process*, 1980, *19*, 237-238.

Satir, V. *Conjoint family therapy*. Palo Alto: Science and Behavior Books, 1967.

Selvini Palazzoli, M. Why a long interval between sessions? In M. Andolfi and I. Zwerling (Eds.), *Dimensions of family therapy*. New York: Guilford Press, 1980.

Selvini Palazzoli, M., Boscolo, L., Cecchin, G., & Prata, G. The treatment of children through brief therapy of their parents. *Family Process*, 1974, *13*, 419-442.

Selvini Palazzoli, M., Cecchin, G., Prata, G., & Boscolo, L. *Paradox and counterparadox*. New York: Jason Aronson, 1978. (a)

Selvini Palazzoli, M., Boscolo, L., Cecchin, G., & Prata, G. A ritualized prescription in family therapy: Odd days and even days. *Journal of Marriage and Family Counseling*, 1978, *4*, 3-9. (b)

Selvini Palazzoli, M., Boscolo, L., Cecchin, G., & Prata, G. Hypothesizing-circularity-neutrality: Three guidelines for the conduct of the session. *Family Process*, 1980, *19*, 3-12.

Silverman, S. The victimizer: Recognition and character. *American Journal of psychotherapy*, 1975, *29*, 14-25.

Slipp, S., & Kressel, K. Difficulties in family therapy evaluation. *Family Process*, 1978, *17*, 409-422.

Sluzki, C. Marital therapy from a systems theory perspective. In T. J. Paolino and B. S. McCrady (Eds.), *Marriage and marital therapy: Psychoanalytic, behavioral and systems theory perspectives*. New York: Brunner/Mazel, 1978.

Sluzki, C., & Eliseo, V. The double bind as a universal pathogenic situation. *Family Process*, 1971, *10*, 397-410.

Solyom, L., Garza-Perez, J., Ledwidge, B., & Solyom, C. Paradoxical intention in the treatment of obsessive thoughts: A pilot study. *Comprehensive Psychiatry*, 1972, *13*, 291-297.

Soper, P., & L'Abate, L. Paradox as a therapeutic technique: A review. *International Journal of Family Counseling*, 1977, *5*, 10-21.

Stampfl, T., & Levis, D. Essentials of implosive therapy: A learning theory-based psychodynamic behavioral therapy. *Journal of Abnormal Psychology*, 1967, *72*, 496-503.

Stanton, M. Marital therapy from a structural/strategic viewpoint. In G. Sholevar (Ed.), *The handbook of marriage and marital therapy.* New York: S. P. Medical and Scientific Books, 1981. (a)

Stanton, M. Strategic approaches to family therapy. In A. S. Gurman and D. P. Kniskern (Eds.), *Handbook of family therapy.* New York: Brunner/Mazel, 1981. (b)

Steiner, C. *Scripts people live.* New York: Bantam, 1974.

Stierlin, D. *Separating parents and adolescents: A perspective on running away, schizophrenia, and waywardness.* New York: Quadrangle, 1974.

Stoltz, S., & Associates. *Ethical issues in behavior modification.* San Francisco: Jossey-Bass, 1978.

Tennen, H. Perspectives on paradox: Applications and explanations. In M. Rohrbaugh (Chair), *Paradoxical strategies in psychotherapy.* Symposium presented at the meeting of the American Psychological Association, San Francisco, August, 1977.

Tennen, H., Rohrbaugh, M., Press, S., & White, L. Reactance theory and therapeutic paradox: A compliance-defiance model. *Psychotherapy,* 1981, *18,* 14–22.

Tomm, K., & Wright, L. Training in family therapy: Perceptual, conceptual, and executive skills. *Family Process,* 1979, *18,* 227–250.

Turner, R., & Ascher, M. Controlled comparison of progressive relaxation, stimulus control, and paradoxical intention therapies for insomnia. *Journal of Consulting and Clinical Psychology,* 1979, *47,* 500–508.

Vogel, E., & Bell, N. The emotionally disturbed child as the family scapegoat. In *A modern introduction to the family.* Glencoe, IL: Free Press, 1961.

Wagner, V. Enrichment and written homework assignments with couples. In L. L'Abate, *Enrichment: Structured interventions with couples, families, and groups.* Washington, D.C.: University Press of America, 1977.

Wagner, V., Weeks, G., & L'Abate, L. Enrichment and written messages with couples. *American Journal of Family Therapy,* 1980, *8*:3, 36–44.

Watzlawick, P. Brief communications. *Psychiatry,* 1965, *28,* 368–374.

Watzlawick, P., Beavin, J., and Jackson, D. *Pragmatics of human communication.* New York: W. W. Norton, 1967.

Watzlawick, P., & Coyne, J. Depression following stroke: Brief, problem-focused treatment. *Family Process,* 1980, *19,* 13–18.

Watzlawick, P., Weakland, J., & Fisch, R. *Change: Principles of problem formation and problem resolution.* New York: W. W. Norton, 1974.

Weakland, J., Fisch, R., Watzlawick, P., and Bodin, A. Brief therapy: Focused problem resolution. *Family Process,* 1974, *13,* 141–168.

Weeks, G. Toward a dialectical approach to intervention. *Human Development,* 1977, *20,* 277–292.

Weeks, G., & L'Abate, L. A bibliography of paradoxical methods in the psychotherapy of family systems. *Family Process,* 1978, *17,* 95–98.

Weeks, G., & L'Abate, L. A compilation of paradoxical methods. *American Journal of Family Therapy,* 1979, *7,* 61–76.

Weeks, G., and Wright, L. Dialectics of the family life cycle. *American Journal of Family Therapy,* 1979, *7,* 85–91.

Wiener, N. *Cybernetics.* New York: John Wiley, 1948.

Wilden, A. *System and structure: Essays in communication and exchange.* New York: Barnes and Noble, 1972.

Wildman, R. Structured versus unstructured marital intervention. In L. L'Abate (Ed.), *Enrichment: Structured interventions with couples, families, and groups.* Washington, D.C.: University Press of America, 1977.

Woodruff, R., Clayton, P., & Guze, S. Is everyone depressed? *American Journal of Psychiatry,* 1975, *132,* 627–628.

Zeig, J. Symptom prescription and Ericksonian principles of hypnosis and psychotherapy. *American Journal of Clinical Hypnosis,* 1980, *23,* 16–22. (a)

Zeig, J. Symptom prescription techniques. Clinical applications using elements of communication. *American Journal of Clinical Hypnosis, 1980, 23,* 23–33. (b)

Index